**FIGHTER
PILOT'S
HEAVEN**

FIGHTER PILOT'S HEAVEN

*Flight
Testing
the
Early
Jets*

Donald S. Lopez

*Smithsonian
Institution
Press*

Washington

This book was edited by Lorraine Atherton and
designed by Linda McKnight.

Library of Congress Cataloging-in-Publication Data

Lopez, Donald S., 1923–
Fighter pilot's heaven: flight testing the early jets /
Donald S. Lopez.
     p.   cm.
   Includes index.
   ISBN 1-56098-457-0
   1. Airplanes, Military—United States—Flight testing—
History.   I. Title.
TL685.3.L67   1995
623.7´464´097309044—dc20   94-21061

British Cataloguing-in-Publication Data is available.

01 00 99 98 97 96 95   5 4 3 2 1

Manufactured in the United States of America

♾ The paper used in this publication meets the minimum
requirements of the American National Standard for
Permanence of Paper for Printed Library Materials Z39.48-1984.

Publisher's note: The descriptions of otherwise undocumented
personal incidents and the recollections of episodes and persons
are entirely the author's. Every effort has been made to verify
details and ensure correctness; inaccuracy if it occurs is regretted.

For my lovely granddaughter
Laura Victoria
who can see air

Contents

Photographs appear after page 100

Foreword

During the Gulf War of 1991 the entire world was amazed at the sophisticated weapons used by the American forces. Television captured vivid pictures of bombs literally flying down ventilation shafts, and there were stories of airplanes that were invisible to radar detection. The conflict displayed wonders of technology put to a destructive purpose. The roots of that technology go back many, many years.

America, between the two great wars, was almost backward in the development of military weapons and certainly primitive in the airborne weapons arena. Civilian airliners of the thirties were faster than bombers. The most sophisticated aircraft of the era were often civilian racing planes. World War II changed all of that. That ultimate effort may well have represented the pinnacle of the American civilization. Vast changes were wrought in the tools of air warfare.

Don Lopez has written one book, *Into the Teeth of the Tiger,* that describes his part in World War II. As a newly commissioned, nineteen-year-old aviator, he fought in China, became an ace, and participated in the early evolution of American air weapons supremacy. Upon his return to the States, before the end of the war, Lope was assigned to Eglin Air Force Base and began a career as a test pilot, proving and improving the aircraft that had done so much to win the war. His days at Eglin were spent in that slow and often dangerous process of test and evaluation. He was one of the first American pilots to fly the Bell P-59, America's first jet aircraft. He participated in every fighter development in the immediate postwar era and, in addition, was selected by the Air Force to attend one of the first classes of the Air Force Test Pilot School at Wright Field in Dayton, Ohio.

In these pages Colonel Lopez describes the beginning of the modern Air Force as only one who has participated in the process could. We fly with him on missions as varied as shooting down captured V-1 missiles to cold-weather testing the P-80 in Alaska. We meet the unwashed characters who silently flew their missions and did their dangerous jobs, often losing their lives in the process. All of this drama is recorded in Lope's engaging style and dry wit. He is, after all, an unusual fighter pilot, with an advanced degree from Cal Tech, a nondrinker, a devoted family man, and a keen observer of his times.

One can only hope that *Fighter Pilot's Heaven* represents the second in a series of books and that the sequel will describe his career from Eglin to the present.

Frank Borman

Preface

From June 1945 through September 1950 I was a test pilot in the Fighter Test Squadron of the Proof Test Group at Eglin Field, later Eglin Air Force Base, Florida, part of the Air Proving Ground Command. Its mission was to determine the operational suitability of the aircraft and weapons systems of the Army Air Forces and later the U.S. Air Force. To accomplish this mission the aircraft and weapon combinations were rigorously tested for function and accuracy, using live ammunition in most instances. Also, the tactics and techniques for the most effective use of the weapons were tested and perfected.

It was a challenging period, as the standard propeller-driven fighters were being replaced by jets that posed many new problems for which solutions had to be found. Also, the military was going through the difficult transition from wartime to peacetime operations.

There has been little if anything at all written about the type of testing done at Eglin, and this book is my attempt to tell at least part of that story. Everything related in the book actually took place, but there might be slight chronological discrepancies that have no effect on the story.

I want to express my gratitude to those who contributed to the completion of this memoir: Ian and Betty Ballantine for their support and suggestions in the beginning phases of the book; Dr. Richard Hallion and his staff at the Center for Air Force History for their assistance in locating photographs and research material; Felix Lowe, Director of the Smithsonian Institution Press, for his encouragement; Dr. Von Hardesty, Barney

Turner, Jim Colburn, George Larson, Pat Trenner, and Bill Hardaker for their helpful comments on various sections of the book.

My wife, Glindel, even more than in my earlier memoir, *Into the Teeth of the Tiger,* played a major role in the composition of this book. In addition to her more mundane roles of spelling specialist, typo tyrant, and grammar guru, she contributed greatly to the content. We were together at Eglin Air Force Base for much of the period covered, and she had firsthand knowledge of the individuals and events described and thus was able to fine-tune my memory. But more than that, her sensitivity and insight in making suggestions in areas I never would have considered made it less an engineering report and more a book.

Prologue

Tuesday, May 11, 1948, Eglin Air Force Base, Florida

The hot Florida sun beat down on my canopy as I circled over Range 52. Maj. Si Johnson was leading our flight of four in a P-84B with Leonard Koehler, Fred Belue, and me in P-80s. Len was flying Si's wing, and I was leading the second element. We were at 5,000 feet waiting for a flight of six B-29s to arrive over the range at 500 feet so that we could make a simulated attack as the final event of a fire-power demonstration.

A voice crackled in my earphones, "Si, this is range control. The B-twenty-nines are two minutes out, altitude five hundred feet, heading zero-niner-zero. You are cleared for your attack."

Si replied, "Roger. We'll hit them just in front of the stands." He started a slow descending turn to position us. When the bombers crossed the boundary of the range, we nosed down into a steep dive to the north and then swung to the right into a curve of pursuit on the bombers. As we completed the pass, we began a steep climbing turn to the right. I thought that it must have looked great from the stands, because Si had timed it right on the money. It's always a good feeling when a mission goes like clockwork.

The good feeling was short-lived, however. My eyes were glued to Len's P-80 when, suddenly, from the corner of my eye, I saw Si's P-84 dis-integrate. The pieces hurtled into the ground, sending up a tremendous cloud of dust and debris. It happened so fast that I couldn't believe my eyes. My first thought was that he must have collided with another airplane, but we were past the B-29s, and our three P-80s were intact. I yelled into the oxygen-mask mike, "What happened, Len?"

"Beats the hell out of me," he replied. "The plane just broke into pieces. Si didn't have a chance."

Just then range control broke in and tersely ordered all planes to return to Eglin and land. I took the lead, and we proceeded back to the field in stunned silence.

1

Fighter Pilot's Heaven

As I finished my combat tour with the 75th Fighter Squadron of the 23rd Fighter Group in China,* the group commander, Col. Ed Rector, one of the Flying Tigers of the American Volunteer Group (AVG), told me I should request an assignment as a fighter test pilot at Eglin Field, Florida, when I got back to the States. I agreed enthusiastically, since that was one of my ambitions. Accordingly, he gave me a letter of recommendation to the commander at Eglin.

I was delighted when, after my leave and stay at the Army Air Forces (AAF) processing center at Miami Beach, I was ordered to report to the 611th Proof Test Group at Eglin for assignment as a fighter test pilot. On June 5, 1945, after a long and boring train trip to Crestview, Florida, via Jacksonville, I reported for duty at Eglin.

Eglin Field was the headquarters of the Air Proving Ground Command. All Army Air Force aircraft, weapons, and flight equipment were tested there for operational suitability. At Wright Field in Ohio and Muroc (later Edwards Air Force Base) in California, aircraft were tested as aircraft, to ensure that they met their design specifications. At Eglin, they were tested as weapons to determine their compatibility with various types of armament and the best method of employment. It was a particularly desirable assignment because of the opportunity to fly many different types of aircraft, including the latest models. Equally exciting was the chance to use

_____
*See *Into the Teeth of the Tiger* (New York: Bantam, 1986).

the experience I had gained in combat to influence the design of the aircraft I was to test.

Eglin Field, with nine auxiliary fields and dozens of bombing and gunnery ranges, is the largest military facility in the United States, covering some 724 square miles of slash pine, scrub oak, and palmetto. It is situated on the Gulf of Mexico about halfway between Panama City and Pensacola. The beaches along that stretch of the Gulf are among the most beautiful in the world, with snow-white sand, reed-covered dunes, and bright blue-green water. Much of the gunnery was done over the water ranges a few miles offshore.

After checking in at Command and Group headquarters, I was told to report to the commanding officer (C.O.) of Squadron 611B, the fighter test squadron. The C.O., Major Muldoon, greeted me with well-disguised enthusiasm, saying, "Not another damn P-forty pilot from China. Doesn't Ed Rector ever quit? Well, I guess I'm stuck with you. Report to the operations officer, Major Schoenfeldt." I thought that was a most unpromising beginning to my career as a test pilot, but as I got to know Major Muldoon I found that though he ran a taut squadron and demanded the best from everyone, he was very fair and had a great sense of humor. He was also in a class by himself as a needler. He had commanded a P-38 squadron in North Africa, and Major Schoenfeldt had served under him there.

Major Schoenfeldt was dark-haired and stocky with a perennial smile. He too was a needler, but not quite in Major Muldoon's class. He greeted me pleasantly and gave me pilot's handbooks for the various types of planes in the fighter squadron, saying that I would have to pass a written exam on each plane before I could be checked out in it. Since virtually all the planes were single seaters, the first flight would, of necessity, be solo.

As I went from Major Schoenfeldt's office into the operations room a familiar voice said, "Well, Lope, it's about time you were getting here." It was Dick Jones, one of my best friends, whom I had known since my first day of active duty and who was my roommate in China. We had both flown the Curtiss P-40 Warhawk and the North American P-51 Mustang in the 75th Fighter Squadron in the 14th Air Force. In fact, we had flown our first air combat on the same mission when we scrambled as part of a group of twelve P-40s to intercept Japanese bombers that were attacking our base at Hengyang. On that flight Dick had shot down two Lily bombers while I had knocked down an Oscar fighter by running into it on a head-on pass for the first of my five victories. Seeing Dick was a pleasant surprise, since I had no idea that he was at Eglin. He had left for the States about a month before I did. He said that Major Cruickshank, also from China, was in the squadron. I began to see what Major Muldoon had meant by his P-40 pilot remark.

The 23rd Fighter Group had been formed in China to replace the Flying Tigers of the AVG when it was disbanded on July 4, 1942. Both Tex Hill and Ed Rector, who commanded the 23rd, were aces with the AVG, and Tex was the commander when I reported as a green, nineteen-year-old second lieutenant.

That night, in the club, Dick introduced me to Maj. Barney Turner, one of the most experienced and best-liked pilots in the squadron. Barney was about six feet tall, handsome, quiet, and very pleasant. He had flown P-40s in North Africa with the 79th Fighter Group of the Desert Task Force and had been at Eglin for about a year. He said his roommate was on temporary duty away from Eglin and I could room with him until he returned. Fortunately his roommate's transfer became permanent, and we roomed together for several years. Barney, Dick, and I became a well-known bachelor threesome and remain good friends to this day.

Dick, with his usual enthusiasm, told me that we had found fighter pilot's heaven. We had P-51Ds and Hs, P-38s, P-47s, P-63s, P-61s, a P-59 (the first U.S. jet), and all the ammunition in the world. What more could a fighter pilot ask?

The next morning I hesitatingly told Major Schoenfeldt that he had given me the pilot's handbook for the Martin B-26 Marauder, a *bomber,* by mistake. He said it wasn't a mistake, that the squadron had a B-26 to tow targets, and all the pilots had to take a turn at flying it. I protested that I had never flown a bomber, but he replied that neither had any of the other pilots in the squadron until they checked out in the B-26. Early in the war the B-26 had a reputation as a very hot and dangerous airplane. It was a bit short of wing area and had almost no margin for error with one engine out. Built in Baltimore, it was nicknamed the Baltimore Whore because it had no visible means of support. I was particularly conscious of its reputation because there was a B-26 group based at MacDill Field in Tampa, my hometown, and its slogan was "One a day in Tampa Bay." The B-26 was later extensively modified, and it compiled a very good record in the war.

A few days later, after an orientation flight as copilot in a CQ-3 (a Beech C-45 rigged as a mother ship for drones), I saw that I was to fly the next morning as copilot with Major Muldoon in the B-26. I carefully reviewed the pilot's handbook and questionnaire, somewhat apprehensive about checking out in a bomber, and with no less than the commanding officer.

Early the next morning I attended the flight briefing and walked out to the B-26 with Major Muldoon. I climbed into the copilot's seat, and after we were strapped in I said, "What do you want me to do?" He said, "Nothing." That was well within my capabilities, so I put my hands in my lap and watched him closely. We took off and climbed toward the gunnery range over the Gulf. It was much quieter and smoother than the B-25 I'd ridden in while in China. He set it on course roughly paralleling the beach, and the tow-reel operator reeled out the target. He then told me to take the controls and hold it on course. When we got to the end of the range he took the controls, made a 180-degree turn, then gave it back to me. Barney Turner was firing on our target with a P-38, and before he went back to re-arm he flew formation with us for a few minutes. I had never been close to a P-38 in flight; it was a beautiful sight with its twin booms and two counter-rotating propellers, all shining in the bright Florida sun. We P-40 pilots liked to tell P-38 pilots that the P-38 was nothing more than two P-40s with a Link Trainer in between, but I chose not to mention that to Major Muldoon.

After about three rather boring hours we landed, and as we walked back toward operations Major Muldoon said, "Well, Lopez, now you're checked out." I asked him, "What do you do if one engine quits?" He said, "In this squadron, engines don't quit!" and he was right. We never had an engine failure in the squadron while he was C.O., although we had several in later years.

It doesn't make much sense, but pilots who were trained on single-engine aircraft worry more about losing an engine in a twin-engine plane than they do in a single-engine. In single-engine airplanes you have only three choices, a dead-stick landing, a belly landing, or a bailout. In twin-engines you often have to fly for long distances on one engine operating under the stress of higher power, and you have to make a proper approach the first time because you usually don't get a second chance. I had a fair amount of twin-engine time before I got over that feeling. Later in my career I lost an engine once in a Douglas A-26 and three times in B-25s but had no trouble landing safely all four times.

The next day the fun began. I checked out in the first of the squadron's fighters, a Bell P-63 Kingcobra. This airplane was much beloved by the Russians, who were furnished them under lend-lease, largely because its 37mm cannon was effective against tanks and because Russians, for reasons known only to God, prefer flying at tree-top level. Low-level capability was what they wanted. The AAF found it unsuitable for combat because it, like its predecessor the Bell P-39 Airacobra, had limited range and poor high-altitude performance. I found it an enjoyable airplane to fly, maneuverable and easy to handle. The Allison V-12 engine was mounted behind the pilot and drove the propeller via a long shaft that went under the cockpit, leaving room in the nose for the cannon that fired through the propeller hub. It was a bit disconcerting when the engine was started because the instrument panel became a blur and the alcohol in the compass was churned to a froth until the engine smoothed out. Sometime later I was checking out one of the bomber pilots in the P-63. When he started the engine and the vibration began, he cut the engine and said, "What the hell is the matter?" I replied, "Nothing. It always starts like that." He didn't reply but quickly got out of the cockpit and walked away, never to return.

That evening I saw to my surprise that I, with a total of three hours copilot time, was to fly the B-26 the next morning with Dick Jones, who had never even been in it as copilot. As we climbed in, Dick jokingly remarked that because we were both single-engine fighter pilots we should each fly one engine. The long-suffering flight engineer, a grizzled sergeant with hundreds of hours in the B-26, knew I'd been in it only once and wondered what ill fate had put him in this squadron of super-hot fighter pilots. He kept a wary eye on us to be sure that we didn't do anything stupid enough to kill him.

A few minutes later he almost had a wary black eye and a concussion as well. Shortly after we started to taxi I applied the brakes to slow down a bit, but to my surprise the wheels locked. We stopped so suddenly that the flight engineer, who was standing between the pilots, was hurled forward onto the console. When I apologized for the sudden stop, he said he should have been ready, as all the fighter pilots did that on their first flight as pilot. Fighter brakes have to be applied firmly, but the B-26 had power brakes that had to be used gently. Automobile drivers who have switched from standard hydraulic to power brakes are familiar with this problem.

After that the flight went smoothly enough, with Dick and me sharing the flying, but I had a bit of trouble in the landing pattern. On my first try I put the base leg in so close that I couldn't make the turn to line up with the runway without making a vertical bank, which none of us, especially the flight engineer, thought was advisable. I went around and on the next approach moved the base leg out a bit and was able to turn onto final with only a 70-degree bank, which felt okay to Dick and me, if not to the engineer. The landing was fine, and I was very gentle with the brakes as we taxied back to the flight line. We parked and cut the engines, and now Dick, too, was a bomber pilot. I'm sure, however, the flight engineer hoped that we would stick to flying fighters.

During the next few weeks I was checked out in the P-47D Thunderbolt, the P-38L Lightning, the CQ-3 (C-45), the P-47N, the P-61 Black Widow, the P-51H, and rechecked out in the P-51D and the AT-6, which we used for instrument training. If this wasn't Valhalla, it was damn close to it.

On June 21, I became a member of a select group of pilots when I was checked out in the Bell P-59A Airacomet, the first U.S. jet. It was powered by two small General Electric turbojet engines based on the design of Sir Frank Whittle, the British inventor of the jet engine, whom I was privileged to get to know some thirty-five years later at the National Air and Space Museum. Aside from being jet powered, it was not an impressive airplane. It was not very fast or maneuverable and had limited range. It even looked rather clumsy and confirmed the pilot's maxim that an airplane that looks good, flies good—not terribly profound, but generally true.

On the day of my checkout I climbed from the large shoulder-high wing down into the bathtublike cockpit, where Barney Turner briefed me on the starting procedure. It was quite simple: you just pressed the button for the left engine, waited until the rpm reached 10 percent, then opened the stopcock. The rise in tail-pipe temperature and engine rpm were the only indications that the engine was running. You could barely hear it in the cockpit when it was at idle rpm (about 35 percent). You then repeated the procedure for the right engine.

I was surprised that almost full power was required to get the P-59 moving. I probably shouldn't have been, since the two engines together generated only 3,200 pounds of thrust and the airplane weighed about 14,000 pounds. I taxied directly to the runway and lined up for takeoff. It seemed strange to eliminate the engine run-up and magneto check that I had performed on every flight until this one.

I ran the engines up to full power, 100 percent (16,800 rpm), and released the brakes. Instead of pushing me back in the seat with its acceleration, it gained speed very slowly. The engines were so smooth and silent that I had the eerie feeling that the plane shouldn't be moving. I felt as though I were in a glider being pulled by an invisible tow plane. Gen. Adolf Galland, leader of the Luftwaffe fighters in World War II and a 104-victory ace, had somewhat the same feeling on his first jet flight in an Me 262. He, however, expressed it much better when he said, "It felt like the angels were pushing." Years later I was to meet and get to know General

Galland, and we have had many long conversations on World War II and aviation in general.

There was only enough fuel for about forty minutes of flight, so I climbed up to 20,000 feet—where fuel consumption was much lower— and ran through a few maneuvers to get the feel of the airplane. It was slow for a jet but cruised much faster than propeller fighters. Its rate of roll was quite slow, which was expected because of its large wing area. It accelerated well in a dive without the drag of a propeller but was difficult to slow down for the same reason. These effects were more pronounced in the P-80, which was a much cleaner aircraft. I returned to the field and found that landing the P-59 was quite easy because of its wide gear and large flaps. Because of its poor performance, only a small number were built, and they were used to initiate pilots into the mysteries of jet flying. Nevertheless, I was proud to have flown the first American jet.

I was now officially a jet pilot, which gave me a sense of accomplishment even though it wasn't much of a thrill. The real excitement came about six months later when I checked out in the Lockheed P-80 Shooting Star, the AAF's first operational jet fighter.

2

Bombs Bursting in Air

One type of mission I particularly enjoyed was chasing, and occasionally shooting down, JB-2s, an American copy of the
German V-1. In the latter part of World War II, the Germans
introduced the first of their so-called vengeance weapons, the V-1 flying
bomb. A forerunner of the present-day cruise missile, the V-1 was a pilotless
airplane powered by a pulse-jet engine. Launched from ramps in German-
occupied Europe by jettisonable rockets, it held its heading and altitude
by means of a gyro-stabilized autopilot. Range was controlled by counting
the revolutions of a rotor, driven by the airflow, until a preset number
had been reached. At that point, the engine was shut off and the V-1 would
dive into whatever was below it, detonating the explosive-filled nose on
impact.

It was not very accurate but was effective against large targets like
London. Its effectiveness was increased by its characteristics. The engine
made a loud, deep buzzing sound that could be heard from a great distance. As long as the people on the ground could hear it, they were safe;
but once the noise stopped, they knew it had started its final dive, and they
had little time to seek shelter.

Although many were shot down by Allied fighters, the menace continued until the Allies had driven the German ground forces so far back
that the V-1s did not have the range to reach England. In those operations,
a number of V-1s were captured intact and brought back to the United
States for testing. Much of the testing of the V-1s and JB-2s was done at

Eglin, for possible use against the Japanese, by the First Experimental Guided Missile Squadron, of which more later.

The captured buzz bombs, as we called them (the British called them doodle bugs), were launched over the Gulf from Santa Rosa Island, a narrow strip of pristine white sand, now filled with high-rise condominiums, between the inland waterway off Choctawhatchee Bay and the Gulf. The fighter test squadron was responsible for providing fighter cover for the buzz bombs until they crashed into the Gulf or were far enough from the shore to no longer pose a threat to the populace. Since the buzz bombs' speed was greater than that of any of the fighters, we were unable to keep up with them in level flight. In order to cover the launches we used two pairs of fighters (P-51s and P-63s). The first two fighters circled at an altitude of about 5,000 feet just inland from the launch site. As the launch countdown began, those fighters began a full-power dive toward the site, timed to be just behind and to either side of the buzz bomb as it was launched. They stayed with the buzz bomb during its short climb to 500 or 1,000 feet. Then they trailed it at full power until their speed began to drop off and they fell out of gun range. At that point, the second pair of fighters, following at about 10,000 feet, would dive down and take up the chase. In that way the fighters were able to stay within firing distance of the buzz bomb until it had reached a safe distance from the coast.

Of course we all hoped for the bomb to malfunction and start to turn so that we could shoot it down. This happened quite often; I shot down two with a P-51, and the next year, flying a P-80, which was faster than the bomb, I shot down two more. The last two had been air-launched from B-17 bombers and were shot down just off the beach as part of our fire-power demonstrations. The JB-2s were much faster than the Japanese Oscars and Tojos I was used to fighting, but fortunately, they took no evasive action and never fired back.

I preferred to be in one of the first two fighters so as not to fly so far out over the Gulf. My engine always seemed to run rougher as the shoreline receded and then smooth out again as I approached the beach. Learning firsthand how to ditch a fighter was definitely not one of my goals.

On one launch, in addition to testing the buzz bomb, we were using it as a target to test a new type of proximity fuse. Our rockets were supposed to explode if they passed within about ten feet of the target, destroying the buzz bomb with shrapnel. In addition to the four regular fighters, I was flying a P-47D armed with eight proximity-fused, five-inch High-Velocity Aircraft Rockets (HVARs). I remained at altitude until the second pair of fighters had taken over, then dived to get into position behind the buzz bomb and fire the rockets. Approaching it, I noticed that I was closing too fast and had to S-turn sharply in order to stay behind it. Its autopilot had gone out of whack, causing it to slow down and fly in a nose-high attitude just above stalling speed. I slowed to about the same speed and tried to get into firing position, but the P-47 was at such a high angle of attack that I had to descend well below the buzz bomb to get my gunsight on the target. As I wallowed along I decided to fire before the target spun in on its own accord. I didn't have high hopes of hitting the target, and my fears were realized. None of the rockets got close enough to trigger the fuses. The buzz bomb flew along in a semistall for about fifty more miles before it ran out of fuel and dived into the sea.

On another occasion the buzz bomb ran amok as the fighter pairs were changing positions, leading to what could have been a disaster. It pulled up suddenly to about 5,000 feet, nearly stalled, then made a diving turn down to 500 feet and headed for the shore. The first two fighters were unable to catch up, and the high fighters lost sight of it momentarily against the water. It continued shoreward, but the fighters were unable to fire for fear of hitting someone. They doggedly continued to pursue it inland for about thirty miles until it crashed near De Funiak Springs, a small town northeast of Eglin. We were greatly relieved when the pilots reported that it had crashed in an open area and no one had been hurt. Shortly afterward, we received three separate reports of the crash through the state police, and two of the witnesses said they had seen the pilot bail out before the crash. So much for the accuracy of eyewitness reports.

The experimental guided missile squadron, or XGM, later did some extensive testing of methods for air launching the buzz bombs from B-17s, as I mentioned earlier, leading eventually to the air-launched cruise missiles in use today.

In addition to the buzz-bomb chases, most of the tests I flew while learning the test-pilot trade consisted of delivering some type of ordnance against ground targets. There was a wide variety of targets on the many Eglin ranges, including airplanes, trucks, cars, buildings, concrete bunkers, and groups of foxholes. We used .50-caliber machine guns, 20mm cannon, all types and sizes of bombs and rockets, and napalm. The type and amount of damage inflicted by each attack were carefully measured by specialists at the ranges.

When we dropped bombs or fired rockets to test the accuracy of the sights and delivery techniques, the impact points of each release were measured by triangulation from towers on the three corners of each range. The range controller would inform the pilot, as he circled into position for another pass, of the accuracy of his previous effort. One day I was firing five-inch HVARs in pairs from a P-51 at a ground target to test a new sight. I had fired four of the ten rockets on two passes and was starting my turn onto the target for the third pass when the controller radioed that my last rockets had been three feet over and one foot left of the target. I replied, "Roger," but instead of pressing the microphone button on the throttle with my left thumb, I pressed the rocket firing button on the stick with my right thumb. Two rockets blasted off in the general direction of one of the range towers. Fortunately, they missed it by a wide margin, but apparently I was shaken up much more than the controller, because he came on the air and calmly said, "Your last rockets were one half mile short and one mile to the right." I apologized and subsequently made certain that the rocket arming switch was turned off between passes.

A short time later Major Muldoon called me in and said that he had received a request from Tyndall Field, an AAF field about sixty miles to the east on the Gulf coast near Panama City, Florida, to make a night napalm drop as a demonstration for an ordnance orientation course. A P-38 had been loaded with two 150-gallon tanks of napalm, and I was to fly it to Tyndall, contact the lieutenant in charge, make the drop at the prescribed time, and return to Eglin. Accordingly, in the late afternoon, I climbed into the P-38, flew to Tyndall, and went into operations to find the ordnance officer. He was waiting there and seemed excited that we had acceded to his request. He had a pilot, a P-38, and 300 gallons of napalm at his disposal.

I told the lieutenant that I wanted to see the target before the demonstration. Much to my surprise, he drove me to a vacant field, 150 feet square, in the middle of the barracks area. It was lighted and lined with bleachers for lectures and demonstrations. He blithely said, "I want you to drop the tanks in the middle of this lot when I finish my lecture. The tower will notify you."

"Lieutenant," I exclaimed, "you must be out of your mind. I don't know if your lecture will be done well, but I know your students will be well done if I drop the napalm here. It will fry everyone in these bleachers and burn up half the base!"

He insisted that I was wrong because he was an ordnance officer and by definition knew more about it than I. Obviously, he didn't realize that a fighter pilot couldn't be wrong on any subject involving flying, especially when arguing with a mere mortal without wings on his chest. I curtly told him that I had dropped a lot of napalm, and there was no way I would drop it there, but I would drop it along the beach if no one was within 1,000 feet. He became angry, insisting that I had been sent there to drop the napalm and that he would take full responsibility. I'd had enough of the discussion, so I said, "Forget it. I'm going back to Eglin." As I walked away he threatened to go to the base commander. "Be my guest," I replied, and returned to the flight line.

I was climbing into the plane when a harried-looking sergeant rushed up and said the base commander wanted to see me right away. As I was being driven to the colonel's office, I hoped he wouldn't order me to make the drop, because then I would have to refuse a direct order, something I had never done and hoped never to do.

When I walked in and saluted he growled, "What in the hell is this all about?" I carefully explained to him that the proposed target for the napalm was too close to the grandstands and barracks for safety, and I refused to make the drop. "I thought you Eglin guys could hit any target," he said.

"Sir, I can hit the target," I replied, "but I can't stop the napalm from spreading to the bleachers and barracks."

He walked to an aerial photograph of Tyndall mounted on the wall and sarcastically asked me to point out this impossible target. When I showed him the small field in the middle of his base he exclaimed, "Jesus Christ!" His manner quickly changed, and he turned to me and said, "When you return to Eglin please give my compliments to your commanding officer and thank him for his cooperation." I saluted, and as I left the office, I heard him telling his secretary to get that pea-brained ordnance officer there on the double.

Approaching Eglin, I asked the tower to have the ordnance men meet me because I still had 300 gallons of napalm aboard. They would have the difficult task of unloading the tanks and disposing of it. I hoped that they knew how to perform this task, since it was unlikely they had ever faced the problem. Napalm is a combination of a gelling compound and gasoline that is mixed just prior to loading. I still don't know how they got the glop out of the tanks. It seemed about as difficult as getting toothpaste back in the tube, but they did it, and I didn't ask how.

A few days later Major Muldoon told me that I would be the test officer for the .60-caliber gun test. The test officer not only flies most of the missions but is also responsible for meeting the goals of the test and forwarding the data and pilot's reports to the project officer. In this case the project officer was Lieutenant Colonel Moon, at Wright Field. A few years later, when I attended the Air Force Test Pilot School at Wright, he was the commanding officer.

The next day I ferried a P-51 to Wright Field and met with Colonel Moon to be briefed on the project. The .60-caliber guns had been ground tested at Wright Field's armament lab, and two of them had been mounted in the nose of a P-38 for preliminary air-firing tests. This weapon was designed with a larger projectile and increased muzzel velocity to make it a heavier hitter and to give it greater range than the standard .50-caliber gun.

When we drove to the flight line to inspect the P-38, I was amazed to see how far the muzzles projected in front of the nose. The normal four .50-caliber machine guns and one 20mm cannon armament of the P-38 did not extend beyond the nose, but these two .60-caliber guns protruded about three feet beyond it. They looked like Kentucky long rifles. I hoped they were as accurate as those frontier weapons were reputed to be.

After being checked out on the operation of the gun switches and recorder cameras, I went back to base operations to file a clearance for the flight back to Eglin and bumped into Barney Turner, who had been at Wright Field for several days on another project. He was walking out to the P-38 with me when we met another pilot just returning from a flight, carrying his parachute back into operations. Barney greeted him and then said, "Lope, I'd like you to meet Chuck Yeager. We flew together at Muroc on the accelerated service test of the P-eighty." We shook hands and exchanged a few pleasantries, then went on our respective ways. Yeager had not yet begun his legendary career as a test pilot, but he was a maintenance officer in the Flight Test Division and as such flew all the fighters. Our paths were to cross many times, and since 1979 he has generously given an annual talk on his experiences, and on various aspects of aviation, at the National Air and Space Museum. Incidentally, his talks are by far the most popular in the museum's lecture series.

Back at Eglin our armorers thoroughly inspected the gun installation and fired a few hundred rounds through both guns on the ground range, which was normal procedure before beginning the flying phase of a test. When they were satisfied, I began flying several missions a day with the object of firing a thousand rounds through each gun, at constantly increasing g-loads, to test the feed mechanism. The gunnery range was over the Gulf, about one mile from shore, with all firing straight out to sea. To accomplish this, especially at the higher g-loads, I had to dive toward the beach from about 8,000 feet down to 5,000 feet, the firing altitude, and roll into a tight turn so that I would have the proper g-load established in a steady state by the time I was heading out to sea. I would then fire a short burst and start climbing back into position for another pass. The test went well, and we had no problems with the guns jamming up through 6 g's, which was the maximum called for by the test program. I had serious doubts, however, about the accuracy of the guns in that mounting configuration. When they were fired, the ends of the barrels wavered wildly through two or three inches. It would have been next to impossible to hit a target at any reasonable range. After I wrote that in my report, Major Muldoon flew one of the missions to confirm my findings. Upon landing he said that the airplane would have to go back to the armament laboratory at Wright Field for new gun mounts before we could start firing for accuracy.

Previously, I had flown several night missions to determine how much the gun's flash interfered with the pilot's vision. That was the first time I had ever done any firing at night, so I had no idea what to expect. I didn't think there would be a problem, because the barrels were so long, but was I ever wrong. Fortunately, Barney had told me to keep one eye closed while firing, so I would retain my night vision in that eye no matter how bright the flash.

I made the flight on a dark, moonless night to achieve the maximum effect. Once over the Gulf range at 5,000 feet, I armed the guns, closed one eye, and pulled the trigger. The sky lit up like the Fourth of July. A flame-thrower would have generated less light. Barney's advice proved essential, because I couldn't even make out the instrument panel with the open eye. I expended the rest of the ammunition on several more firing passes, then circled for about fifteen minutes—until my night vision returned—before landing.

Shortly thereafter, Colonel Moon came to Eglin and, following a discussion of the firing results, decided to take the P-38 back to Wright Field to modify the .60-caliber gun system. The armament lab, however, after studying the data, decided to cancel the test. The extensive modifications and further testing that would have been required were deemed unlikely to produce a new operational weapon before the war ended.

I had been so busy since arriving at Eglin that I hadn't given much thought to the war. Although the war in Europe had ended, it was still raging in the Pacific. The B-29s from Tinian and Saipan, under Gen. Curtis E. LeMay's innovative leadership, had burned out many Japanese cities with incendiary bombs while Army and Navy fighters were attacking the coastal cities. Even though there was little doubt that Japan would be defeated, its fanatical defense, to the last man, of Iwo Jima and Okinawa earlier in the

In the early sixties I was assigned to the Air Force War Plans Division in the Pentagon and regularly briefed General LeMay, then the chief of staff. Along with most of the briefing officers, I was in awe of the general and much relieved each time I escaped unscathed from another briefing.

In June 1990, General LeMay lectured on strategic bombing at the National Air and Space Museum. In that lecture he said that the only two Americans who could speak with authority on successful strategic bombing campaigns were Gen. Jimmy Doolittle and himself, and since he was the youngest, at 83, he was delivering the lecture.

He spoke with visible emotion on the great disparity in the results of the bombing efforts against Japan and against North Vietnam. In Japan, the 500,000 tons of bombs that were dropped brought Japan to the point of surrender, and he was convinced that the surrender would have come within a few months, even without the atomic bombs. In Vietnam some 6.5 million tons of bombs were dropped without any decisive effect. The crucial difference was target selection: the Japanese targets were selected by the military commanders on the scene, but the Vietnamese targets were selected by civilians in Washington with little or no military experience.

At a small dinner preceding the lecture I saw another side of General LeMay. When the bread was served, one of the guests who knew him well mentioned that General LeMay baked fresh bread nearly every day. Since I too bake bread regularly we got into a discussion on various types of bread. He asked if I baked French bread, and if so, did I spray it every five minutes during its baking. When I said that I did, he asked what I used as a sprayer. I said, "I use an old Windex bottle." He smiled and said, "So do I." Sadly, that lecture was his last public appearance. He suffered a heart attack and died in September of that year.

year indicated that the planned invasion of the Japanese mainland would be a long and bloody struggle. I fully expected that after completing a year at Eglin I would again be assigned to a combat fighter squadron to continue my war with the Japanese, but I hoped I would be flying something a little more advanced than the P-40. With the skills and experience attained in a year at Eglin, I was sure to be a more formidable antagonist.

On August 6, 1945, the first atomic bomb was dropped on Hiroshima, and on August 9 a second hit Nagasaki. Although it was difficult to comprehend how a single bomb could have the destructive power of some 20,000 tons of TNT, we realized that no country, however fanatical, could stand up to that kind of destruction. We didn't realize it at the time, but a whole new era, the atomic age, had begun. An all-out nuclear war could not only win a war but also destroy both sides, if not all life on Earth. A new vocabulary, previously used only by scientists, came into being. Words like "fission," "fusion," "radioactivity," "gamma ray," and "megadeath" became common.

At Eglin, life went on as usual until the night of August 15, when, in the middle of a party at the beach club, our group commander was called to the phone. Upon concluding the conversation, he asked for our attention and announced, "Japan has surrendered. The war is over!" After a brief, stunned silence, the cheering and hilarity began. Lieutenants were pouring drinks on majors; people were singing and kissing and toasting and drinking and drinking. Although I had never felt there was a good enough reason to take a drink before or during the war, this occasion seemed to warrant one. At the urging of many friends I filled a tumbler with bourbon and drank it using a borrowed brier pipe as a straw. It made me, and several of the observers, sick. To date I have never found an event worthy of another drink. Although we believed the news, it was several days before the reality sank in that the killing had ended, and we had not only won but also survived the war.

The war had lasted almost six years. Millions, a shocking two thirds of them helpless civilians, had been killed or maimed. Thousands of square miles of territory had been devastated, including magnificent cities, cathedrals, and monuments that had survived for centuries. The ocean bottoms were littered with shattered ships, submarines, airplanes, and the bones of their crews. Mankind hoped that the atomic bomb would make future wars impossible. It was not to be, but so far at least, it has been a deterrent to world wars.

3

Tigercat Performance

t first, nothing much changed with the ending of the war. The great war machine that the United States had forged in the last few years had too much momentum to stop instantly. The production miracle that had armed the U.S. troops, along with most of the Allies as well, would have to make a transition to peacetime production. There was a great demand for all types of civilian goods, since their production had practically ceased during the war. Automobiles, tires, large and small appliances, and many other so-called necessities were unobtainable and would remain so until the factories could make the transition.

The armed services, too, would have to return to peacetime status, which would entail a great reduction in manpower and equipment. The government planned to carry out this reduction in an orderly manner, keeping enough troops to meet our occupation requirements in Europe and Asia with a large enough establishment in the ZI (Zone of the Interior—which is what the Army, for some reason, calls the United States) to support the overseas troops. At the time we thought that the occupation would be relatively short-lived. I'm sure no one had any idea that almost fifty years later we would still maintain large forces in the countries of our allies and former enemies Germany and Japan.

The United States, however, had no strong tradition of peacetime military service, and within a month of the surrender, members of Congress were besieged with letters urging them to bring the boys home and get them out of service so they could take up their lives where they had left off.

Sadly, there were many homes to which the boys would never return. The government was forced to release all the eligible servicemen and -women just as fast as they could be processed. Eligibility was determined by a system of points awarded for total service, overseas service, combat, wounds, and decorations. Because of congressional pressure the number of points required for discharge was steadily reduced. By the end of 1945 entire units had been dissolved and the military services had been depleted almost to the point of becoming nonfunctional. It took about a year for the remaining units to regain full strength.

Many of the officers and the majority of the enlisted personnel left the service as soon as possible to return to college or to resume their previous careers. A major factor that influenced the rapid exodus from the service was the G.I. Bill of Rights, passed by the Congress and signed into law by President Franklin Roosevelt on June 22, 1944. In addition to low-cost loans for homes and businesses and unemployment benefits, it provided discharged servicemen with subsistence and tuition for higher education and other approved training for a period equal to the time spent in service plus twelve months. Some seven million veterans took advantage of either the education or training assistance, to the great benefit of the veterans and the country. The education benefits especially allowed many thousands of veterans whose prewar circumstances could never have financed a college education to enter the professions and achieve goals that would have been beyond their reach otherwise.

My squadron was left with only the career enlisted men and a few short-time draftees to perform the aircraft maintenance and other vital squadron functions. Fortunately, we had some outstanding master and tech sergeants who by great effort allowed us to maintain our test flying schedules at almost the same level as during the war.

Two that I remember in particular were Billy P. and Daniel T. Brannon, identical twin master sergeants who were line chief and hangar chief respectively, or vice versa. They were master sergeants in every sense of the word. What they didn't know about aircraft maintenance wasn't worth knowing. Their knowledge, dedication, and attitude made them the rarest of individuals, truly indispensable. Many years later, when I was teaching thermodynamics at the Air Force Academy, a young doolie (freshman) came to see me. He was the son of a retired Master Sergeant Brannon, and regardless of which twin it was, I jumped at the chance to tell him how much I thought of his father and how invaluable he had been to our squadron.

I had no intention of getting out of the Army Air Forces. My job as an Eglin test pilot was one of the choice assignments in the AAF and far exceeded my boyhood dreams. I knew the jets were coming, and I wanted to be in on the ground floor. I intended to make the Air Force my career, as did my closest friends, Dick Jones and Barney Turner. So for us, the end of the war had almost no effect on our daily lives; the flight testing went on as before.

As young bachelors and fighter pilots our lives were almost idyllic. We lived in bachelor officer quarters just a short distance from both the flight line and the officer's club, where we took our meals. On weekends we had a choice of personal cross-country flights, dancing at the club with lovely southern belles, or swimming and sunning at the beach club and admiring those same belles. Often, flying to other cities to see different belles (southern or northern) won out.

Also, many of the married pilots and their wives—Schoeny and Jean Schoenfeldt, Pete and Carol Bedford, and Bill and Emmy Cavoli in particular—saw to it that we ate properly by regularly inviting us to dinner. We spent a lot of time with them at their homes and at the beach. Bill and Emmy had no children at that time and sort of adopted us. Emmy, being a good Italian, thought that if you could walk away from the table, she had not fed you enough. Often, what I thought was the full meal was just the appetizer.

We had no major duties other than flying many different fighters. If there was no specific test flight scheduled, we could always find a reason to take up the planes for an hour or so of aerobatics or rat racing.

The Gulf coast has large buildups of cumulus clouds almost every afternoon in the summer, and they gave me some of my fondest lifetime memories. Often at the end of scheduled flying for the day, Barney, Dick, and I would take off in three fighters of the same or different types, climb up in formation to near the top of the clouds, and then peel off into a rat race (aerial follow the leader), diving into cloud canyons, zooming up over cloud mountains, rolling over the top, and then diving down again. As we flew between the clouds and the sun, we could see the shadow of the airplane on the cloud surrounded by a rainbow-colored halo. If I had to choose one thing to do for the rest of my life, that would be it. Who knows, when fighter pilots die maybe they fill the heavens in their favorite airplanes, encircled in rainbows. If so, most of my best friends will be there, and we'll have one hell of an eternal rat race.

In early August three Navy fighters had been delivered to Eglin for us to test for possible AAF use: a Grumman F7F Tigercat, a Grumman F8F Bearcat, and a Ryan FR-1 Fireball. The Tigercat was a powerful, heavily armed twin-engine fighter powered by two 2,000-horsepower Pratt & Whitney R-2800 engines, the same engines used in the P-47, B-26, P-61, and Douglas A-26 Invader, as well as the Navy's Grumman F6F Hellcat and Chance Vought F4U Corsair. Ours was a single-seat version, but there was also a two-seat night-fighter model. It did not see action in World War II, but the night fighter was later used by the Marines in Korea.

The F8F, a small fighter that is still flown today, consisted of a large propeller and an R-2800 engine dragging a small cockpit and wings along for the ride. Delivered to the Navy in 1945, it never saw combat in World War II, but with various modifications it has been a regular winner on the unlimited air-race circuit and has set many speed and time-to-climb records, flown by pilots like Darryl Greenamyer and Lyle Shelton. It was flown to Eglin by a Grumman test pilot who then demonstrated its performance by doing an Immelmann (a half loop followed by a half roll) on takeoff. It was quite impressive, since most fighters did not have a high enough power-to-weight ratio to perform that maneuver.

The FR-1 was a hybrid fighter powered by both a reciprocating and a jet engine. It mounted a 1,350-horsepower Wright R-1820 engine in the nose and a General Electric J-31 jet engine with 1,600 pounds of thrust in the tail. Even with both engines at full power, its performance was unimpressive. Its principal use, it seemed, was for the shock value of flying past bombers with the propeller feathered. Often we would fly over to the Navy air-training area near Pensacola, get in formation with an SNJ trainer, feather the front engine, and pull away from it. An SNJ was about the only plane it could outrun with only the jet engine running.

I had an interesting experience on my checkout flight in the FR-1 Fireball. It had been at Eglin for a week or so before it could be flown, undergoing a complete inspection by our maintenance crews. I was on the flight line one morning while the FR-1 crew chief was trying to remove the upper half of the engine cowling. When he pushed up on the cowling, the nosewheel came off the ground and the airplane settled back on its rubber tail skid. As I helped him get the nose back down, he told me that the weight of the jet engine in the tail put the center of gravity almost directly over the main landing gear, making it easy to tilt it back on its tail.

A few days later I was given a cockpit check and took it up for my first flight. All went well until I peeled up to land and lowered the landing gear. The green lights for the main gear came on, but the nosewheel light did not, indicating that the wheel had not locked down. I pulled out of the landing pattern and cycled the gear a number of times with the same result. Several more attempts under both positive and negative g and while rocking the wings proved fruitless. I flew by the tower at low speed to give the tower operator a chance to look with his binoculars. He said the wheel did not look locked to him. Capt. Dick "Superhot" Scott was completing a mission in a Mustang, and I asked him to fly alongside and take a close look. He confirmed that the nosewheel appeared unlocked. By this time I was running low on fuel and would soon have to land. Knowing that the airplane would sit back on its tail without much provocation, I decided to try to land and bring it to a stop on the main gear and tail skid so the nosewheel did not touch down at all. I notified the tower of my intention and asked them to have a vehicle follow me down the runway, with some men aboard to sit on the horizontal stabilizer when the plane stopped and to remain there until the nosewheel could be locked down. I touched down in a nose-high attitude, rolled the canopy all the way back, leaned back in my seat, and gently lowered the tail skid to the runway, not touching the brakes but letting the drag of the tail skid coupled with the nose-high attitude slow me down. Three men from the fire truck chased the plane as it slowed and jumped onto the horizontal stabilizer, where their weight kept the nose up until a couple of crew chiefs, who had followed the fire truck in a jeep, locked the nosewheel in place and then gently lowered it to the ground. I was relieved that my plan had worked but was concerned that it had looked to the crowd watching, which included the group commander, like a Keystone Kops routine. Back at the squadron, however, Col. Thomas McGehee (the group commander) congratulated me on avoiding an accident and said it was lucky I was so experienced in the plane. I replied, "Thank you, sir."

Lieutenant Colonel Muldoon, who had recently been promoted, assigned me as test officer for the F7F. I was pleased to be considered a good enough pilot to be assigned to a performance test. Since this was the initial AAF testing of the airplane, we started off with some basic performance tests before beginning the operational suitability phase. Colonel Muldoon had been checked out by the Navy pilot who delivered the plane, and he in turn gave me a cockpit check before my first flight.

I found the Tigercat a delight to fly. It was quite maneuverable for so large a plane, and its two big engines provided good acceleration and climbing ability. I was already familiar with the engines, since I had flown the R-2800-powered P-47, the P-61, and the B-26. The F7F had a control stick, which I preferred, instead of a wheel, which is common to most twin-engine aircraft. Only the rudder, which was exceptionally large, was hydraulically boosted. One feature concerned me, though. It had folding wings to facilitate parking on the crowded decks of aircraft carriers. Although it was supposed to be impossible to fold them in flight, I wanted an extra safeguard, so I had the crew chief wire the control handle securely in the extended position.

Because turbulence increases, especially at low altitude, as the air heats up during the day, performance speed runs and timed climbs were made at first light. The sea-level speed runs were made over the water on a measured course at a height of about 100 feet. Flying at high speed at low altitude is both exciting and dangerous; a small error can be fatal. The tests proceeded smoothly until the first timed climb using water injection. The water-injection system allows the engine to provide 10 to 15 percent more power by injecting a small amount of water into the cylinders, increasing cooling and preventing detonation and the consequent engine damage. The F7F carried enough water for about five minutes of operation.

On the morning of the first climb test, I taxied to the end of runway 6 at about five-thirty, ran up my engines, checked the mags, and lined up for takeoff. The test called for me to run the engines up to full power while holding the brakes, cut in the water injection, simultaneously release the brakes and start my stopwatch, then climb at the optimum climbing speeds up to the service ceiling of the F7F, about 40,000 feet, noting the elapsed time on my knee board at 5,000-foot intervals.

Everything went as planned until I released the brakes. The airplane leaped ahead like its namesake springing after a gazelle, snapping my head back against the armor plate and causing me to haul it off the ground before I was ready to fly, although it clearly was. I exceeded the permissible wheels-down speed before I could retract the gear. All that was disconcerting enough, but more important, I had forgotten to start my stopwatch, making the test a mission impossible. Turning back, I landed and returned to the parking area where the puzzled mechanics were waiting, wondering what was wrong with the airplane. Embarrassed, I told them of my problems, while they quickly topped off the fuel and water tanks. I tried again and, since I was ready for the sudden burst of power, completed the mission without difficulty.

On a later mission, I was making a series of speed runs at 5,000-foot intervals with two 150-gallon external tanks installed on pylons between the fuselage and the engines. The runs were made without incident until I completed the one at 30,000 feet. A bit low on fuel, I was making a rather steep dive back toward the field. At nearly 300 miles per hour indicated airspeed and about 25,000 feet, the airplane began a porpoising motion that steadily increased in amplitude, jerking the stick out of my hand. I immediately chopped the power, and as the airplane slowed, the porpoising decreased and then stopped. I continued back to the field at a lower speed and landed without difficulty. When I reported the problem, Colonel Muldoon decided to repeat the descent under the same conditions to see if he obtained the same results. He did, and we repeated the dives without the drop tanks. There were no problems right up to the redline (maximum permissible) speed. It was obvious that the tanks were interfering with the airflow. We reported the results to the Grumman technical representative at Eglin, who in turn reported to the company. Shortly thereafter we received new pylons that were several inches longer than the originals, thus moving the tanks several inches farther from the lower wing surface and creating a smoother airflow in that area. They solved the problem, and we were able to dive at any speed with tanks on without porpoising. The modified pylons became standard on the F7F.

Just before the end of August, Colonel Muldoon assigned Barney Turner and me to fly two of the P-51Hs we were testing to the North American Aviation plant in Los Angeles and bring back two new ones that had been modified. The H was a lightweight version of the P-51D Mustang. Although it had slightly better performance than the P-51D, I didn't like it as well as the D. It never felt quite right to me. Also, it had disc brakes on small wheels, and the brake pedals were tilted toward the pilot so much that it was easy to ride the brakes unknowingly while taxiing, causing them to burn out with great frequency. The unmodified H's cockpit arrangement was poorly designed. Something was wrong with the relationship between the seat and the stick. It felt like the stick was about six or eight inches too long, putting your stick hand almost level with your face. It was very uncomfortable, especially on long flights.

Despite those problems I was quite excited about the prospect of flying to California. The western half of the country would be all new. I had never been west of Russellville, Arkansas, and was there only on a cross-country flight in basic-flying school. I hoped there would be time to see the famous corner of Hollywood and Vine and perhaps even a movie star. I was also eager to see Texas, the scene of so many of the cowboy films and books I had always enjoyed.

We took off early in the morning with a couple of uniforms and toilet articles stuffed under the seat. The flight would cover almost 2,000 miles, and we would have to land twice along the way, as we weren't carrying external fuel tanks. Barney led the first leg across the flat lowlands of Alabama, Mississippi, Louisiana, and East Texas to Ellington Field, near Houston. I led the next leg, and my wish to see Texas was more than fulfilled. The whole second leg was over Texas, from Houston to Biggs Field, at El Paso. It was flat, dry, and featureless over the whole route until we approached El Paso, when a range of mountains appeared northwest of the city. Just west of the city was the mountain pass that gives El Paso its name.

We ate a quick lunch while the planes were being refueled and then took off for California. The mountains and deserts of New Mexico, Arizona, and California were majestic in their beauty, especially as the visibility was so good in the clear air. I flew a loose formation so I could watch the scenery, instead of Barney's plane.

When we crossed the last range of mountains before entering the Los Angeles Basin, there was too much haze to sightsee, and I closed in on Barney as we descended toward the coast. It was a good thing Barney was leading, because I don't think I could have located Mines Field (now Los Angeles International Airport). The haze was not the only problem; the North American factory adjoining the field and the runways was camouflaged—covered by large nets with fake houses and shrubbery on them— and the runway was disguised in trompe l'oeil depicting houses and trees. They really tromped my oeils. I didn't know what Barney had in mind as we dived toward the trees and houses and peeled up to land. I figured he must know since he was flying with such precision, and when he lowered his wheels I did the same. As we got lower I could begin to make out the runway and landed, following Barney all the way in. After parking the airplanes we were met by one of the AAF plant representatives, who told us that the new P-51Hs would not be ready for two days. In the meantime he had booked us into a nearby hotel and arranged for a car to take us there. He said that a couple of engineers from the P-51H program would pick us up at seven and take us to dinner. They showed up right on time, and as we drove to the restaurant, we discussed the flying characteristics and cockpit arrangement of the unmodified H. They thought we would find the new arrangement much more satisfactory, and later, upon inspection, we did. The cockpit of the modified P-51H was much better arranged, but I still was never as comfortable in the H as in the D. Recently Chuck Yeager and I were discussing P-51s and discovered that we shared the same feelings about the P-51H.

The next day Barney and I wandered around Hollywood and were somewhat disappointed. Hollywood and Vine looked much like any other intersection, and we saw nothing remotely resembling a movie star. We did see the Brown Derby and Grauman's Chinese Theater, which was impressive in a gaudy way, and the famous footprints in the concrete out front. That night we were taken to Earl Carroll's Vanities for dinner and a spectacular show featuring gorgeous showgirls, who really opened my oeils, and comedy skits, similar to today's Las Vegas shows.

Early the next morning, we took off for Eglin. It was a bright day, and I could see Los Angeles, the beautiful coastline, and even Catalina Island clearly. I was astounded by the extent of the city, although it was far smaller than today. I would get to know the city better in 1956, when I returned with my wife and two children, as a graduate student at Cal Tech.

We flew back by a more northern route, landing at Albuquerque, New Mexico, and Shreveport, Louisiana. The terrain was much more mountainous along the first part of the route, and we saw the meteor crater just north of Route 66 in Arizona and also had a glimpse of the spectacular Grand Canyon. I didn't fully appreciate its magnificence until, en route from Cal Tech to the Air Force Academy, we spent several days there. It was also a relief to look at something other than partial differential equations, Laplace transforms, Bessel functions, and complex numbers.

The trip back was uneventful, and we landed at Eglin just before dark. The flying time for the trip was about eight and a half hours each way. Somewhat weary, we ate dinner in the club snack bar that night. The fare and the surroundings were much simpler than those of the two previous nights, but it was good to be home.

4

Top Guns in Texas

When we reported to the flight line at seven in the morning on August 9, Colonel Muldoon called Barney Turner, William Vandersteel, and me into his office and said, "Get right over to operations at the Very Heavy Bomber Squadron. They have a B-twenty-nine ready to fly you to Mitchel Field. Get the base ops people there to drive you to the Republic Aviation plant at Farmingdale, where you'll pick up new P-forty-seven Ns. I expect you back before dark."

The P-47N was a bigger, long-range version of the P-47D, developed for the long overwater flights in the Pacific theater. It had been tested at Eglin months before I arrived, and there were several in the squadron. During the tests, Barney had flown a simulated long-range combat mission of twelve and a half hours. The flight surgeons were quite interested in the physical effects on the pilot of a flight of such long duration in a fighter. They were flabbergasted when they weighed Barney at the end of the flight and found he had gained weight. However, when they learned how much food he had carried with him in the cockpit, they were surprised he had gained so little.

Since I had never ridden in a B-29, I was given the bombardier's seat in the nose, between and just forward of the two pilots. After going through what seemed like an interminable checklist, we finally started the takeoff roll. The B-29 accelerated well, but I was surprised that we took off in a flat attitude, with the nosewheel only slightly off the ground. We climbed in almost the same attitude, and when I inquired why the climb wasn't made at a steeper angle, I was told that the nose was held low to keep the climbing speed higher and improve engine cooling. I was intrigued by the actions of the pilot during the takeoff and initial climb. He was moving the control wheel forward and back and from side to side with no apparent effect except the production of a great deal of creaking. As far as I could tell, the airplane was flying smoothly. A year or so later, when I made some takeoffs and landings in the B-29, I could feel through the control wheel the need for all those adjustments, to keep the wings level and maintain the proper climb angle, though it had not been apparent to me as a passenger.

When I had first seen a B-29 in April 1944, in Karachi, India (now Pakistan), I never dreamed that I would someday fly one of those monsters. In fact, at that time they were heavily guarded, and we mere fighter pilots were not allowed anywhere near them. We were pleased to see them nevertheless, since we knew they were to bomb Japan from bases in China.

We took off at about seven-thirty and about four hours later flew over New York City on the way to Mitchel on Long Island. It was a clear day, and from the bombardier's position in the nose I had my first view from the air of the city where I had spent the first fifteen years of my life. Instead of looking for the famous landmarks like the Statue of Liberty and the Empire State Building, I searched out the beach on Jamaica Bay in Brooklyn from which I took my first airplane ride at the age of seven, and Floyd Bennett Field, where I spent many weekends scrounging flights in Buster Warner's cabin Waco. He was a family friend, which greatly increased his scroungability.

We descended and landed at Mitchel. Though it was a fairly short field for a B-29, it was no problem for our experienced pilots. Base operations fixed us up with a car, and we grabbed a sandwich while we waited for it. We were taken directly to the AAF office on the flight line at the Republic plant, where we signed for the P-47s, inspected them, climbed in, and were on the way back to Eglin within an hour of our arrival at the plant, with Barney in the lead and Vandersteel and me following in loose vic (V) formation. The long-range Ns could easily make it to Eglin without refueling.

Our Ns were equipped with autopilots, the first I had seen in a single-engine fighter. In fact, they were three of the first to be so equipped and were to be tested at Eglin. Barney told us to spread the formation still wider and try the autopilots to see if they were functioning. I turned mine on and found that it worked quite well, holding altitude, heading, and airspeed within close tolerances. It worked quite well, that is, until somewhere over Virginia, where I caged my directional gyro, which controlled the autopilot heading, to make a correction of almost 30 degrees. When I uncaged it, the P-47, which had been docile until then, reared up into a violent wingover and plunged toward the ground, rapidly gaining speed. Evidently, the autopilot could not make an instantaneous correction of that magnitude without overreacting. My first instinct was to take over the controls and pull it out manually, but the autopilot vetoed that suggestion. It was too strong to overpower. I had to shut it off before I could regain control. It was fortunate that Barney had spread us out, or I might have run into Vandersteel, which, among other things, would have frosted Colonel Muldoon. For the remainder of the flight the autopilot and I declared a truce, and we landed at Eglin well before dark, after a flight of about four and a half hours.

The P-47 was a delight to fly. The cockpit was roomy and quiet since the engine exhaust went through the turbosupercharger near the tail before being discharged. The 2,000-horsepower Pratt & Whitney R-2800 engine is one of the most dependable engines ever made. The airplane was quite stable, and its wide landing gear made it easy to land and almost impossible to ground loop. The cockpit was so roomy that supposedly, when a pilot was under attack, he could run around the cockpit and yell help every time he passed the radio.

A short time later I received orders to attend a one-month course at the Fighter Gunnery Instructors School at Foster Field in Victoria, Texas, along with a newly assigned pilot named Tom Holstein. This was the Top Gun program of its day, where pilots learned not only the latest methods for weapons delivery but ways to teach those methods. Actually there were more differences than similarities between the current USAF Red Flag and Navy Top Gun programs and our school, but it was the best we had at the time. We fired at targets using no radar and what were essentially the same type of gunsights used in World War I. The modern programs send groups of fighters on simulated combat missions where they can be attacked at any time by aggressor fighters simulating enemy aircraft and tactics. In addition to the very high rate-of-fire Gatling guns, the weapons used are radar-guided missiles and heat-seeking missiles. Of course the students don't actually fire their weapons, but the combination of airborne and ground-based radars, video recorders, and computers makes it possible to analyze the tactics and relative positions of the combatants and determine who would have shot down whom. This can be done in real time, allowing the range controllers to tell a pilot when he has been destroyed and must disengage. In the earlier days all the pilots involved in practice dogfights could argue that they were the victors, and they invariably did so. This modern equipment has added an unwelcome element—truth—to the program and has taken away one of the fighter pilot's favorite weapons, exaggeration.

Although I was already quite proficient in gunnery and didn't plan to instruct, it was important that I learn the most up-to-date methods in order to test weapons systems properly. I was overjoyed to get the chance to attend this school and thereby move closer to the top of author Tom Wolfe's ziggurat of "the right stuff." In peacetime, firing at targets is what being a fighter pilot is all about. All of the flying training and practice is to improve the pilot's ability to get into position to hit a target. I had always loved gunnery and looked forward eagerly to a month or so of it.

Competition in gunnery is always stiff, because gunnery scores are one of the few ways a fighter pilot can demonstrate tangible evidence of his skill. P-51s and P-47s were used at the school, but the P-47s were D models. To train in the aircraft we would be testing, we flew there in two of our P-47Ns. I led the flight to Victoria with Tom on my wing. It was a clear day, and we flew at 2,000 feet to stay below headwinds at the higher altitudes. The only thing of interest we saw was the San Jacinto Monument near Houston, a 570-foot obelisk honoring Sam Houston's victory over the Mexican general Santa Ana. After a flight of a little over three hours, we landed at Foster Field. It was a typical World War II AAF airfield with three runways, a large ramp filled with fighters, and wooden buildings. We checked into the BOQ (Bachelor Officer's Quarters) and were told to report to the headquarters of the school at seven-thirty the next morning.

Eager to get started, Tom and I arrived early. We were divided into two groups, P-51 pilots and P-47 pilots, and each group was further broken into flights of three and assigned an instructor. Tom and I were in the same flight, under Captain Bumgardner, a top-notch instructor as well as a pleasant man. We learned that we would spend half the day flying and the other half in ground school learning theory, weapons, and techniques. We would also be reviewing our gun camera film with the instructors, who would assess our passes and suggest methods of improving our techniques. I was pleased to find out that we would spend quite a bit of time on the skeet range. The course would include air-to-air and air-to-ground gunnery, air-to-ground rocketry firing five-inch HVARS, and dive-, glide-, and skip-bombing. Gunnery missions were scored by the straightforward method of counting the holes in the targets, and rocketry and dive- and glide-bombing were scored by triangulation. In skip-bombing, large vertical targets were used, and hits were scored by penetrating the targets.

The first thing on the schedule was air-to-ground gunnery. The targets were set up on Matagorda Island on the coast, a strip of sandy beach a mile or two wide and thirty-five miles long about forty miles northeast of Corpus Christi. They were arranged in groups of four, with one group for each flight and one target for each pilot in the flight. Each target consisted of a wooden frame, about ten feet square, covered with cloth on which a bull's-eye was painted. They were placed about twenty feet apart and were tilted back about 15 degrees.

Although the P-47 had eight .50-caliber machine guns and the P-51 had six, only two guns were loaded during these training missions. This saved a great deal of ammunition and target damage and was quite effective for training since the other guns would hit the same area as the two that were fired. Each gun was loaded with two hundred rounds of ammunition for each mission, air-to-air and air-to-ground.

The first two missions were flown with gun cameras only, allowing us to practice the proper spacing on the passes and, by observing the film, to see how well we were holding the sight pipper on the target. There was an indicator on the film to show if we were skidding or slipping during the passes. If the ball was not in the center, the bullets would not hit the target even though the sight was right on it.

Two safety rules were stressed both in the ground school and by Captain Bumgardner. The first was to maintain sufficient spacing between the firing planes to be sure the first plane could complete his pull up and turn before the next plane fired, thus preventing ricochets from hitting the plane ahead. We were told that more than one plane had been shot down by the following plane when this rule was not observed. I don't know if it was true, but it certainly got my attention.

The second rule was to avoid target fixation; that is, don't concentrate so hard on getting hits on the target that you fly into the ground. It was a relatively common error, especially in combat. We had lost several pilots in China that way, and we nearly lost my favorite pilot, me. According to my wingman, I had cleared the roof of a building I was strafing by at least an inch. Despite this warning, a few days later one of the pilots in another P-47 flight hit the ground with his propeller, damaging it so badly that he had to shut down the engine. Fortunately, he was able to make a safe belly landing on a wide stretch of beach.

To qualify as an expert aerial gunner a pilot had to score 50 percent on air-to-ground gunnery and 30 percent on air-to-air. I scored well above 50 percent on all my air-to-ground missions and up into the eighties on early morning flights when the air was smooth. Turbulence made it difficult to keep the pipper on the target for any length of time. The trick was to fire a short burst when it was on the target. I had always been a good gunner, having qualified as an expert as a cadet, but part of the reason for my high scores was the practice I had been getting at Eglin for the past three months.

The bulk of the training in the course was devoted to air-to-air gunnery, which was by far the most difficult of the skills to master. The problem of deflection shooting (all air-to-air gunnery except firing from head on or from directly behind) is far from simple because the pilot is firing from a moving platform at a moving target and both are capable of movement in three dimensions. The amount he must lead the target is constantly changing as the angle between the firing plane and the target changes. In skeet shooting or bird shooting the shooter is stationary while the target is moving. Although the problem is much simpler, it is about the best practice available on the ground, since a different amount of lead is required at each of the firing stations.

The target for the aerial gunnery missions was a piece of heavy wire mesh six feet by thirty feet with a metal pipe and a lead weight on the front end to make it fly in a vertical position. It was attached to a tow plane, an A-26 or a P-47, by a long cable. Since four planes would be firing at the same target, the tips of the 400 rounds of ammunition in each plane would be dipped in a different color paint (red, yellow, blue, or green). The paint had a soft wax base that would mark the bullet hole as it passed through the target. Following each mission the target was laid flat on the ramp and scored by the pilots and the instructor. Occasionally there were arguments over whether the paint trace was blue or green, but generally the scoring was simple. Each hole was daubed with black paint after scoring so that the target could be reused.

On firing and gun camera missions the tow ship climbed to about 5,000 feet and flew parallel to the coast a few miles offshore and then reversed course periodically to stay within the range boundaries. The flight of four fighters would fly in echelon 1,000 feet or so above and abreast of the tow plane and about half a mile closer to shore. One by one they would peel off toward the target, then reverse the turn into a curve of pursuit and start firing when within range, inside 250 yards. The pilot had to cease firing at about 30 degrees off the target so the bullets would not endanger the tow plane. Also, he had to break off early enough to avoid colliding with the target, because hitting it could severely damage a fighter. The fighters then pulled up toward the shore and got into position for another pass. It was easy to tell if a pilot had fired from too narrow an angle, because his bullet holes would be elongated. If that happened more than once, the instructor and the tow pilot, especially the tow pilot, would chew him out. As in ground gunnery, the first few missions were with gun camera alone, so gross errors in technique could be eliminated before actual firing began. Gun cameras were used, however, along with the guns on all firing missions to evaluate technique.

The air-to-air firing went smoothly—all of the pilots were experienced, and there were no safety violations. It was a joy to take off in a formation of fighters, climb into the bright blue Texas sky, rendezvous with the tow ship at about 5,000 feet over the even bluer Gulf of Mexico, and then peel off individually to set up our firing passes. Watching the other P-47s make their passes was almost as enjoyable as making my own firing pass. They curved down toward the target and emitted a long trail of smoke as they fired. When they pulled up from the pass in a tight turn, the wing tips generated graceful white streamers in the moist Gulf air.

After landing, the pilots gathered on the ramp waiting impatiently for the return of the target. As soon as the jeep brought in the dropped target we eagerly pored over it, looking for our colors in the bullet holes. Then we scored the target officially, with two pilots calling off the hits by color. They had to be in agreement on the color before the third pilot could enter them on the score sheet. My scores were quite good, usually well above 50 percent.

Since this was an instructor's school, we were drilled on how to spot errors of technique both on the films and in the air and were taught how to correct the errors. The ground school stressed the teaching of the theory behind all of the weapons delivery methods we were learning.

Although the flying in the course was a fighter pilot's dream, it and the ground school were very demanding. Our days began at seven-thirty in the morning and frequently ended at seven-thirty in the evening. If weather interrupted the flight schedule during the week, we made it up on Saturday.

Except for the base theater, there was little or no recreation available in Victoria. There were few young women who were willing to waste their time with officers who would be there for only a month. Athletic equipment was available in abundance, so we played softball and basketball for hours in the evenings and on weekends. We had a simulated world series between the Jug (P-47) pilots and the Mustang (P-51) pilots. The real World Series was going on at the time, and on one weekend we were glued to the radio, with the same enthusiasm that glues today's sports fans to the television, while the Chicago Cubs battled the Detroit Tigers. It was an exciting series, all the more so because it was the first most of us had heard since 1941. The Tigers won in seven games. We also became great fans of the local high school football team and attended all its home games. I doubt that they ever had a louder or more loyal cheering section.

An interesting break in the school routine came when Admiral Nimitz, a native of Texas who commanded the forces in the Pacific in World War II, returned to the United States and was honored with a major parade in Dallas. All of the fighters at Victoria as well as aircraft from several other Texas bases were assigned to participate in an aerial parade. We flew to Carswell Field at Fort Worth early on the morning of the parade and were briefed on the formation we would fly, time over target, and radio procedures. The parade flight went well, but since there were about two hundred airplanes, it was difficult to maintain good formation in all the turbulence they generated. It also was more difficult for those farther back in the formation, both because of the extra turbulence and because small corrections in power at the front of the formation were magnified in the rear. Fortunately, I was in a flight of four near the front.

As we crossed over the heart of Dallas with its hundreds of thousands of cheering spectators, I thought how fortunate we were as Americans never to have experienced the horror and devastation caused by aerial bombing that so many cities in Europe and Asia had endured.

When we landed back at Carswell to refuel for the flight home, one of the P-51s, piloted by a character named Majalowski, landed too fast and too long, ran off the end of the runway, and then ground looped intentionally to avoid hitting the fence. He raised a great cloud of dust but didn't damage the airplane.

The control tower operator radioed, "P-fifty-one that just landed, are you having trouble?"

As he taxied back to the runway Majalowski replied, "No, I always land this way."

Once we were back at Victoria, the remaining ten days of the course seemed to pass rapidly. We spent about half the time in bombing and the other half in rocketry. About the only thing new we learned was the wing line method of determining dive angle on bombing and rocketry passes.

This system had been developed by the school, and it worked quite well despite, or perhaps because of, its simplicity.

The system consisted of a series of parallel lines painted on the wings, all starting at the leading edge and extending back about two feet. The lines were labeled 20, 30, 40, 50, and 60 degrees, with the line farthest from the cockpit labeled 20 and the closest one 60. Regardless of altitude, if the pilot flew so that the target on the ground passed under the 20-degree line and he rolled into a dive as the target disappeared under the wing, he would be in a 20-degree dive, the same being true for the other angles. Since the amount of lead used in bombing varied with the angle of the dive, it was helpful to be as precise as possible. Without the wing lines the pilot had to estimate the angle of dive from whatever clues were available, which was far less accurate.

Suddenly the course was over, the last bomb dropped, the last rocket fired, and we said our good-byes to the instructors and new friends and dispersed to our respective bases. Schools like this ensured that in time a pilot would have friends at most of the fighter bases, which is one of the good features of a military career.

The next morning Tom and I climbed into our airplanes and headed back to Eglin. We had been gone just over a month and had logged some fifty hours each in the P-47N, which had turned out to be a very stable gun platform.

A few weeks after my return Colonel Muldoon called me into his office and handed me the report of my grade in the course. It was Superior. He was effusive in his praise. He said, "Well, Lopez, at least you didn't disgrace us."

5

Fighter on First Base

One of the things that Colonel Muldoon stressed in the squadron was sports. He may have been ahead of the day's psychologists by recognizing that athletics is good for relieving stress and for making an organization more cohesive, or maybe he just liked sports. In any case, the fighter squadron had a team in the group officer's softball league that played two or three times a week on a field just off the southeast end of runway 13-31, the runway running southeast and northwest. (The actual runway headings were 130 degrees and 310 degrees.) This runway was seldom in use, because the north-south runway was much longer and wider. We also had a bowling team in the group league. When baseball was out of season, we played pickup basketball and volleyball in the base gym and touch football at the beach or on one of the fields on the base.

Dick Jones was the star of our bowling team, scoring on average about fifty pins higher than anyone else in the league, so our team won several trophies. I was a below-average bowler, never having bowled before, but the league gave me one of the trophies anyway, a typical one with a bowler mounted on a stand. Once when I was away on a trip, some of the pilots removed my trophy from its stand, broke off its arms, screwed it to the top of my jet helmet, and painted on the helmet, "Look, no hands!" It looked a bit like a German pickelhaube. On my return, I donned the helmet without comment and tried to wear it in a P-80, but with the seat lowered enough to close the canopy, I could not see out of the cockpit. I had to remove the ornament.

Dick was also a fine catcher on the softball team, and I was an adequate first baseman. If my baseball ability had matched my love for the game, I would have been a major leaguer. I grew up in New York and was an avid Yankee fan, thanks largely to a kind uncle who often took me to Yankee games. I was fortunate to have seen Babe Ruth, Lou Gehrig (who was my idol), Bill Dickey, Joe DiMaggio, et Al (Al Lopez, that is).

Colonel Muldoon was the shortstop, Major Schoenfeldt the pitcher, and Barney Turner the third baseman. Fortunately, slow-pitch softball had not yet been introduced, and none of the pitchers in the league was a real hotshot, so the games were well balanced and enjoyed by all. At times some of the secretaries stopped by to watch the games, which were played just after work, inspiring us bachelors to do our best. Some of the base organizations that worked in shifts played softball on those same fields in the early afternoon, and thereby hangs a tale.

One afternoon I was testing, in a P-47N, a new engine-control regulator and a pressure-demand oxygen mask, both of which had to be tested above 40,000 feet. Although the temperature on the ground was about 90 degrees, at 40,000 feet it was minus 65, so I was dressed in heavy winter flying gear. When I reached 41,000 feet the test program called for me to try a number of different throttle settings to determine the manifold pressure at which insufficient air flow would cause the turbosupercharger to stall. When it stalled, the engine power dropped about 50 percent, and the airplane lost several thousand feet before I could regain full power. After repeating the test three times with identical results, I proceeded to the test of the oxygen mask. I had switched the oxygen system to the pressure position above 35,000 feet as prescribed by the operating instructions. Oxygen must be supplied under pressure above that altitude, because even if the pilot is breathing 100 percent oxygen, the atmospheric pressure is too low to force the oxygen from his lungs into his bloodstream. The pilot may become hypoxic (oxygen starved), lose consciousness, and eventually die.

The pressure-breathing system forces oxygen into the pilot's lungs under pressure, which is difficult to get used to: the pilot must force the air out of his lungs to exhale, and as soon as he relaxes his diaphragm muscles, his lungs fill up again. Besides testing the general functioning of this equipment, we were to determine how effectively a pilot could communicate on the radio with oxygen being forced down his throat. The answer was, not very well. I made several calls to the ground radio, but no one could understand a word. It sounded garbled in my earphones, and I doubt that I could have understood it. Some pilots in my squadron were airborne at the time, and I received several derogatory remarks, including, "Lope, you're not supposed to eat peanut butter when you're transmitting," and, "If you're drowning, Lope, I'll drop you a life raft."

Other pilots using this system had the same problem, although some were able to develop a technique for speaking clearly enough despite the pressure. I never could, however. My technique was to turn off the pressure while I was speaking, which worked quite well. In the next few years, cockpits in jet aircraft were pressurized, and we seldom if ever had to use the pressure system in the oxygen masks again.

Anyway, after completing the tests I dived back toward the field for landing. The main north-south runway was under repair, requiring me to land on runway 13, to the southeast. I came in at about 100 feet and peeled up to the left for a standard circular fighter pattern and made my usual great three-point landing. About halfway down the runway I began to apply the brakes gently. The left brake reacted normally, but at the first touch, the actuating cylinder broke off from the right pedal, and the pedal itself flopped loosely forward. Suddenly, what had been a routine roll out after landing turned into a potential accident. If I didn't use the brakes the plane would run off the end of the runway; if I applied the good left brake it would run off the side of the narrow runway into the soft sand and either nose over or rip off a landing gear. I was too far down the runway to take off again, which wouldn't help anyway, since the brake couldn't be repaired in the air. I would still have to land with only one brake.

Knowing that the softball field at the end of the runway was hard-packed clay, I opted to run off the end of the runway, where I would be moving as slowly as possible, then unlock the tailwheel and ground-loop the airplane. I had immediately pulled back the mixture control to shut off the engine, and when I had passed the end of the runway and reached the outfield area, I unlocked the tailwheel and stomped on the left brake. When the nose started swinging to the left I saw to my horror that the field was full of players running in all directions as this monstrous airplane chased them in circles with the propeller still windmilling. I hadn't been able to see them earlier because the nose of the P-47 completely blocks the pilot's forward view when the tail is down. I was afraid I might complete my first unassisted triple play, the permanent kind, but by the grace of God, and because I started my ground loop in the outfield, the team remained intact. Instead of a triple play I had twirled a no-hitter.

When the plane finally came to a stop the players all ran toward it and stood there, sweating in their shorts and T-shirts, gaping as I opened the canopy and clumsily climbed out of the cockpit in my heavy, sheepskin-lined flying gear. I felt foolish as I apologized for breaking up the game, but since no one had been injured, they took it in good spirit and even seemed to enjoy the adventure of seeing the P-47, and a genuine Arctic explorer, up close and personal.

During my first year at Eglin I had my only experience with the military justice system, when I was appointed to a general court-martial board that had been convened to try a number of cases. General courts-martial handle major cases such as murder, desertion, stealing, and embezzlement, while special courts-martial deal with lesser offenses including absence without leave (AWOL) and drunkenness. The court-martial board comprises five to seven officers, all of whom must be of equal or higher rank than the defendant, and acts as both judge and jury, determining guilt or innocence and the sentence, if guilty. Col. Thomas McGehee, the 611th Group commander, was the president of the general court-martial board, Major Schoenfeldt was appointed defense counsel for general cases, and Capt. Dick Jones was made a defense counsel for special cases. Neither Schoeny nor Dick had any legal training, but the trial judge advocate (prosecutor) was a lawyer. That was not as unfair as it seems, because the cases were thoroughly investigated and reviewed by lawyers before formal charges were made and went through several higher reviews after sentencing. Because of the appearance of bias against the accused, however, the Uniform Code of Military Justice now provides that the defense counsel must be a lawyer if the prosecutor is a lawyer.

Dick had to defend a large number of AWOL cases and, since they were all cut and dried, lost them all. In fact, none of the AWOL cases was won by the defense, regardless of who was defending them. Nevertheless, it was somewhat embarrassing for Dick whenever we went to the post exchange (PX). At that time the base stockade was right next to the PX, and as he approached, a large percentage of the prisoners would wave and shout, "Hi, Captain Jones, have you won any cases yet?"

We tried about a dozen cases over the several months of my tenure on the board, but two of them stand out in my memory. The first was a particularly pitiful case involving a young, illiterate, enlisted man who had to depend on his squadron mates to read items on the bulletin board for him, including the daily bulletin, required reading for all personnel. During this period, shortly after the end of the war, soldiers were getting discharge orders almost every day. One day, as a cruel joke, the other soldiers informed him that he was discharged and that he should go home and wait for his discharge papers.

His home was on a farm about twenty miles north of Pensacola, Florida, which is forty miles west of Eglin. On the stand he said, "When they told me I was discharged, I hitched a ride to Pepsicoly, and my folks picked me up. I waited for two months, still wearing my uniform, awaitin' my orders, and then the MPs [military police] come to take me back." He was accused of desertion because of the length of his period of AWOL, but he was obviously not a deserter. He was convicted of being AWOL, but the sentence was suspended, and he received an honorable discharge and went back to the farm near Pepsicoly, where I hope he has had a good life in those more gentle surroundings.

The second case was more serious. A lieutenant, in an enlisted man's uniform, had visited a bar off-limits to officers in the nearby town of Crestview for reasons he never made clear. He probably would have gotten away with that, but he got drunk and started a large fight, or a small riot, in which a lot of furnishings and windows were destroyed. Then to top it off, he tried to get away in his car and promptly collided almost head-on with another car. Fortunately there were no serious injuries. He was arrested, however, and turned over to the MPs for trial by general court-martial.

One of the first witnesses was an old man from Crestview who had been in the bar and seen the whole fracas. After the trial judge advocate (TJA) had established that fact, he asked the witness if he could identify the lieutenant, and if so, would he point him out to the court. To the consternation of the TJA and to my astonishment, the witness pointed at me. I think he must have suffered a whiplash as the TJA spun him around to face the accused, whom he subsequently identified as the bad guy. I was about the same build and height as the accused, and we both had dark hair, but the similarity ended there. Besides I was a captain. That tended to discredit the witness, but as there were four others to identify the lieutenant, correctly this time, it didn't hurt the case, and the defendant was found guilty on all counts and given an appropriate sentence. Shortly after that my legal career came to an end with the appointment of a new board, and I was able to go back to full-time flying, at which I was much more proficient.

In early January I was excited by the prospect not only of visiting New Orleans for the first time but also of flying in my first airshow. Both were in conjunction with the opening of Moisant Field (now Moisant International Airport) in New Orleans. Moisant Field, just west of New Orleans, was scheduled for completion and opening in the second week of January 1946. It was named for John B. Moisant, a wealthy sportsman and pioneer flier who won a number of air races in 1909 and 1910 and was a public idol. He was killed in a crash in New Orleans on December 31, 1910, while attempting to win the Michelin Prize for flight duration. His sister, Matilde, was one of the better-known woman pilots during that period.

Although the field was far from ready for opening, the city fathers decided to have the ceremony on schedule but not to open the field to traffic until sometime later. They asked Harding Army Airfield, near Baton Rouge, Louisiana, to provide AAF aircraft and Naval Air Station (NAS) Pensacola to provide Navy aircraft for both static display and fly-bys for the ceremonies. NAS Pensacola, a training base, had no first-line operational aircraft for the show. Therefore, they arranged for a Grumman TBM Avenger torpedo bomber from NAS Opa Locka and a pair of fighters, a Grumman F6F Hellcat and a Vought F4U Corsair from NAS Jacksonville, to participate. Then, for the sake of the airshow, the Navy swallowed its pride and asked Eglin if it would fly the three latest naval aircraft, the F7F and F8F and the FR-1, in the show. Since the Navy is one of our allies, the commanding general of the Proving Ground Command approved the request, and Dick Jones, Bill Greene, and I were chosen to fly them.

Consequently, on January 11, we took off—Dick in the FR-1, Bill in the F8F, and me leading in the F7F—for the fifty-mile flight to Bronson Field, one of the Pensacola training fields, where the Navy planes would assemble and where we would be briefed. After being cleared by Bronson tower, we approached the landing runway at about 250 mph and a height of about 100 feet. At the beginning of the runway we peeled up to the left out of our right echelon formation and made a standard AAF fighter approach, which is essentially a loop except that instead of being in the vertical plane, it is about 40 or 45 degrees from the vertical. The gear and flaps are lowered, and the plane is slowed to landing speed and rolled onto the runway heading just as it crosses the end of the runway. This was a much different pattern from the one the Navy pilots fly. They fly long, low, straight approaches used for landing on aircraft carriers.

After we parked we were taken to meet Comdr. Harold Funk, the commander of Bronson Field, who was in charge of the airshow detachment. He was a fighter ace from the Pacific, where he had flown Grumman F4F Wildcats and the version built by General Motors, the FM1, which he called the Housecat. He was intrigued by the F8F Bearcat, which he had not seen before. After looking it over, he said he would like to fly it, and after a brief huddle we agreed that he could. It may have been the only time a Navy commander (equivalent rank to a lieutenant colonel in the Army) asked an Army Air Force captain for permission to do anything, especially to fly a Navy airplane. Bill gave him a short briefing and a cockpit check, after which he took off and put on a great show. Starting with a steep climb after takeoff, he performed a series of well-executed loops, Cuban eights, and vertical rolls, ending with a top-speed low pass followed by a double Immelmann. All of the spectators, AAF included, were duly impressed.

Today's pilots could never get away with giving a pilot from another service, or their own service for that matter, a spur-of-the-moment check-out. Of course, the World War II aircraft were orders of magnitude simpler, and less expensive, than today's aircraft. A P-51 cost about $60,000 in 1944; today a Grumman F-14 Tomcat runs about $30 million. Things were much looser then, so there were no repercussions.

While Commander Funk was flying, we were on an observation balcony just below the tower with a group of Navy pilots. The Hellcat and the Corsair had arrived earlier, and the Avenger was expected momentarily. A few minutes later it came into view just over the trees on a long final approach. At that distance it seemed to be barely moving, although the engine sounded like it was at fairly high power. When it was about five feet above the end of the runway, the pilot cut the power, and the Avenger (or Turkey, as the pilots call it) seemed to stop in midair and drop straight down onto the runway, after which it rolled a surprisingly short distance and came to a stop. I thought the pilot made a terrible landing and hoped that he wouldn't be ahead of me in the landing pattern at Moisant. Since he didn't start to taxi to the ramp, I assumed that he had either blown both tires or broken the landing gear. The Navy pilots, though, were quite impressed and said that he must be an old pro because that was a great landing. Sure enough, when he taxied in we learned that he had been delayed by a radio problem, the landing gear were in perfect shape, and he was an experienced pilot with hundreds of hours in the Avenger.

If a P-51 or a P-40 had landed that hard, the impact would have driven the wheels up through the wing, but Navy aircraft have extremely rugged landing gear, designed to withstand the shock of carrier landings.

Speaking of carrier landings, even though it is de rigueur for Air Force pilots to belittle Navy pilots, and vice versa, I have the utmost respect for anyone who can put a fifteen-ton jet on the heaving deck of a carrier on a black night, or on a bright day for that matter. I would hate to know that after completing a tough night combat mission that the most dangerous

During the Vietnam war my brother-in-law, Comdr. Doug Barton, flew several combat tours in Douglas A-4 Skyhawks on various carriers. He had one of the hairiest experiences I've ever heard of. After a night bombing mission over Vietnam, the A-4s were offshore returning to the USS *Coral Sea* when his wingman approached too fast and ran into him, knocking off a large section of the trailing edge of his wing. The wingman's plane went out of control, and the pilot was forced to eject, landing in the sea, where, miraculously, he was located and rescued. Doug retained control of his plane, but it was losing fuel rapidly through the ruptured tank and severed fuel lines. He knew he couldn't make it back to the ship but was able to rendezvous with a Douglas A-3 Skywarrior tanker on station for emergency refueling. After hooking up with the tanker he found that the inflowing fuel could barely keep ahead of the leaks, so he stayed hooked up until they were in the carrier landing pattern, then disengaged and landed safely on the first try despite the wing damage. One try was all that he had because his fuel was almost exhausted. It was, to say the least, a masterful piece of airmanship.

part of the flight, landing on the carrier, still lay ahead.

A few years ago I was privileged to be aboard the carrier *America* observing night landing operations, and it was frightening even to watch the planes hurtle out of the darkness at about 150 mph, hit the deck, and either catch the wire and stop or hurtle back into the darkness at full power to try again. In my book, and this *is* my book, carrier-qualified pilots are all pretty high on the ziggurat of the right stuff.

We spent that night in the visiting officer's quarters (VOQ) after getting acquainted with the Navy pilots over dinner in the club. The next morning Commander Funk flew a group of mechanics to Moisant Field in a Beechcraft SNB, a small utility transport known to the AAF, to general aviation, and to Naval aviators as the C-45, the Twin Beech, and the Bug Smasher, respectively. They were to act as the ground crew for the Navy detachment, which in this case included our three aircraft.

A few hours later we, along with the three Navy pilots, took off for the one-hour flight to New Orleans. As we had been told, the airport was far from ready for operations; the runways, ramp, and taxiways were complete, but the areas between had not been landscaped and were a sea of mud. The terminal and hangars were still under construction. The condition of the field and the cold, damp weather with low-hanging clouds did not bode well for the open house and airshow that were to begin the next morning and continue for two days. We parked in the section of the ramp assigned to the Navy, guided by the ground crews who had been flown in a few hours earlier. After tying down the planes and ensuring that they would be under guard when we were not present, we got into a Navy bus and were driven to NAS New Orleans, on the shore of Lake Pontchartrain, and moved into the VOQ. Since it was now raining we decided not to go into the city but spent a quiet afternoon and evening at the officer's club and the base theater.

The rain had stopped, but the low clouds were still in place as we left for Moisant early the next morning for the first day of the airshow. We were in our best uniforms, because while on the ground we would be standing in front of our planes to answer questions. We wore our forest-green blouses (in the Army, what would be a civilian suit coat is called a blouse), pink trousers, and khaki shirts and ties. Sadly, pinks and greens are now seen only in World War II movies. We took our flying clothing along in what turned out to be a vain hope of flying.

We did no flying at all because the bad weather persisted throughout the show. We became so cold standing in front of the airplanes that contrary to all regulations, we wore our leather A-2 flying jackets over our uniform blouses with the lower part of the blouses sticking out below the jackets. Few visitors came to the opening and even fewer ventured onto the windswept flight line to view the planes. While I commended their good sense, I wished more people would gather around to shield us from the blustery, cold wind, if nothing else. At long last, things took a decided turn for the better. A nice-looking stewardess walked up in her Chicago and Southern Airlines uniform (the airline is long since a part of Delta), stared at my odd outfit for a minute, and commented, "That's a nice peplum you're wearing."

I said, "Thank you. What's a peplum?"

"It's that little dark green skirt sticking out below your jacket," she replied.

I unzipped my jacket and showed her the rest of the blouse, explaining that I had to wear the jacket because of the cold wind and that it wouldn't fit under the blouse. She told me that her airline had a heated trailer farther down the flight line where we could get coffee and sandwiches. It was an offer I couldn't refuse—food, females, and Fahrenheit—and I must admit, for that brief period at least, Fahrenheit was paramount.

I assigned some of the Civil Air Patrol cadets on the flight line to take charge of the airplane and accompanied her to the trailer, picking up the well-chilled Dick Jones and Bill Greene on the way. There were several other hospitable stewardesses there, and we spent the rest of the day in their company, with occasional forays out to check on our planes. We asked Miss Peplum and two others if they would show us the town, and much to our delight, they agreed to pick us up at the Naval air station that evening. We had a great time—dinner at Arnaud's, dancing at the Court of Two Sisters, then to one of the New Orleans all-night coffee-and-doughnut bars. The evening was so enjoyable that we did essentially the same thing the next night.

But the next night I committed a major faux pas with Miss Peplum. We were talking about our flying experience, a constant subject of discussion among fighter pilots, and she asked me how many flying hours I had. When I estimated my time at about 900 hours, she said, rather haughtily, "That's not very much. I have more than fifteen hundred."

It is a taunt that fighter pilots are accustomed to hearing from bomber or transport pilots, and without thinking I blurted out the standard riposte, "But how much time do you have on your back?" I of course meant inverted flying, but she misunderstood, turned red, and stomped off. I caught up with her, and after I explained what I had meant, she rejoined the group at the table. When they had recovered from their fit of laughter, Jones and Greene confirmed that those words were standard in the fighter pilot's lexicon but could easily be misconstrued by nonpilots. She graciously accepted their explanation, and all went well for the rest of the evening.

The weather continued to be lousy, but there was another high point to the airshow, in addition to Chicago and Southern's contribution. Lt. Gen. Jimmy Doolittle delivered the dedication address. I don't recall what he said, but I do vividly remember shaking his hand when he came down to the flight line to greet the pilots. He always had been, and still is, one of my heroes, even before he led the Tokyo Raid, because of his exploits as a race pilot. He was the only man to win all three of the principal air races: the Thompson, the Bendix, and the Schneider. Even more impressive, he had a Ph.D. in aeronautical engineering from MIT and was the only pilot

In late 1973, as assistant director for aeronautics at the National Air and Space Museum, I visited General Doolittle at his home in Santa Monica to decide what items of his memorabilia the museum wanted for its collection. He greeted me when I arrived at seven-thirty in the morning, introduced me to his wife, Joe, took me to his den, and left for his office. Upon completing my list of items at about eleven-thirty, I thanked Mrs. Doolittle and told her I was leaving. She said that General Doolittle had called and asked that I stop by his office in downtown Santa Monica to look at a few more items.

When I arrived at the office, he said it was time for lunch and gave me the choice of eating out or allowing him to fix something. I chose the latter; he disappeared into a tiny kitchen and soon emerged with a tray bearing our lunches. We each had a six-ounce cup of soup made from Cup-a-Soup mix, the same size cup of Dr. Pepper, and a large Pepperidge Farm chocolate layer cookie filled with white cream, sort of a designer Oreo. When we had finished, which didn't take long, he went back into the kitchen and shouted to me, "Do you like Ding-Dongs?" I told him I didn't know what Ding-Dongs were. He brought out two Twinkie-size choco-late cakes rolled around a white cream mixture, which I knew, in the east, as Ho-Hos. We polished them off in short order and went back to our work. It was as unbalanced a meal as I had ever eaten, but I can't knock it, because General Doolittle lived well into his nineties.

to survive the deadly Gee Bee Super Speedster, winning the Thompson in it in 1931. I never dreamed that much later, as deputy director of the National Air and Space Museum, I would not only get to know him well but would also interview him in a Smithsonian film.

The evening after the dedication we were told that since the airshow was over, there would be no security at the airport; it would return to con-struction mode. We couldn't leave the planes unguarded at night, and the weather was too bad to fly back to Florida. Commander Funk decided we could fly the planes to NAS New Orleans and remain there until the weather cleared. He called the station commander to get permission for the move and then called all the pilots together. I was a bit irritated when he said that he had received permission for everyone to land except me. It appeared the station commander didn't think an AAF pilot could land a big airplane like the F7F on that short (less than 3,000 feet) runway. Recently, a Marine pilot had landed there in an F7F and had run off the end of the runway into the lake.

I was insulted that anyone would think that an AAF pilot, especially this one, couldn't make a short field landing. I told Commander Funk that in China I had often landed a P-40 carrying almost a full load of fuel and two 500-pound bombs on a 2,500-foot strip with ten-foot-high raised embankments on both ends and thought nothing of it. I said that I could land the F7F and stop easily within 3,000 feet and that I would take full responsibility. Of course we both knew that as the pilot I had full reponsibility anyway, especially to Colonel Muldoon.

Commander Funk called back and obtained permission for me to land with the rest. I said I would land last, so when we got in our planes and taxied out, I brought up the rear. It was a short flight to the Navy field, and I circled while the others landed. I made a long, low approach and dragged it in to the end of the runway holding my airspeed between the power-off and the power-on stalling speed. Airplanes stall at a higher speed with the power off than with the power on because of the additional airflow over the wings generated by the propeller. I came over the end of the runway about three feet high and chopped the power. The F7F stalled instantly and dropped straight down, hitting the runway extremely hard on the main gear. I quickly put the nosewheel on the runway and got on the brakes. I believe I could have turned off at the intersection, but rather than risk overheating the brakes, I decided to leave well enough alone. I did make it obvious, though, that I had to add power to taxi to the end of the runway. When I parked and climbed out of the plane, my Navy companions said that my landing would have been a great carrier landing, boosting my ego to an even higher than normal level.

We spent that evening at the club, and the next morning the weather had cleared. We said our good-byes and took off for Eglin, where we rejoined the Air Force.

6

Unstuck in a Shooting Star

Early in February 1946 I saw one of the most thrilling sights of my life. Colonel Muldoon had gone to Muroc, California (later the site of Edwards Air Force Base), to ferry a Lockheed P-80 Shooting Star back to Eglin to begin operational suitability testing. The squadron was notified that he would be arriving at Eglin early on Sunday morning. Barney Turner, Dick Jones, and I arose at dawn and checked with base operations for Colonel Muldoon's estimated time of arrival (ETA). We were told he would arrive in about an hour. Since our quarters were close to the runway, we decided to walk out onto the airfield and wait alongside the landing end of the runway for the arrival.

About half an hour later we heard the then unfamiliar sound of the jet's roar in the distance. Scarcely a minute later a beautiful, sleek gray airplane with a most unusual shape flashed by about fifty feet above the runway at a speed of almost 600 mph and zoomed up to three or four thousand feet in an instant. It was like nothing I'd ever seen. The wings were set far back on the fuselage, well behind the cockpit, which was covered by a tiny bubble canopy, and the external fuel tanks were faired onto the wing tips. At first glance it looked to me like something out of *Buck Rogers in the Twenty-fifth Century* (a prewar comic strip and radio series).

The P-80 came by again in another high-speed pass; then, on a third slower pass, it peeled up into a landing pattern and touched down right in front of us. We hustled to the ramp and arrived just as Colonel Muldoon was climbing out of the cockpit and sliding to the ground. Sliding is the right word, since we didn't yet have the special ladder that hooked over the side of the cockpit, and the wing was too far aft to step on. Showing rare excitement, he said it was a great flying airplane and that Jones and I would be checking out in it as soon as the acceptance inspection was completed. Barney had checked out in the airplane some months previously at Muroc.

During the next week, Dick and I memorized the dash-one section (pilot's operating instructions) of the P-80 tech order and were briefed by Barney and Colonel Muldoon on the flying characteristics. As soon as the P-80 was back in the hangar, we spent several impatient hours in the cockpit familiarizing ourselves with the instruments and controls. Although Dick and I had both flown the P-59, the P-80 was to be the first U.S. operational jet, and it had far better performance than the Airacomet.

On February 20, with great anticipation, I climbed up the ladder, which had finally arrived, and settled myself in the small cockpit for my first flight. It felt like a fighter should feel, with its tight cockpit and the gunsight jammed in front of the pilot's face. The stick had a nonstandard grip that was twisted slightly counterclockwise and a large, three-position thumb switch on the top that controlled the elevator trim. There was no trim-position indicator, but a green light on the panel was illuminated when the elevator trim was in the neutral position. The elevator had a spring balance that partially held the stick in the full forward or full aft position while the plane was not in motion; however, it was not noticeable in flight. The ailerons were hydraulically boosted, with a ratio of fifteen to one, to reduce the stick force needed to roll the airplane (much like power steering in an automobile). The aileron trim was a right-left switch on the left console. There was no rudder trim, since without the torque of a propeller, the rudder requirements were minimal. A second altimeter on the left console indicated the cabin altitude, which, since the cabin was pressurized, was normally 10,000 or so feet below the actual altitude if the plane was above 20,000 feet. These first P-80 cockpits were not equipped with ejection seats; to bail out, the pilot released the canopy and dived over the side or rolled the airplane upside down and pushed forward on the stick. His chances of success were slim if he had to get out at high speed.

The starting procedure in the early model P-80 was best described as sporty to the pilot and spectacular to the outside observers. The throttle was set in the full-open position, and the fuel tank switches were turned on. The wing tanks fed through the fuselage tank, so it remained full when the others ran dry. The external power unit was plugged in because the aircraft battery was barely able to rotate the engine fast enough for the start.

The starter switch was held in the on position until the engine tachometer read 9 percent, about 1,050 rpm (100 percent was 11,800 rpm). Then the emergency fuel pump switch (called the I 16) on the left cockpit wall was turned on, and the fuel stopcock was moved forward to the on position. As soon as the pilot heard the loud rumble of the burning fuel, almost an explosion, and the tail-pipe temperature started to rise, which occurred instantaneously, the I-16 was turned off and the throttle snatched back to the idle position to keep the tail-pipe temperature from exceeding 900 degrees centigrade, which was considered a hot start. If that happened, the engine had to be shut down immediately and inspected before another start could be attempted. To the observer, the starting rumble was accompanied by a visible streak of flame coming out of the tail pipe. If the start was not hot, the starter switch was held on until the engine rpm reached 16 percent and then released. The rpm would increase rapidly from that point until it reached idle rpm, 35 percent. As the rpm increased to idle, the tail-pipe temperature dropped back into its normal operating range, below 715 degrees.

We often took advantage of this spectacular start sequence to astound the observers, most of whom had little or no knowledge of jets. The Eglin pilots did not originate this practical joke—some unknown genius deserves the credit—but we used it whenever the circumstances were right. During many of the airshows, we spent a good bit of the day at static displays, that is, with the P-80 parked on the ramp with the pilot beside it to answer the public's questions, generally concerning the speed, the armament, and what made it move. The most common misconception was that jets are propelled by the force of exhaust gases pushing against the air. Actually thrust is produced by the airplane's reaction to the ejected gases as described by Newton's Third Law: for every action there is an equal and opposite reaction. When it was time to fly, the crowd was moved back to a safe distance, and the pilot climbed into the cockpit and initiated the start sequence. When the engine rpm reached 9 percent, the pilot nodded to the crew chief, who would light a piece of newspaper and put it into the tail pipe. As soon as the pilot saw in the rear view mirror that the crew chief was clear of the tail pipe, he opened the stopcock, and the engine started with an explosive roar. No doubt there are still some people who believe that the jet had to be ignited with an open flame.

When the pilot was ready to taxi, he closed the dive brakes (sturdy flaps that extend at an angle of about 60 degrees from the bottom of the fuselage below the cockpit) using a switch on the left cockpit wall behind the throttle. (In later models this switch was on the throttle.) To start taxiing, he opened the throttle to about 80 percent rpm and then reduced it to about 50 percent once the plane was moving. All the ground steering was done by differential braking, but the P-80 handled well on the ground, and this presented no problem.

Jet aircraft require no warm-up or engine check before takeoff, and since fuel consumption is so high on the ground, they always had first priority for takeoff. This tended to irritate some of the bomber pilots as we taxied in front of them onto the runway, sometimes with rude gestures to increase the irritation. While taxiing into position, we closed and locked the canopy by means of a long handle on the right side and lowered the flaps to the takeoff position of 80 percent. Once the airplane was lined up with the runway, the engine was run up to 100 percent rpm, and if all the instruments were in the normal range, primarily the tail-pipe temperature and the oil pressure, the pilot released the brakes and began the takeoff roll. Acceleration was much less than in a propeller airplane but considerably more than in the P-59. Unless there was a crosswind, little brake or rudder was needed, as the speed increased, to stay on the runway centerline. The stick was pulled gently back at about 80 mph to rotate the airplane around the main landing gear and raise the nosewheel slightly. After a run of some 4,000 to 5,000 feet, at about 120 mph, the plane lifted off, or as the British so aptly put it, unstuck.

It continued to climb at about the same shallow angle until the airspeed reached 160 mph, then the flaps were milked up slowly in increments of about 15 percent to preclude the sudden loss of altitude that would occur if they were fully retracted immediately. As soon as the plane was high enough to clear all obstacles, it was held in level flight until it accelerated to 330 mph, the optimal climbing speed at sea level. The high climbing speed, about double that of propeller-driven fighters and in fact considerably higher than their cruising speed, was a novel but much-enjoyed feature to jet novices because they could legally buzz along at about 100 feet until that speed was attained.

Another major difference between jet and propeller flight was the need to fly at what were then very high altitudes much of the time. Jet-engine fuel consumption is at its highest at sea level and decreases markedly with increased altitude. In the P-80 it was about three times higher at sea level than at 30,000 feet. Consequently, much of our flying, especially cross-country flying, was done at or above 30,000 feet. With the jet's internal fuel of 432 gallons, low-altitude flying time was limited to less than one hour. A Mustang, with about 250 gallons internal, could fly for at least four hours.

The crash helmet, or brain bucket, that had replaced the soft helmet worn up to then, was a necessity in the P-80. The pilot's head was so close to the small canopy that at high speed in turbulent air it was constantly rapped against the Plexiglas. Later, as more P-80s entered the inventory, a beat-up, chipped helmet was the mark of an experienced pilot. When we first started flying jets at Eglin the crash helmets were still under development so we had the squadron personal-equipment technicians affix tank-driver helmets to our standard soft helmets. They did the job well until regular helmets were issued.

On my first P-80 flight, on February 20, 1946, it took a few minutes to become accustomed to the boosted ailerons. I flew along gently rocking my wings after takeoff because of overcontrolling. Luckily, there were no other planes nearby (rocking one's wings is the signal to join formation). Actually it wouldn't have mattered, because no one could have caught up with the P-80, being the only jet in the sky. I soon overcame that tendency and found the ailerons responsive, giving the airplane a high rate of roll. I could perform a quick roll by just moving the stick sharply in the direction I wished to roll. No rudder at all was used, very different from the aileron-rudder coordination required to slow roll in propeller airplane.

The P-80 was a delight to fly. All the controls and instruments were where they belonged, and the control pressures were well balanced. The elevator trim button on top of the stick was a great innovation. All the elevator trimming could be done without taking my hand off the stick. The ailerons required little or no trim changes, but the aileron trim was put on the top of the stick in later P-80s. The elevator trim switch was most appreciated when the dive brakes were operated, especially at high speed. When they were lowered, the nose pitched up sharply. The reverse occurred when they were raised, so rapid trim changes were necessary.

I ran through a series of stalls both clean and in landing configuration (dive brakes down, landing gear down, and full flaps) and learned that the airplane started mushing and buffeting about 10 mph before it stalled. The stalls were normal, with no wing drop unless they were held too long; recovery was clean using standard procedures (stick forward and add power to increase airspeed). Accelerated (high-g) stalls also gave ample warning by buffeting; the airplane recovered immediately when back pressure on the stick was relaxed.

After a few rolls and loops, I headed back to the field for landing. As I had been told, the P-80, even with everything down for landing, did not decelerate like a prop airplane with the power off, because the propeller acts as a brake at idle power. Consequently, the approach had to be much flatter; with a steep approach, the pilot couldn't slow it down for landing within a reasonable distance. It was quite easy to land, and I taxied to the ramp with the comforting feeling that now I was a real jet pilot, notwithstanding my previous flights in the P-59.

My feelings during that first P-80 flight are difficult to describe but are more difficult to forget. The name "Shooting Star" fit the P-80 well. I felt as though I were riding on a shooting star, that all my training and flying up to now were to prepare me for this airplane. I felt as though I were, at least for the moment, king of the sky. Later I made the transition into newer and faster jets, but none of my later first flights matched my first P-80 flight for pure exhilaration and joy.

The good performance and handling characteristics of the P-80 were a tribute to designer Kelly Johnson and his Lockheed team. The project details for the P-80 were completed in one week, and Lockheed promised delivery of the first plane within 180 days. On January 4, 1944, 143 days after the contract was let, it made its first flight. The Germans and the British were much farther along with the Messerschmitt 262 and Gloster Meteor, respectively. They both became operational in 1944. After a great deal of testing and modifying, there were four P-80s overseas—two in England and two in Italy—in 1945, but a tragic accident involving one of them caused them to be grounded, and they never saw combat. Maj. Fred Borsodi, an experienced Wright Field test pilot, was demonstrating one of the 80s in England when, unknown to him, a fire started in the engine compartment. The aft section of the airplane burned off, and he was killed. His death was not completely in vain, however, for his accident resulted in the installation of a fire warning sensor in the engine compartment, which saved the lives of a number of pilots.

During the next few months after my P-80 flight, I was engaged in a series of armament tests flying mostly P-51s and P-47s. It was quite a letdown for a real jet pilot, but the one P-80 was spread pretty thin among fifteen eager pilots. The gun tests involved firing 5,000 rounds per gun at various altitudes and g-loads with a new model of the .50-caliber machine gun to test its durability and the dependability of the belt feed system. Firing at high g-loads (4, 5, and 6 g) was extremely enervating, especially in hot weather at low altitude. After three of these flights I felt, and looked, like a dishrag. I thought that was tough duty until a few months later, in midsummer, when we started the same tests with the P-80. The early models that we were flying were not equipped with air conditioning and, because

Many years later, in 1989, I was able to get a ride in a two-seat version of the General Dynamics F-16C Fighting Falcon with the Vermont Air National Guard. The visibility, performance, and handling were astounding, to say the least. It had been twenty-five years since I had flown a jet fighter, as I had retired from the USAF in 1964.

I was well aware of the performance of modern fighters, but until I experienced it I did not fully appreciate it. When not fully loaded, the thrust exceeds the weight, and thus the F-16 could climb vertically. It could pull and sustain 9 g's, and the seat was tilted back at a 30-degree angle to help the pilot retain consciousness at that g-load. The heads-up display projected the gunsight, radar scope, and all required flight and armament data onto the windscreen, so the pilot didn't have to look down into the cockpit. The HOTAS (Hands On Throttle And Stick) allowed the pilot to fly the airplane and operate all its systems without removing his hands from the stick and throttle. There are nine buttons and switches on the stick and seven on the throttle. A saxophone player would feel at home with the system. In contrast, the P-80A had only a trigger, bomb release button, and trim tab switch on the stick and a microphone button on the throttle.

The emergency warning system on the F-16 is considerably improved from that in the P-80, which consisted of a few analog gages with red lines on the faces indicating trouble (such as low oil pressure or high tail-pipe temperature) and a fire warning light. In the F-16, a female voice, known as Bitching Betty, repeats, "Warning! Warning!" in the pilot's earphones while a red signal on an annunciator panel lights up the proper panel to define the emergency. This table outlines the performance of the two airplanes:

	F-80A	F-16C
Gross weight	14,500 lbs	25,071 lbs (for air-to-air missions)
Static thrust	4,000 lbs	29,000 lbs
Maximum speed	558 mph	1,320+ mph
Rate of climb	4,580 ft/min	35,000+ ft/min
Service ceiling	45,000 ft	50,000+ ft
Range	540 miles	1,100+ miles

of the heat generated by the friction of the high-speed airflow on the fuse-lage, had cockpit temperatures that ran from 120 to 140 degrees Fahren-heit. When I came into operations after a flight I would take off my anti-g suit and wring out a considerable amount of water. Several visitors accused me of passing through the shower on my way to operations; I hadn't, but it sounded like a good idea. Later models of the P-80 included air-cycle air conditioning. (Hot air was tapped from the compressor and passed through a small, high-speed turbine that removed enough energy to lower the temperature of the air, which was then delivered to the cockpit.) It made flying the P-80, especially at low altitude, much more pleasant, but there was a disconcerting side effect. In the high humidity of the Gulf coast, when a jet was about halfway down the runway on takeoff, small clouds of steam began pouring out of the vents on either side of the rudder pedals. The steam was harmless and dissipated almost immediately, and we became used to it—so used to it that we often forgot to mention it to new pilots checking out in the P-80, and it would cause them to abort their takeoffs.

Barney Turner had a close call on one of these low-altitude armament tests. He was over the Gulf at about 5,000 feet when the fire warning light came on. He reduced power immediately, but the light remained on, caus-ing him to follow the mandated procedure and shut down the engine. He zoomed to gain as much altitude as possible and turned back toward land and the field. He thought he could just make the runway, but with the en-gine not turning, he had no hydraulic pressure to lower the landing gear and to power the aileron boost. Without boost the stick felt as though it were mounted in rapidly hardening concrete; it took both hands to bank. Despite this he managed to hold a steady glide while pumping the gear down by hand and fighting the stick when he tried to turn. He made a good landing on the field, but only the nose gear and the right main gear were locked down. The left gear folded, and the airplane skidded off the side of the runway and stopped with no injury to Barney and minimal damage to the P-80. Barney was a fine pilot, and he did a masterful job of saving the airplane when he would have been fully justified in bailing out.

About two years before the P-80 crash landing, Barney was on his checkout flight in the Bell XP-77 prior to starting its test program. The XP-77 was a plywood fighter powered by a Ranger V-12 575-horsepower en-gine. Designed to dogfight with the Japanese Zeroes, it was more than 1,000 pounds lighter than the Zero, but it came out long after they had ceased to be a major threat. The only thing Zero about it was its worth to the AAF.

After checking its general handling and stall characteristics, Barney dived to pick up speed and started a loop, but he fell out of it at the top into a flat spin. Recovery from a flat spin can be difficult; without a rudder it becomes impossible. Unknown to Barney, the rudder had torn free from the vertical stabilizer. He tried everything he knew to break the spin, until, almost too late, he dived over the side and pulled the ripcord without counting to ten. If he had, the numbers from five to ten would have been recited posthumously. The chute opened; he swung once and hit the ground on the downswing. The XP-77 landed flat, about fifty feet away. The prop had chewed all the branches from one side of a scrub oak. When he didn't return from the flight, the squadron began a search of the area he had been flying over, and after several hours a pilot spotted the wreckage on the ground. Barney's parachute was nearby, but he did not see Barney. A short time later, a jeep was directed by radio to the wreck and found Barney ensconced in the upper branches of a nearby tree that he had climbed to escape the hordes of voracious Florida mosquitoes. Barney said he had waved when the plane came by looking for him, but the pilot evidently was not looking for him in a tree, especially as his chute was on the ground in plain view. At the time, Barney thought the fall had only knocked the wind out of him, but in later years he developed severe back problems that required a major operation to correct them.

In June I was checked out in my first night fighter, the Northrop P-61 Black Widow. It was the first airplane designed as a night fighter; all previous night fighters were modifications of aircraft originally designed for another purpose. It looked almost foreboding on the ramp, with its all-black paint and two big 2,000-horsepower Pratt & Whitney R-2800 engines. It was armed with four forward-firing 20mm cannon in the belly (lower fuselage) and with four .50-caliber machine guns in the top turret. The machine guns could be locked to fire forward as fixed guns operated by the pilot or used as moveable turret guns by the gunner, whose position was behind and above the pilot's cockpit. The radar operator sat in the back of the fuselage, facing forward, between the tail booms. He had no forward visibilty and not much to the sides. My brother Carl trained as a P-61 radar operator in Fresno, California, and he remarked that the only way he knew they were landing was when he saw the Roma Wine sign go by.

It was large for a fighter, with a wingspan of 66 feet and a gross weight of about 30,000 pounds, but it handled like a smaller plane. The flaps were long, reaching almost from wing tip to wing tip, and the ailerons were tiny, with a span of about 4 feet, but they were only to provide control feel for the pilot. Roll control was achieved by spoilers that rose out of the top surface of the wing; they reduced lift on one side or the other, causing the airplane to roll.

I had already completed the written test on the aircraft systems, so after a cockpit check by one of the other pilots, I started up and taxied to the end of the runway. Since this was my checkout flight, I was flying without a crew. The P-61 accelerated well at takeoff power, and it lifted off easily. I reached forward to raise the landing gear lever, careful not to ease the wheel forward unconsciously. I had been warned about pilots who nosed into the ground while raising the gear, especially at night. Just as I was congratulating myself for avoiding that pitfall—fighter pilots have to congratulate themselves since they are the only ones aboard—there was a loud impact behind me that I both heard and felt. I cut back to climb power and started a turn to stay close to the field in case something was amiss. All the instruments had their proper readings, and the airplane felt okay. To be on the safe side, I asked one of our pilots who was approaching the field in a Mustang to look the P-61 over and see if anything was loose or had fallen off. He assured me everything was all right, so I continued with the flight.

After landing I went back into ops and told the pilot who had checked me out about the noise and impact. He said with a smile, "I must have forgotten to tell you that the nosewheel slams into the up position, right under the pilot seat, when it retracts. It's perfectly normal." I found out later that every pilot being checked out was intentionally not told about the nosewheel so that he, too, could be surprised. Of course I followed the same procedure later when I checked pilots out in the P-61.

I had a sad duty to perform late in June. The Grumman F7F Tigercat tests were completed, and the airplane was declared surplus to the requirements of the AAF. I was detailed to fly it to the Aberdeen Proving Ground in Maryland, where it was to be used as a target for gun and rocket tests. It was in excellent condition with little more than a hundred hours of flying time, and it seemed wasteful to destroy it. I thought we should give it back to the Navy, but they wanted only the two-seat night fighter version. If I could have hidden it away somewhere, today it would be worth several hundred thousand dollars to the avid collectors of warbirds. Before I took off for Aberdeen I had to sign a form stating that the aircraft clock was installed and working. After an uneventful flight with one landing at Spartanburg, South Carolina (I didn't need fuel but wanted to make an extra landing and takeoff), I landed at Aberdeen, where the operations officer signed for the clock and, incidentally, for the F7F. It was only one of the disappointments I experienced during this period.

About a month earlier, Colonel Muldoon had assigned me as test pilot for the Japanese Kawasaki Ki-61 Hien (Swallow) that had been brought to the States following the war. It was better known to Americans by its code name "Tony." I had never encountered one in combat, although a few had been reported in China. I was looking forward to flying it and was excited when I learned it was to be flown to Eglin from Wright Field in a few days. Unfortunately, the engine failed during the ferry flight, and the pilot had to make a belly landing. He was not injured, but the airplane was not reparable without more effort than it was worth. As a result I lost what I thought would be my only chance to fly a foreign airplane, but in 1993 in France, I flew two Russian planes, an Antonev An-2 and a Yak-11.

Early in July, one of the married pilots in the squadron, who considered it his duty to keep abreast of such events, announced in operations that two new good-looking blondes were now living on the base. The arrival of two blondes was big news. Eglin was in such a sparsely populated area that young women hired as secretaries often lived too far away to commute. The base housed them in dormitories, enclosed by high metal fences, that were off-limits to men (an old-fashioned idea). The young ladies had to meet their gentlemen callers in a small building outside the fence. A few days later I saw them from a distance but couldn't tell much except that our intelligence seemed to be correct.

I didn't know how correct until two weekends later when I was introduced to them at the officer's beach club. They were both very good-looking. One of them, Ann Coleman, was at the club with a squadron mate, Maj. Spider Webb, whom she later married. The other, Glindel Barron, had that Lauren Bacall look, tall and willowy, with a great suntan. Much to my dismay, she was accompanied by an equally suntanned fugitive from Muscle Beach, an ordnance officer attached to our squadron. But he was a ground pounder, and I knew that a real jet pilot like me would have no trouble turning inside him if it became necessary. Eventually it did.

7

Travels by Yo-yo

During the summer and fall of 1946 I flew on two short but interesting tests and took two long trips, one to Alaska and one to California. The first test involved a new large fighter-bomber developed by Boeing for the Navy, the XF8B. It had been sent to Eglin to see if the AAF had any interest in it. The XF8B was much larger than the fighters of that time. The wingspan was 54 feet, 2 feet more than the Lockheed P-38 Lightning, which was the largest AAF day fighter. It was powered by the 28-cylinder, 3,250-horsepower Pratt & Whitney Wasp Major engine driving counter-rotating propellers. In size it closely resembled the Douglas A-1 Skyraider, which was used with great success by the Navy and the Air Force in Vietnam. One of its distinctive features was a bomb bay, which allowed it to carry bombs internally, with less drag, instead of on the wings as they are on most fighters.

The first couple of flights were spent in feeling the plane out, checking its stall response, and trying a few aerobatic maneuvers. Because of the counter-rotating props, there was no torque to correct for on takeoff; it seemed strange in a propeller aircraft, although flying jets had prepared me for the feeling. The sun shining through the counter-rotating props formed intricate, changing kaleidoscopic patterns that were almost hypnotic. I thought that might create a problem for already fatigued pilots on long flights.

Despite its size and weight (18,000 pounds) it handled like a much smaller plane. I was most conscious of its size while taxiing and on landing.

The plane had a long landing gear, and the cockpit was above the bomb bay, putting the pilot about twelve feet above the ground at touchdown, which took some getting used to, especially since the P-80 cockpit was quite close to the ground.

My first test mission was to drop some practice bombs in level flight to check the functioning of the winker bomb bay doors. On a glide-bombing or skip-bombing run, the pilot would normally have to open the doors, release the bombs, and then close the doors; the winker doors allowed the pilot to do all that just by pressing the bomb release, at which time the doors would quickly open, the bombs release, and the doors close immediately. The Boeing technical representative told me the enemy would never know where the bombs came from. I thought the enemy might suspect that they came from the airplane that had just completed a run on them, but I didn't say anything.

As briefed, I climbed to 10,000 feet over the Gulf range, accelerated to 300 mph in level flight, and notified range control that I was ready to release the first bomb. Upon receiving clearance, I pushed the bomb release button on the stick while peering through the glass peephole in the floor of the cockpit, which allowed me to monitor the opening and closing of the door. The doors partially opened and then closed as programmed, but the bomb release hit the right door, which had not opened far enough, and bent it badly. I could see that the bomb was gone. In fact, I saw the smoke marker when it hit the water, but since I could also see the Gulf through the peephole, I knew the door had not closed completely. I reduced my speed as much as possible, returned to the field, and landed. After the door was repaired, we ran some tests without bombs to determine the problem with the doors. There were two difficulties: the airflow over the doors at the higher speed created a low pressure inside the bomb bay, and the springs that aided the opening were not strong enough. Small aerodynamic spoilers and stronger springs corrected the problem, and we made a number of successful drops. Later, we did some firing at ground targets. The six 20mm cannon practically dissolved the targets.

We suddenly were ordered to discontinue the tests and return the airplane to the Navy. Both the Navy and our test team thought it would be an effective fighter bomber, with its range of greater than one thousand miles and its 6,400-pound internal bomb load, but with the end of the war there was no longer a requirement for it.

I had a rather hairy experience on another test that was run in conjunction with the equipment lab at Eglin. One morning Colonel Muldoon told me to get my helmet and report to Dr. Graves at the equipment lab. He said I would not need my parachute. Wondering what was in store, I left for the lab. I had met Dr. Graves a few times at the club. He was tall and extremely thin (we told him he would have to tread water in a test tube) and well liked, with a Ph.D. in aviation physiology. He was totally dedicated to his profession and determined to make flying as safe and comfortable for the aircrews as possible. At this time he was trying to find ways to make fighter pilots more comfortable on long flights, especially long flights over water. When there was an appreciable body of water to be crossed, the pilot's normal seat cushion was replaced with a packed life raft. Since the pilot cannot move around in the cockpit, six or eight hours of sitting on a life raft becomes extremely uncomfortable. The pilots often commented that the raft didn't bother them; it was the propeller on the outboard motor that really hurt.

The lab staff had devised a hammock seat that would keep the pilot suspended a few inches above the parachute and, by conforming to his body contours, provide comfortable yet sturdy support. The rig consisted of a rectangular piece of heavy canvas, about four feet long and eighteen inches wide, attached firmly to the inside of the parachute harness at four points, two at the top of the pilot's shoulders and two at the front of the parachute pack under the pilot's knees. There was sufficient slack in the canvas to provide a hammocklike seat. The canvas had a metal grommet in each corner and a larger hole in the center of the lower end for the parachute leg straps to pass through.

In the P-51H to be used in the test, the seat had been removed and a metal framework about the size of a seat installed. The seat belt and shoulder harness were attached to this frame, and there were four L-shaped pins or hooks on the frame, two at shoulder level and two at the knees. When I got into the cockpit I had to brace myself with my feet on the rudder pedals and with my back against the armorplate rear wall of the cockpit until Doc Graves and one of his henchmen slipped the grommets over the four pins and the hammock would support my weight. The lab staff had already completed many hours of ground testing and knew that the seat met the comfort requirements. My job was to test it under combat maneuvers, including positive and negative g-loads, to determine its utility.

I took off and, as directed, flew generally straight and level for two hours before beginning the combat maneuvers. I had to admit that the seat was comfortable during those two hours. I had no problems under high g-loads and during turns, dives, and rolls, but when I pushed over at the top of a zoom, the negative g lifted the left shoulder grommet off the hook. When I leveled out, there was no support on that side, my parachute hit the floor, and I dropped below the cockpit rim with an absurd tilt to the left and my knees still up. I knew it would be virtually impossible to land safely in this ridiculous position, since I could barely see out, so I somewhat frantically tried to get the grommet back onto the hook. I couldn't get my feet under my body to lift up, and I could barely touch the canvas with my hand. I decided that my best chance would be to do a series of pushovers and hope to slip the grommet over the pin. After several futile attempts, I succeeded—succeeded, that is, in lifting the right shoulder grommet off its hook and dumping myself on the floor of the cockpit with my knees up. I was so inclined that I was in the recommended position to do sit-ups, had I been so inclined.

Now I was in a real predicament; I couldn't see out of the cockpit except straight up, and that is no help in landing. Hoping that I wouldn't have a midair with someone also sitting on the cockpit floor, I settled down and tried to figure a way out of this fix. After ruling out having another pilot guide me to a landing, making an upside-down approach and rolling out just before touchdown (I gave that minimal consideration), and bailing out, assuming that I could from that position (Colonel Muldoon would never understand why I had abandoned a perfectly healthy airplane), I decided on the following. Using my feet, I was able to move the rudder pedals to the full aft position, that is, as close to me as possible. Then I braced my feet on the pedals and pushed forward hard on the stick. When my body rose to the right height, I pushed back and braced my back against the armor plate. I managed to stay in this position until I had landed and taxied off the runway. By that time my legs were quivering so badly under the strain that I shut off the engine, opened the canopy, sat on the floor, and waited for Doc Graves and his team to help me out of the cockpit. After I explained to him what had happened, he said he would put catches on the hooks to keep the grommets from slipping off inadvertently, but I told him they might also make it impossible to bail out. It was back to the drawing board for Dr. Graves and his team and back to the squadron for me. I never heard of the seat again, so perhaps the idea was abandoned.

When I got back to operations looking somewhat the worse for wear, I was asked, "What happened to you, Lope?" I said I had just become the first person to land a P-51 while standing up.

Not long afterward, I was told to report to the base commander's office at nine the next morning in Class A uniform for an award ceremony.

Two other squadron pilots, Maj. John Hudson and Capt. Bill Greene, received the same orders. John said we were to be awarded medals that we had won during the war but had not received. The next morning the base commander, Col. John F. Whiteley, pinned medals on seven officers after a formal reading of the citations by the base adjutant. I received the Silver Star and the Soldier's Medal. The Silver Star was awarded for repeatedly attacking a group of Japanese Oscar fighters that were providing top cover for a flight of Val dive bombers, even though I was out of ammunition and had been ordered to return to base. My attacks had kept the Oscars busy, allowing others in the squadron to shoot down three of the dive bombers. I received the Soldier's Medal for my part in rescuing crew members from a burning B-25 that had crashed on our airfield in China.

I couldn't help but contrast the formal ceremony at Eglin with the award of the Distinguished Flying Cross and Air Medal in China. I had received copies of the orders for the medals, but not the medals, and hadn't given it much thought. Just before I left China for the States, I stepped into the 23rd Fighter Group operations office in Luliang to say good-bye to some friends, and one of the ops officers asked me if I had received my medals yet. When I said no, he reached into a drawer, brought out a DFC and an Air Medal, both in boxes, and threw them across the room to me. I caught them, put them in my musette bag; and left. In retrospect, it was rather an appropriate presentation, since they were both flying medals.

A few days after the awards ceremony, Colonel Muldoon told me that I might be taking a P-80 to Alaska that winter and that I would be leaving in two days, on July 22, for Alaska in a B-25 with Lt. Col. Bob Bowden, the commanding officer of the medium and light bomber test squadron, to familiarize myself with the route. Sure enough, on the afternoon of the twenty-second, we took off for Ladd Field, near Fairbanks, Alaska. We made the trip in easy stages, spending the first night at Memphis and the second at Tinker Field in Oklahoma City, where Colonel Bowden had to check on the progress of some modifications to the fuel tanks of an Eglin C-54 transport (Douglas DC-4).

I had been checked out in the B-25 a few months earlier, so Colonel Bowden let me have the left seat on the leg from Memphis to Oklahoma City. I made a good landing, but it turned out to be my last of the trip. He didn't say anything, but I don't think he thought much of my steep, power-off landing approach. From then on he just climbed into the left seat as a matter of course, although he split the flying time evenly. Later, when I had more experience in the B-25, I found that his technique of a flatter approach with a little power was best suited for the B-25. Occasionally, even a fighter pilot can learn something, but I never admitted it to Colonel Bowden.

Our next stop was Offutt Field, south of Omaha, where we spent the day examining a crashed Fairchild C-82 Flying Boxcar that was assigned to the cold-weather test detachment at Ladd Field and discussing the crash with the pilot. He said that he had encountered a severe downdraft as he approached the end of the runway, causing him to hit the ground so hard that both of the tail booms broke and the fuselage was badly crushed despite the application of full power. It might have been the same wind-shear phenomenon that has caused a number of serious crashes in more recent years.

The next day we flew to Great Falls, Montana, via Denver, Colorado, and Hill Field, near Ogden, Utah. I had never been in this part of the country before, and the vast open spaces and the variation in scenery were a revelation. There seemed to be no end to the wheat fields in the Great Plains. Although the country was flat, it was gradually rising toward the Rocky Mountains, and by Denver the elevation was one mile above sea level. As we approached Denver, in the then crystal-clear air, the majestic peaks of the Rockies came into view, including Pikes Peak near Colorado Springs. Little did I realize that some twelve years later I would see it every day as one of the original faculty members of the new Air Force Academy.

From Denver to Ogden we had to fly at 15,000 feet to top the mountains that rise above 14,000 feet in that area. As we neared Great Falls, our last stop in the United States, the tall smokestack of a copper-smelting plant was visible from about one hundred miles. We spent a couple of days at the air base in Great Falls while the radio was being repaired. It had been operating erratically for several days, and we wanted it fixed before we left the country. We chose not to go into town, because we were expecting the repairs to be completed momentarily. The technicians couldn't locate the problem, so they replaced the set.

From Great Falls we flew to Whitehorse, Yukon Territory, with a reueling stop at the Royal Canadian Air Force field at Fort Nelson, in the northeast corner of British Columbia. We crossed most of the province of Alberta on the way to Fort Nelson, roughly paralleling the Canadian Rockies as we headed northwest. The country was rough and hilly but not mountainous. The airfield at Whitehorse is on a plateau that looks down on the town. Because there were no quarters on the airfield, we stayed in town at the only hotel. Whitehorse was much like the Yukon gold-rush towns I had seen in *Call of the Wild* and other frigid classics. The sidewalks were made of wood planking, and there were many huskies roaming the streets. The hotel was small, and the rooms were of unfinished wood and sparsely furnished. There was one bathroom on our floor and, I assume, one on the next floor as well. I was intrigued by the local movie house, which was located in a private home. The hotel clerk suggested that we go see the movie after we had finished dinner. He tried to point out the location, but we didn't see anything that remotely resembled a theater. He patiently explained that it was in a house just down the street. We went to the house, knocked on the door, paid the admission, and sat in chairs set in rows in the living room. There were only about ten other patrons, and I believe the owner was waiting for us because he started the film almost immediately. It reminded me of the film arrangements in China. The film was sixteen millimeter, and there was a rather long pause every time a reel had to be changed. During the lull, the patrons questioned us about our trip and were quite interested to hear that we had come all the way from Florida. We enjoyed the film and the pleasant company, and when we left the theater, I was surprised to find it was still bright daylight even though it was nearly ten o'clock.

The next morning, we had a most hearty and excellent breakfast, a year's supply of calories and cholesterol by today's standards, but that was 1946 B.C. (Before Cholesterol). We staggered away from the table and took off for our final destination, Ladd Field, Fairbanks, Alaska. Just out of Whitehorse I saw Lake Lebarge, where the cremation of Sam McGee took place in Robert W. Service's poem of the same name. The rest of the two-hour flight was over hilly terrain through which the Alcan Highway twisted and turned.

After landing at Ladd, which with Fairbanks is in a valley in a bend of the Tanana River, I checked into the visiting officers quarters and was handed a wire from Eglin ordering me to return to Great Falls as soon as possible since a B-25 from Eglin would be coming through and would bring me back. Somewhat disappointed that I would not have a chance to see more of the area, I went back to base operations to see if I could catch a ride to Great Falls. Unluckily, a C-47 was leaving the next morning, so my stay at Ladd was a short one.

I arrived at Great Falls on August 2 and spent four boring days waiting for the B-25—another standard hurry up and wait situation. One of the pilots was from Helena, Montana, and they had spent several days there before picking me up. Since the other pilot was the deputy commander at

Eglin, I vouchsafed no complaint. With two pilots already aboard, I was free to spend most of the flight in the nose compartment sleeping or observing the country below, which is always fascinating when you are low enough to see it clearly. On the first leg of the flight, I was dozing in the sunny nose when I was awakened by the bail-out alarm bell—the prearranged signal for me to don the headset. The pilot told me to look out on the right side, and there, practically at the same level, were the presidents' faces on Mount Rushmore. It was a magnificent sight, and we circled several times for further viewing. I didn't say anything, but I was completely surprised to see the faces, since I had been told many years before that they were on the Hudson River palisades in New York.

Back at Eglin I found that drastic changes had taken place in the fighter test squadron. The much larger test squadron from Pinecastle, Florida, had been merged with our squadron. Their C.O., Lt. Col. Dewey Slocumb, had become our C.O. Colonel Muldoon was going to Alaska to command the Eglin cold-weather test detachment. Dick Jones had left for Wright Field, Ohio, to attend test pilot school, and about a dozen new pilots had joined the squadron, along with many new aircraft and maintenance personnel. Most of these pilots, including Don Dessert, Len Koehler, Ray Evans, Fred Belue, and Hank Pashco, became my good friends later. I knew before I left that this transfer was contemplated, but I didn't expect such an early consummation.

Barney gave me the good news that he and I were to take two P-80s to Alaska for cold-weather testing, which meant we would be working for Colonel Muldoon. We were not to leave for Alaska until October, giving us about two months to prepare the test programs and read up on Arctic flying.

While I was gone, a new night fighter had been delivered to the squadron, a North American P-82C Twin Mustang, the perfect name for two stretched P-51H fuselages joined together by a mutual wing center section and a mutual horizontal stabilizer. It had been designed as a two-pilot, long-range fighter to operate over the Pacific, but a number of them were converted to the night-fighter configuration by the addition of radar housed in a long nacelle that protruded from the center section forward, extending beyond the arcs of the counter-rotating propellers. It immediately acquired the nickname "the Dong." The pilot's controls in the right cockpit were replaced by the radar operator's gear. It was armed with six .50-caliber machine guns in the wing center section and was powered by two 1,350-horsepower Merlin V-1650 V-12 engines. Painted shiny black, it looked rather strange on the ramp with its four-wheel landing gear. Each fuselage had a main landing gear and a tailwheel.

As soon as possible, I read through the pilot's operating instructions and arranged a checkout flight. The cockpit was identical with that of the P-51H with the exception of the dual engine controls and instruments. I decided that the best way to fly it would be to ignore the right fuselage, except while taxiing, and fly it like a P-51. That worked well, and I felt quite comfortable with the airplane as I put it through its paces. I found it considerably heavier on the controls than the Mustang, but the performance was roughly the same.

All went well until I came in to land. I was looking forward to my first four-point landing, but instead I made four one-point landings. I peeled up into a normal fighter pattern for a P-51, but as I was holding it off the runway waiting for the stall, the nose dropped sharply despite full back stick (up elevator). I hit on the left main gear, then bounced to the right tailwheel, the left tailwheel, and then the right main, as best I could tell. By then it had stalled, and all the wheels stayed on the runway. By good fortune I had landed on the cross runway, so no one in the fighter squadron had seen me dribble the airplane down the runway, thereby avoiding the loss of yards of face.

After some thought, I decided that the radar nacelle's forward location caused the center of gravity to move too far forward for the elevator to have full control at landing speeds, although no one had mentioned it in my briefing for the flight. On my next flight I left a little power on, about ten to twelve inches of mercury, which took care of the problem. Some time later, when I flew the day-fighter version of the F-82, sans dong, I had no trouble holding the nose up without power.

My brother Carl, who had trained in P-61s, had not seen combat in World War II because of the end of the war, but he made up for it in Korea. He was stationed in Japan with the 68th Fighter Squadron (All-Weather) as a radar observer in F-82Gs. On June 27, 1950, his pilot, Lieutenant Hudson, and he were covering the air evacuation of Seoul when a group of North Korean Yak-9s appeared. The F-82s attacked and drove them off, and Lieutenant Hudson and he shot one down, scoring the first USAF victory of the Korean conflict.

In mid-August I was told that I would be going to the Lockheed field at Van Nuys, California, to pick up one of the first two P-80s to be equipped with a radio compass as soon as it came off the assembly line, and that in October I would take it to Alaska. A radio compass has an indicator on the instrument panel with a needle that rotates through 360 degrees. When a radio beam or commercial station is tuned in, the needle indicates the heading to the station. Turning the airplane to align the needle with the fixed marker at the top of the dial heads the airplane toward the station. The range of the radio compass depended on both the strength of the station signal and the altitude of the airplane and could be more than a hundred miles. Since the instrument worked in the low-frequency band, it was almost useless around thunderstorms, unless you were interested in the heading to each flash of lightning.

The test of the radio compass was added to the test program, and it would help in navigation on the long flight to Alaska. The only other radio navigation aid in the P-80 was a Detrola low-frequency receiver that could be used to receive the radio beams. It was of little use because it was located on the floor in an awkward position, was unreliable, and because a P-80 usually would not have enough fuel to go through the procedures required to determine the transmitter's location and then make a range approach.

On Thursday afternoon, August 26, we were advised by Lockheed that the P-80 was ready for pickup. An Eglin B-25 was leaving for Los Angeles early the next morning, and I was to be on it. The squadron adjutant sent me to base headquarters with a request for orders to be cut for the trip before the end of the day. (Mimeograph stencils had to be cut to print orders in those primitive days.) By great good fortune the young lady assigned to cut my orders was Glindel Barron, the blonde I had met at the beach and been impressed with earlier in the summer, so I had the opportunity to regale her with an inventory of the many sterling attributes of fighter pilots as opposed to mortals.

The next day, Friday, after a boring, noisy flight, I was dropped off at Van Nuys by the B-25 crew. When I checked with the Army Air Force duty officer, he told me that the airplane would not be ready until Wednesday or Thursday and that a room had been reserved for me at the Biltmore Hotel in Los Angeles. After I checked into the hotel, I stopped at the ticket agency in the lobby and asked what was going on that weekend in the way of sports. I bought tickets to a college football game on Saturday, UCLA versus Oregon, and a professional game on Sunday, Rams versus Eagles. Both games were in the Coliseum, about a two-mile walk from the hotel. The tickets were ridiculously cheap compared with today's prices, less than $5 each. The agent said there were thousands of tickets available for the pro game. That was before television created pro-football mania. Now I have as much chance of obtaining a ticket to a Redskins game as I have of playing for the Redskins.

The weather was pleasant, and I enjoyed both games, especially the Eagles-Rams game. The Eagles were one of the best teams in the league at the time, with such stars as Steve van Buren, Tommy Thomas, Pete Pihos, and Bucko Kilroy. The Eagles won handily, although the game was the much-heralded first professional appearance of Tom Harmon, the great Michigan halfback. He was of special interest to me. I had last seen him in Hengyang, China, dressed in coolie clothes. He had just been shot down in a P-38, had parachuted behind Japanese lines, and been brought out by Chinese guerrillas. He looked better in the Coliseum than he did in China, but the Eagles were harder on him than the Japs would have been, constantly smearing him for big losses.

That evening I was in the hotel restaurant seated right next to the main aisle. As I was polishing off a gigantic banana split, an older gentleman stopped and said, "I wish I could eat one of those." I didn't understand his problem, since he looked as though he could afford it, but now that I have reached his age, I do understand his problem.

On Wednesday I got the welcome news that the P-80 would be ready to go the next morning. It came none too soon, as I was almost out of patience, money, and clean clothes. The next morning, when I went to sign for the plane after inspecting it, I asked that tip tanks be installed so I wouldn't have to land so often. I was told that not only were there no tip tanks available but also the pump in one of the leading-edge tanks was inoperative—instead of the 755 gallons I was expecting, I would have only 381. If I chose to wait for a new pump to be installed it would take three or four days. Since the airplane was to undergo a complete inspection at the Eglin maintenance subdepot, I opted to take the airplane and leave immediately.

I changed into my flying suit, stuffed my toilet kit and dirty clothes in the ammunition boxes in the nose, and carefully folded my last uniform under the seat. I climbed in and began yo-yoing my way across the country. With so little fuel my range was limited to about 350 statute miles. I would take off, climb on course to about 35,000 feet, and almost immediately begin a slow descent to the next stop. At that time all aircraft being ferried were prohibited from flying at night or in instrument weather, so after landing at March Field in Riverside, California, Luke Field in Phoenix, Arizona, and Biggs Field in El Paso, Texas, I was overtaken by darkness and had to spend the night at Midland, Texas. Jets were still something of a rarity in the country, so refueling took much longer than it should have because of all the interest in the airplane and its cockpit. I had planned to spend the night at Carswell Field in Fort Worth but, because of the delays, couldn't make it before dark. Midland was not a regular base, and although it had some spartan quarters available, there was no place to eat that late. Retrieving my uniform, I went to the latrine to change and found to my horror that my new Parker 51 fountain pen, guaranteed not to leak in flight, had been completely incontinent, leaving me with a six- to eight-inch black spot on my shirt just below my wings. I debated skipping dinner but was starving, so I went to town on a shuttle bus and found a small restaurant. It seemed that every person I passed on the street and all the diners in the restaurant told me that my pen was leaking. I'm still trying to come up with a clever retort.

The next morning I took off bright and early, and after landings at Carswell, Barksdale Field in Shreveport, Louisiana, and Brookley Field in Mobile, Alabama, I arrived back at Eglin. The entire flight had taken only five hours and thirty minutes of flying time, with eight landings. The same flight, in a Mustang a year earlier, had taken eight and a half hours with two landings.

Besides the sense of accomplishment and the enjoyment of my first cross-country flight by jet, the five and a half hours increased my total jet flying time by 25 percent, to twenty-five hours. The eight landings had allowed me to make many more yards of face than the three landings with tip tanks would have, because so many more nonjet pilots got the chance to see a real jet pilot. I was looking forward eagerly to my next cross-country, which would be from Florida to Alaska, but I hoped to have a full fuel load, including tip tanks, for that 3,500-mile trip.

8

Snow-Bound

The P-80 I flew in from California went immediately to the Eglin subdepot for its acceptance inspection, and then it and the P-80 Barney was to fly were winterized for their upcoming cold-weather tests. Many of the fuel, oil, and hydraulic line seals were replaced with low-temperature seals, and lighter lubricants and hydraulic fluid replaced the standard fluids. The outer sections of the wings and tail assembly were painted bright red to make the aircraft more visible if they were forced to land, or crashed, on the snow-covered terrain.

Barney and I test-hopped the P-80s after the winterization was completed, and they both seemed as eager as we were to get the show on the road. The ammunition cans were removed from the noses, they were shipped up separately, and their spaces were packed with emergency gear, including sleeping bags, snowshoes, and flare pistols. Since the weather wouldn't be too cold until we arrived at our jumping-off point to Alaska—Great Falls, Montana—we stored our heavy parkas, fur-lined trousers, and mukluk boots in there as well. We would also be required to carry Colt .45 automatic pistols while flying over Canada and Alaska, but they would be issued to us in Great Falls.

In late morning on Saturday, October 19, we taxied away from the fighter squadron ramp, waving good-bye to the pilots who came to see us off, and took off for Barksdale Field, Shreveport, Louisiana, the first stop on our 3,500-mile journey. Since I had the radio compass in my plane, I was leading the flight. As we climbed on course for Barksdale, I tuned the radio compass to the Mobile, Alabama, range station to check it out. I could hear the range signal clearly in my headset, but the indicator needle just spun slowly in circles. It did the same when I tuned in other nearby stations. I turned it off, and it turned me off. I told Barney it wasn't working and continued on course, navigating by time and distance and pilotage (visual reference to landmarks on the ground). We flew through a small rain squall en route, which removed most of the paint on the leading edges of the wings. I knew this would irritate the crew chiefs, who would join us in Alaska, but since flying back through the rain wouldn't put the paint back on, there was nothing to be done.

We landed at Barksdale to refuel, which took quite a bit of time in the P-80. The leading-edge tanks in the wings were so long and narrow that the fuel backed up unless it was added at a low flow rate. We postponed any attempt to have the radio compass repaired till our next stop, Tinker Field in Oklahoma City, which had a major repair and modification depot. After takeoff I tried the radio compass again, without much confidence, but it remained inoperative.

At Tinker I wrote up the problem in the Form 1A, carried in all AAF aircraft to record malfunctions and repairs, and asked the chief of transient maintenance if it could be repaired. He said that he could have a radio specialist there the next day, even though it was Sunday, who would try to locate the problem. We checked in at the VOQ, changed into civilian clothes, and went into Oklahoma City for dinner. As was our custom in those days, the only thing we considered ordering when eating off-base was a big steak (still B.C.). Unfortunately, the sizzling steak I ordered was sizzling so violently that it spattered grease all over the front of my new tan poplin jacket. I guess that was better for my health than eating the grease, but I didn't think so at the time.

The next morning we met the radio technician in the hangar where the P-80 was parked and explained the problem, which was quite simple: the radio compass didn't work. After copying the type and model numbers from the instrument, he went to the technical library to get the maintenance handbook, but since this was a new design, it had not yet arrived.

Undaunted, he said it couldn't be too much different from the earlier model, so he brought up his testing equipment and went to work. After spending the rest of the day trying various fixes without success, he admitted defeat and said he couldn't repair it without the maintenance handbook. We thanked him for his efforts and decided to go on without it rather than delay the flight any longer; we had already lost several weeks waiting for the specially equipped P-80 to come off the production line. Although the radio compass would have been of great value, especially over the sparsely settled country in northern Canada and Alaska, we were confident that our navigational skills were sufficient for the task.

The next morning we took off for an airfield at Kearney, Nebraska, which had closed some months earlier but would have a tank truck of JP-1 jet fuel available for our use. We landed in a strong crosswind on the only open runway. It would have been dangerous to land a P-40 or a P-51 in that wind, but the tricycle gear on the P-80 made it relatively safe. The fuel truck was there, and we were refueled in the normal time, but the external starting unit wouldn't start. We had to wait about four hours while they fixed it. Because of the delay, we had to spend the night at the AAF field at Rapid City, South Dakota, instead of Great Falls.

After arriving at Great Falls the next day, October 22, we learned that the weather was too bad in Canada to allow us to fly to Edmonton, Alberta, under visual flight rules (VFR) as required by AAF regulations for ferrying aircraft. Even worse was the news that it was expected to remain socked in for several days. We made the best of it, however, and checked into the VOQ. We changed into our civilian clothes and caught a bus into town.

Great Falls, on the Missouri River, was then a city of some 25,000. I guess there must have been a great falls somewhere nearby, but I never saw it. The country was flat and windswept, and the view was dominated by the tremendously high smokestack of a copper-smelting plant. There were evidently cattle ranches in the vicinity because many of the local citizens wore cowboy clothes that did not seem to be for show.

After dining on immense steaks in the hotel dining room, we explored the main street. In an unimpressive building that may have once been a saloon, there was a large collection of paintings by the famous western artist and sculptor Charles Russell. Up to then I had seen only a few small prints of his works in books, but these large originals were magnificent; all of them were western scenes, and I was amazed that so much action could be captured on canvas and in bronze. The scenes were incredibly lifelike and displayed the knowledge he had acquired as a working cowboy. We both went back to visit this museum several times before we left Great Falls.

Farther down the street we found a sporting goods store with a large selection of guns on display. After looking around, we decided to buy High Standard .22-caliber sporting pistols to carry on our flight. The Colt .45s we had been issued were not very accurate in the hands of unpracticed shooters. I had barely qualified with the .45, and that had been several years ago. I was certain that a rabbit could hop past me with impunity, if he didn't mind the sound of a gun. I wasn't going to try to shoot a bear with anything smaller than a bazooka, so a .22 would be ideal for my needs. It had the added advantage of being smaller and lighter than a .45 and easier to carry in a shoulder holster. Also I could carry several hundred rounds of .22 ammunition in the space required for fifty rounds for the .45.

The next morning we were informed at base operations, much to our dismay, that it was necessary to be cleared by the hospital before leaving the country. They were only interested in checking our immunization cards to make sure we were caught up on our shots. I was horrified to find I needed several shots, all for warm-weather diseases like yellow fever (with which I was always afflicted at the approach of a needle) and typhoid. I argued that I was unlikely to contract any of them in Alaska, but to no avail. The medic who was to administer the shots didn't look too sharp, but his needle did. He didn't know whether the first shot should be intravenous or intramuscular, so he made it intraboneous. The needle hit the bone in my upper arm and nearly stuck there. It was extremely painful, but undaunted, he wrenched it out and tried again, this time with more success. By the time he finished the series of shots, my arm had turned red and started to swell.

By evening, the combination of the shots and the medic's boner had taken its toll. I had a fever, a swollen and tender arm, and was for the first time praying for the bad weather to hold so I wouldn't have to fly for a few days. Fortunately, the weather cooperated. I was feeling well enough by the twenty-eighth, when we were notified that the weather was marginal but that we might be able to make it to Edmonton VFR. We took off and made it as far as Lethbridge, Alberta, just across the Canadian border, before the weather closed in and we had to return to Great Falls.

Finally, on October 30, the weather broke, and we made the 435-mile flight to Edmonton in just over an hour. After being requested to make a low, high-speed pass in our then wondrous jets and readily acceding, we landed and parked on the RCAF ramp. In the base operations office we received the disheartening news that we would probably have to remain there for several days to wait out the bad weather along our route. We checked into the RCAF visiting officer's quarters and, since it was early in the day, took the bus into town, hoping to check out some of the southern Canada belles.

Edmonton is the capital of the province of Alberta, but at that time it was not a large city. The country is much like the Great Plains in the United

States, with an enormous expanse of flat prairie. As we wandered through the city I had one of my illusions shattered. On a corner was a department store that looked just like a Sears Roebuck, but the sign proclaimed it to be the Hudson Bay Company. All through my youth I had read stories of the Canadian Northwest and the Yukon, and the trappers always traded in their furs and bought supplies at the frontier outposts of the Hudson Bay Company. I had always envisioned them as primitive log cabins in the wilderness—it was quite a letdown.

Since we had to check the weather almost hourly, most of the daylight hours for the next six days were spent on the flight line waiting for it to break. The day after we arrived, ten P-51Hs landed and were parked on the ramp close to our P-80s. They were flown by ferry command pilots who were taking them to a fighter squadron in Anchorage, Alaska. They, too, had to wait for the weather to clear.

While we were having lunch in the operations snack bar on Friday, an RCAF wing commander approached us and said that there was to be an open house and small airshow on Sunday. He asked if we could fly the P-80s in the show. We explained that these were test aircraft and thus couldn't be flown in the airshow, but they could be used as part of the static display and we would be glad to answer visitors' questions. He accepted our offer with thanks and then asked the leader of the ferry pilots if any of the Mustangs could participate. The leader willingly accepted the invitation, saying that eight of them would fly in the show provided they could practice on Saturday. That, too, was acceptable to the wing commander, who no doubt envisioned a special treat for the locals. "Special treat" was hardly the proper term for what ensued.

The next morning, we went to the flight line with the ferry pilots to watch them practice. All ten of them were going to fly, and I suppose the leader was going to select the eight best or, as it turned out, eliminate the two worst. The selection was made easier when they started their engines. One of the engines ran up to full power as it started, causing the Mustang to nose over and destroy its propeller on the concrete. This was a problem with the P-51H if the pilot pushed the throttle full forward when he shut off the engine. The throttle controlled the carburetor by means of hydraulics, and when the engine was restarted with the throttle back in idle position, the carburetor was still in the full-power setting until the hydraulic pressure built up. There were many warnings about this danger in the pilot's operating instructions as well as on a small placard in the cockpit. Since the ferry pilots flew several types of aircraft, the warning must have slipped this pilot's mind.

After that commotion died down, the rest of the Mustangs took off and another commotion began. Keep in mind that ferry pilots were not trained as fighter pilots but were trained to fly fighters, and other aircraft, from point to point. I had some misgivings when, instead of starting their practice at a safe altitude, they came over the field at about five hundred feet in loose trail (follow-the-leader) formation and tried slow rolls. Each of them made the same mistake in varying degrees: they didn't apply enough forward stick while inverted and dished out in the second half of the roll, losing several hundred feet in the process. Barney and I thought that a couple of them were going to hit the ground, but they managed to recover at about fifty feet. Somewhat chastened or frightened, they did the next set of rolls higher. These rolls were as bad, but at least there was more room to recover.

The loops were no better, being egg-shaped at best, because they pulled too few g's going up and too many coming down. Several never made it around the loop, falling off to the side as they stalled. Their formation, if it could be dignified by that name, was laughable, loose and ragged, and becoming even worse in the turns.

Despite the lousy performance, they seemed to be well satisfied with the results of the practice. Barney and I, concerned that USAAF would lose so much face in front of the Canadians with such inept flying, spoke to the ferry leader in private, telling him that we both had many hours in the Mustang as well as a great deal of aerobatic experience and if he would lend us two of the Mustangs we could put on a first-class airshow. But he wasn't about to give up what might be his only chance to fly in an airshow, and he wasn't about to take any advice from two jet jockeys. He obviously thought he was a fighter pilot. This attitude is common among pilots when they get in a fighter cockpit and is the cause of many fatalities.

The next day they flew as scheduled, but I'm sure somebody up there liked them, because none of them crashed. The flying was no better than it had been in practice, and it was embarrassing to us to be in the same air force.

Finally, on November 5, our old Florida friend the sun appeared, and we were able to fly the next two legs of our journey. We landed first at Fort Nelson in the northeast corner of British Columbia, a small RCAF base on the Alcan Highway, where we refueled and had a lunch of beans and bacon. We then took off for Whitehorse, Yukon Territory.

The weather was not as good as forecast, and there was a solid cloud deck at our cruising altitude. Since our trip had dragged on so long and the sky was reported clear over Whitehorse, we bent the ferrying rules and flew on instruments for about an hour, breaking into the clear as we started our letdown to Whitehorse. As usual the tower asked us to make a low pass before landing, and as usual we were glad to comply. I knew from my previous visit that there was a U.S. contingent on the west (left) side of the field and an RCAF facility on the east. Barney said that he would go down the right strip, I could take the left, and we would show them what these Shooting Stars could do. We dived down to the deck and crossed the field at about 550 mph. My taxiway had an unexpected 45-degree jog to the left before it joined the ramp in front of the hangars. I turned to the left, then saw that the hangars were about to join me in the cockpit, so I rolled into a vertical bank to the right until I was past the hangars and then zoomed up away from the field and joined formation with Barney for landing.

After parking we were surrounded by a group of ashen-faced Americans from the cold-weather test detachment at Ladd Field. They were in Whitehorse while their B-17 was being repaired and had been on the second floor of the hangar watching the low pass. They said that I had gone by the front of the hangar in a vertical bank and had cleared the wall by about ten feet, causing them to dive away from the windows. I had no idea that I had been so close but indicated that it had been intentional, thus enhancing my reputation as a hot jet pilot.

At base operations we got the bad news that the jet fuel for our planes had not yet arrived. Most bases at that time did not have jet fuel available, and it had to be delivered in drums. Poor road conditions had delayed the shipment, and it did not arrive until two days later. We required about 700 gallons each, which meant twenty-eight fuel drums. They were brought to the planes on sleds pulled by tractors, and the fuel was transferred to our tanks by hand pumps, a slow process. By the time we were finished refueling, the weather nailed us again, and it was three more days before we could take off for the last leg of our trip.

In Whitehorse we stayed in the same hotel as on my previous visit on the B-25 flight, not because it was so good but because it was the only one. While we were sitting in the combination restaurant and bar one evening, a grizzled old prospector walked in, sat at the bar, and started a conversation with the bartender. He pulled out a small pouch and dumped a couple of gold-streaked rocks on the bar. Curious, we got up to take a better look and asked him if that was really gold. He put the rocks back in the pouch and snapped, "What the hell do you think it is: horseshit?" as he stamped out of the bar. That and a recent incident in which a large brown bear decapitated a man whose sons had wounded it with a .22 rifle are what passed for excitement in Whitehorse. Five days in Whitehorse were pretty grim unless you were hooked on huskies. I shared the sentiments of W. C. Fields: I would rather be in Philadelphia.

On the evening of November 9, the weather was forecast to be clear enough for us to leave the next day. We packed that night and early the next morning went to the flight line hoping that the forecast was correct. The meteorologist said that the sky would be clear for the first half of the 550-mile trip, but then we would run into a solid overcast at about 25,000 feet, which would gradually lower to 10,000 feet over our destination, Fairbanks. We decided that by flying at 35,000 feet until we ran into the overcast and then staying just below it until we reached Fairbanks, we would have a safe fuel reserve.

After takeoff, all went as planned for the first half of the flight, and the overcast appeared precisely as forecast. Soon, however, we found that we were descending much quicker than planned and were below 10,000 feet with about 150 miles to go. Fairbanks was still reporting a 10,000-foot ceiling, so since we didn't have enough fuel to get back to Whitehorse, we continued on course, hoping for the best. The ceiling kept dropping, and it began to snow heavily, further reducing the already poor visibility. Soon we were flying at only a few hundred feet following the Alcan Highway, which fortunately paralleled our course. We slowed down a bit to make it easier to follow the curves. The snow was so heavy that we were considering landing on the highway if we couldn't get through to Big Delta, an airfield about 85 miles from Fairbanks. Just when I was considering getting into the kneeling position, I spotted the field. We circled once to make sure the runways were clear, forgoing our usual high-speed pass, and landed. I don't think that any two Floridians were ever so happy to be on snow-covered ground.

The field appeared to be deserted, but the runways had been cleared of all but the snow that was falling. We taxied to the front of the hangar and climbed out, barely resisting the impulse to follow Pope John Paul II's deplaning routine, but were afraid we might freeze our lips kissing the snow. Leaving the engines running, we entered the hangar through a small door and found it empty but well heated. We were able to open the main doors, climb back into the cockpits, taxi into the hangar, shut off the engines, and close the doors. Shortly thereafter, a member of the caretaker force appeared, saying he hadn't expected anyone to be flying in such rotten weather.

A phone in the hangar connected directly with base operations at Ladd Field, and we reported that we were down safely at Big Delta. Colonel Muldoon came on the line and said, "What in the hell took you so long? Did you taxi here from Eglin?" He added that he would be down as soon as the weather cleared with fuel and a starting unit. A few hours later the snow stopped, and we had a ceiling of about 10,000 feet. Colonel Muldoon came in with a C-46, bringing the fuel and the P-80 crew chiefs who had been impatiently awaiting our arrival at Ladd. They discovered that Barney's electrical system had a short that had drained his battery; while that was being repaired my plane was refueled. As soon as it was ready, Colonel Muldoon said I should leave immediately and Barney would follow as soon as possible.

For some reason, probably the 25-below-zero temperature, I started the engine in the hangar with the doors closed, and when the engine lit up several windows shattered. I hurriedly taxied out and took off for Ladd before Muldoon could make me replace the windows. About fifteen minutes later, after the final obligatory low pass (I had done so many lately that I thought of changing the pronunciation of my name to lo-pass), I landed at Fairbanks, ready at long last to begin the cold-weather tests. Barney landed an hour or so later, and our seemingly endless journey was finally over. It had taken us twenty-three days, but only eleven hours and fifteen minutes of that time had been in the air. Most of the delay was due to ferry command rules prohibiting weather flying and night flying.

Today an F-14, 15, or 16 could make the trip with one refueling in less than six hours; an SR-71 could make it in about two hours.

9

Cold-Weather Testament

The specifications for Army Air Force aircraft required that they be capable of operation in all temperatures from minus 65 to 120 degrees Fahrenheit. The mission of the cold-weather test detachment was to determine if the aircraft and support equipment could meet the low-temperature end of this requirement. Accordingly, since 1942, all new types of aircraft and equipment were sent to Ladd Field in Fairbanks each winter season, roughly October through February, and put through their paces. In addition to the facilities at Ladd Field, there was a complete range for bombing and gunnery testing about thirty miles from Ladd at Blair Lake.

Besides our P-80s, the test aircraft included a North American P-51H Mustang, a North American P-82 Twin Mustang, a Republic P-47N Thunderbolt, a Fairchild C-82 Flying Boxcar, a Boeing B-29 Superfortress, and a Sikorsky R-5 and an R-6, both helicopters. Lieutenant Colonel Muldoon commanded the flying test group, and Colonel Shanahan, from the armament lab at Wright Field, commanded the detachment. Colonel Shanahan was a well-respected armament specialist with a great deal of experience in arctic operations. The other groups of the detachment were testing clothing and ground equipment such as starting units, portable heaters, and motor vehicles.

Most of the pilots were from the flight test group at Eglin, so I felt right at home. Capt. Brad Brown was the helicopter pilot, Capt. Leonard Koehler flew the P-47, Capt. Lippy Lipscomb flew the Mustang, and

Captains Jim Bauer and Joe Cotton flew the B-29. The P-82 pilot was Lieutenant Colonel Buchert from Wright Field. Barney Turner and I had the P-80s, and Barney had the additional duty of operations officer.

In addition to the AAF detachment, an Army Ground Forces group, Task Force Frigid, was there to test tanks, trucks, artillery, and other equipment. Our detachment would support the task force with aircraft when required.

The permanent buildings at Ladd were well designed for the climate. They were connected by tunnels that housed the steam pipes and sheltered personnel traffic. The officer's quarters, in the hospital building, were roomy, well furnished, and warm. There were not enough rooms for all the officers, however, so only majors and above were accommodated. Captains and below were housed in Quonset huts that were connected in pairs by a latrine. No doubt these huts were perfectly satisfactory in a normal winter, but the winter of 1946–47 was anything but normal; it was the coldest ever recorded in Alaska to that time. The temperature dropped to 67 below zero one day, and there were several days in the minus sixties. For a stretch of about ten days, it never rose above minus 50. In a nearby town with the unlikely name "Snag," the temperature hit 83 below. On the good side, there was virtually no wind, so windchill was not a problem. Task Force Frigid sent a powerful message back to Army Ground Forces headquarters by way of a photograph of the new cold-weather lubricant that had been sent there to be tested. In the photograph, a soldier with an axe was chopping a piece of it off a solid block.

The Quonsets were heated by kerosene-burning space heaters that were less than adequate on the coldest days, since the space they heated shrank as the outside temperature dropped. We junior officers had to move the beds closer and closer to the heaters, somewhat reminiscent of Boy Scouts around a campfire. A bottle of Vitalis hair tonic (with a high alcohol content) that was out of the circle of heat froze solid one night. The Vitalis wasn't mine (I had a crew cut), but anyone with the wet look would have had the ice look in that climate.

After about a week under these conditions I developed a bad cold. Colonel Shanahan was nearby when I let loose a few of my kamikaze sneezes, and he called me into his office to ask how I had caught cold. I said it might have been caused by the cold Quonset huts. Concerned, he immediately picked up the phone and asked for the housing officer. He said that one of the two *jet pilots* in the detachment had caught a severe cold from living in the Quonset huts and that he wanted me moved into the main building because, being a *jet* pilot, I was under terrific strain. He put his hand over the mouthpiece and said, "Lopez, go up and see the housing officer, and look jetty." I went to the housing office and looked as jetty as I could, but evidently it wasn't jetty enough to move the housing officer, because he didn't move me. With fifty more hours in jets, I could probably have made it.

The humidity in the Fairbanks area was very low, and this along with the wool rugs in the main BOQs made static electricity a problem for most of us, but for Colonel Muldoon it was an opportunity. When we went to his office or room for meetings or for other reasons, he delighted in sneaking up behind someone while scuffing his shoes on the rug and popping an inch-long blue spark off the victim's ear. His rank was an insulator against reciprocity.

During extreme cold weather there was a phenomenon in the Fairbanks area known as ice fog. Ice crystals formed a dense fog that was only some twenty feet thick but that reduced the visibility essentially to zero. Occasionally, when the visibility was unlimited, something would trigger the atmosphere, and the fog would form almost instantaneously. The first time I took off in a jet from Ladd, the fog formed behind me and closed the field, causing me some concern. Fortunately it had dissipated when I came in to land an hour later, and I had no difficulty. Some time later it was to be the cause of a tragic accident involving Colonel Shanahan.

The cold-weather test detachment maintained a bombing and gunnery range about thirty miles from Ladd near Blair Lake. As soon as the Tanana River had frozen solid enough to support a loaded Weasel (a small tracked vehicle used to move personnel and cargo over rough terrain), Colonel Muldoon led a group of three Weasels to carry the bombing range crew and supplies out to Blair Lake. Barney and I rode with him in the lead Weasel, which was breaking the trail. It was about 30 below zero, and we had flying suits, winter flying pants, and parkas over our uniforms and mukluks on our feet. The cold wasn't too noticeable inside the Weasel, but once we crossed the river and entered the heavily forested area, we had to get out so often to clear fallen trees and debris that we decided to ride on the outside to save time. I was extremely cold until I found a warm spot over the exhaust pipe to sit on. After that, the rest of the four- or five-hour trip was a piece of cake, albeit ice cream cake. Colonel Shanahan spiced up the journey by roaring over our heads periodically in a UC-64 Norduyn

Norseman (a single-engine, high-wing utility or bush airplane), leaning out of the cockpit window, and waving wildly while clearing the tree tops by at least an inch.

After we arrived at the cabin at Blair Lake range we fueled and lit the kerosene stoves and started a fire in the fireplace. When it got warm enough I removed my winter outer gear and found out why I had been so comfortably warm on the Weasel. The heat from the exhaust had burned completely through the seat of my outer pants, and my flying suit seat was scorched as though a hot iron had been left on it. Luckily, layer number three, my uniform trousers, had escaped unscathed, because layer number four was tender epidermis—mine. I was accustomed to flying by the seat of my pants, but not in a Weasel. The return trip the next morning was un-eventful, quicker, and much more comfortable, since I was inside and not on the hot seat.

In the next few months I flew several missions in the Norseman as copilot and kicker, thereby acquiring a new MOS (military occupational specialty). We were delivering food and cans of fuel to the Blair Lake crew, and lacking a place to land, we had to air-drop the supplies. When we ar-rived over the range I went to the rear of the cabin where the door had been removed, tied myself to cabin strong points, and kicked the cargo through the open door on the pilot's signal.

Since the food in the officer's mess wasn't the best, three or four times a week Colonel Muldoon, Barney, two or three others, and I would go into Fairbanks and have steak dinners at the Model Cafe, which I believe was the only eating place in town. The decor was early nothing, but the food was quite good, especially when compared with the fare at the mess. It be-came our custom, at Colonel Muldoon's instigation, to match coins to see who would pay for all the meals. The steak dinners were inexpensive by today's standards, about $3, but salaries were commensurately low too, and paying for five or six meals regularly would have been a strain on a captain's pay. However, the laws of probability did not seem to be affected by the cold, and the costs were spread pretty evenly among us over the course of our stay.

My first flight from Ladd in the P-80, with the temperature at 20 below zero, was uneventful, but my next flight, about a week later at 50 below, was eventful. When I started the engine it rumbled and took much longer to reach idle rpm than normal, but since it seemed to be running all right, I took off. After about 45 minutes, while at 35,000 feet, I heard a strange rubbing noise from the engine and could also feel a vibration in the fuselage. The engine instruments were in the green, but I throttled back and returned to the base to land. The plane was heavier than the normal landing weight, because there was still fuel in the tip tanks, so I added a few mph to my approach speed. As I started to flare, the bottom suddenly dropped out; the airplane stalled about three feet in the air and hit the runway hard. Fortunately the P-80 was extremely rugged, and the only damage was to my pride. Later, the crew chief found that the static ports had iced up, causing the airspeed indicator to read high, thereby restoring some but not all of the face I had lost.

When the engine was removed, it was revealed that the turbine wheel had been rubbing against its housing, which had most likely warped during the engine start. Since it couldn't be repaired in the field, the engine was replaced, a relatively simple task in the P-80. The airplane was removed from the hangar and cold-soaked for several days at below minus 50 degrees. When the crew chief started the engine, it reacted the same way that it had on the last flight. He immediately closed the fuel stopcock and shut it down. The airplane was towed back into the hangar, and after it had warmed up the engine was pulled and inspected. Again the turbine housing had warped, and the blades would have rubbed if the engine hadn't been shut down so promptly. Colonel Muldoon wisely decided to ground both P-80s until we got a handle on the problem. The Lockheed technical representative who was there for the tests asked that Allison, the manufacturer of the engines, send an engineer to Alaska for consultation.

With the P-80s grounded, Barney and I were out of work as far as our primary tests were concerned. To continue to fly, I rode as copilot with Colonel Muldoon in a Curtiss C-46 Commando on a cargo flight to Great Falls and back; we logged more than twenty hours, and I was checked out as first pilot. It was quite a switch from the P-80 I had been flying for the last few months. It weighed more than 55,000 pounds to the P-80's 14,500, and it had two reciprocating engines and was a tail dragger—the P-80 had one jet engine and a tricycle landing gear. Most noticeable, however, was the difference in the height of the cockpit. In the P-80 the pilot's eye level in the landing attitude was about eight feet above the runway; in the C-46 it was seventeen feet. On the plus side, I had a fair amount of twin-engine time and had flown the same engine-propeller combination (Pratt & Whitney 2,000-horsepower R-2800 engines and Curtiss Electric propellers) in the B-26, the P-47, and the P-61. My landings were pretty good, too, because Colonel Muldoon announced before each one that it would cost me a steak per bounce.

Much to my surprise, I enjoyed flying the C-46 and found it handled quite well, especially with no cargo aboard. It handled so well, in fact, that once when testing it after some maintenance, with no cargo and about half full of fuel, I made a creditable fighter peel up and circular landing pattern, to the consternation of the tower and raised eyebrows from Colonel Muldoon. I just couldn't resist the temptation to look jetty.

Since we weren't doing much flying, several of us decided to try skiing for some excitement. Naturally, the group consisted of three Floridians—Barney from Miami, Brad Brown from Lake Worth, and me from Tampa—who had never skied or even been on a mountain before but were undaunted by our lack of experience. One Saturday morning, bright and early, we drew skis, boots, and poles from special services, borrowed a Weasel, and drove to Birch Hill, the Army ski slope just a short distance from Ladd. Walking along jauntily with our skis on our shoulders, we tried to look like old hands but blew it almost immediately. There was a sign in front of the ski slope office that said in large letters, "Fill in your sitzmarks!" Being old soldiers, used to filling out forms for everything, we thought a sitzmark was a form. Brad went in to get them and came out almost immediately. With a sheepish grin he informed us that sitzmarks are the divots skiers make in the snow when they fall, and they fill them in with snow to keep the slope as smooth as possible.

Feeling somewhat deflated, we carefully put on our skis and taxied slowly to the beginning of the rope tow that pulled skiers to the top of the hill. It looked tricky, but after watching a few experienced skiers, we thought we could handle it. Brad went first, then Barney, and I brought up the rear, with intervals of about fifty feet between us. All went well until the slope steepened dramatically about halfway up. I noticed that Barney and I were gaining on Brad. His grip had loosened and the rope was slipping through his gloves. Seeing that Barney was about to collide with him, Brad made a spectacular bailout into the snow, but his ski clipped Barney's, causing Barney to tumble into the snow alongside the tow path. Fortunately, or unfortunately as it turned out, I was able to get by safely and make it to the top of the hill. I was feeling rather superior until I worked my way to the beginning of the downhill run and realized I would have been much happier if I, too, had fallen. It looked twice as high and three times as steep looking down as it had looking up. Also, there was a 30-degree dogleg about halfway down, and I had no idea how to turn. I could see Brad and Barney struggling through the waist-deep snow from the tow path to the slope and wished I were with them.

I stood at the top looking down, trying to muster the courage to launch myself into what looked like oblivion. I might still be there but for some ten-year-olds who made three runs while I stood by. They were beginning to look at me with disdain. The kid in me wanted to yell, "You might be able to ski, but I can fly jets," but I resisted the impulse.

I finally bit the bullet and, hoping not to bite the dust as well, started down. Instead of S-turning across the slope as the real skiers did, I went straight down like a kamikaze pilot, leaving a trail of melted snow. When I reached the dreaded turn I went straight off the slope, up the hill into the deep snow where Barney and Brad were waiting, and did a nice hammerhead stall, ending up almost on top of them.

When we had recovered our respective composures, we went gingerly onto the slope. We precisely aimed ourselves down the less-steep second half of the run and, when there was not a soul ahead of us, pushed off. We all managed to remain upright until we got to the level stretch at the bottom, where we ran into our aiming point, some waist-deep snow that brought us to a stop. Greatly relieved, we gathered our dignity and our ski equipment, turned in the latter, and gave up the sport, swearing to stick to something safer in the future, like test flying.

Later in my career as a member of the faculty at the Air Force Academy, I was one of the officers-in-charge of the cadet ski club. I did quite a bit of skiing in the Colorado mountains on some of the best slopes in the world and learned why skiing can become addictive.

"There are strange things done neath the midnight sun by the men who moil for gold, and the Northern Lights have seen queer sights," reads a line from one of Robert W. Service's Yukon poems, *The Cremation of Sam McGee*. Barney and I were not moiling for gold, but we saw a strange sight late one afternoon in front of the base operations building. We were on the second floor checking some weather maps when we heard a C-54, the military version of the Douglas DC-4 transport, taxi onto the ramp and shut down its engines to discharge passengers. We went to the window that overlooked the ramp to see who was arriving. Seeing no one we knew, we stayed at the window and watched the flight engineer enter the cockpit to start its four engines before they got too cold (it being 50 below zero), preparatory to taxiing the aircraft to the parking area.

The number-one engine, outboard on the left wing, started with no trouble, but the number-two engine kept firing and cutting out. He continued his efforts until finally it flooded and caught fire inside the cowling, and smoke began pouring out. The assistant engineer quickly opened a hatch in the fuselage and climbed out onto the wing carrying a fire extinguisher. He opened an inspection plate on the top of the cowling, through which flames could be seen, and began discharging the fire extinguisher at the flames. They seemed to be diminishing when a fire truck roared up and stopped just short of the wing. One of the firemen was manning a water cannon on top of the truck. He aimed the cannon at the visible fire and turned it on full force. The powerful stream hit the unsuspecting assistant engineer full in the chest and swept him off the wing into some fairly deep snow, where he was instantly transformed into a human icicle.

Water is not the recommended agent for extinguishing gasoline fires, and we soon saw why. Instead of going out, the fire grew steadily larger. The engineer wisely shut off the number-one engine and abandoned ship. The fire continued to grow until it was blazing fiercely, totally out of control. The firemen now directed their efforts to ensuring that the operations building didn't catch fire. They were successful in that endeavor, and one out of two ain't bad.

The C-54's wing eventually burned through, the landing gear collapsed, and the plane was totally destroyed. It was quite a fire, and many of the spectators had the same feeling voiced by Sam McGee's corpse as it sat in the blazing furnace: "Since I left Plumtree, down in Tennessee, it's the first time I've been warm."

When the fire had been extinguished and the wreckage had cooled, the plane was towed away to the base boneyard. It snowed heavily that night, and in the morning there was no visible sign that there had ever been a fire. A few inches of freshly fallen snow can cover a multitude of sins.

In January, near the end of my stay in Alaska, Colonel Shanahan and several staff members were scheduled to attend a meeting back in the States (Alaska was not yet a state). They were to leave one evening in a C-54, which had sufficient range to make the trip nonstop. An ice fog had dropped the visibility to near zero, but Colonel Shanahan, who was in the process of being checked out in the C-54, decided to fly as first pilot with the instructor pilot in the right seat.

No one knows exactly what happened during the takeoff roll, but the C-54 veered to the right and ran off the runway, continuing in a slight curve across the field until it ran into the side of a large hangar. It never lifted off the ground, but the power must have been reduced during the run across the field, because had it hit with full power it is likely that all aboard would have been killed. Only the nose of the plane penetrated the hangar wall, and Colonel Shanahan's leg was crushed against one of the girders.

There was no radar control at Ladd, and the tower operator assumed the aircraft had taken off safely, since he was unable to see it at any point in its run. The plane had cut the phone lines in the hangar, and it was some time before a mechanic, who by great good fortune was working in the hangar, was able to make his way through the almost impenetrable fog to the fire station. Still more time was lost as the fire trucks and ambulance crept cautiously through the fog to the hangar. Had the mechanic not been working, it is unlikely the crash would have been discovered in time, and Colonel Shanahan might not have survived.

The crew and passengers were removed from the plane and taken to the hospital, where their relatively minor injuries, mostly frostbite, were cared for. Colonel Shanahan, however, remained trapped in the cockpit for several harrowing hours while the wreckage was cut away. At the hospital the surgeon was forced to make the heartbreaking decision to amputate his leg, because it was so badly mangled. In fact, the surgeon later told us that the extreme cold had saved the colonel's life. The wound had frozen and stopped the bleeding before the loss of blood became fatal.

Upon learning of the accident the next morning, we were shocked and saddened by Colonel Shanahan's loss but were relieved that there were no fatalities and no other serious injuries. He was popular at Ladd and well respected throughout the Army Air Forces, and the knowledge that he would have to give up flying and leave his beloved Air Force depressed us all. When we were allowed to see him in the hospital, however, he was in good spirits and said he would continue to work with armament as a civilian.

A few days later he was airlifted back to a major military hospital in the States, and Colonel Walker, his deputy, assumed command of the detachment. Colonel Muldoon asked me to see that all of Colonel Shanahan's belongings were packed for shipment back to his home in Dayton, Ohio. I moved into Colonel Shanahan's warm room for several weeks while attending to the packing—the room of the same colonel who had tried so many times before to get me moved into the main BOQ.

Packing his belongings was much more of a chore than I had anticipated. He wasn't much for collecting duplicates, but he had one of everything. His specialty was armament, and he had more guns, ammunition, and assorted accessories than I had ever seen. Included were several homemade rifles made from Browning .50-caliber machine gun barrels. Admittedly, I took my time packing so I could stay in the comfortable building as long as possible, but even with my best effort it would have taken quite a while. I carefully packed everything but his papers in a large wooden crate, but when two muscular GIs came to move it, they could not budge it. It was back to square one. I had to unpack it and repack it in several smaller crates before it could be moved and shipped. Sadly, when it was moved out, so was I.

Time was beginning to weigh heavily on me. My main duty was test flying, and I was doing precious little. As much as I love reading, even that was beginning to pall. I was so bored that I was almost tempted to brave the ski slopes again.

My last flight in the P-80 had been on November 22, and now, near the end of January, neither P-80 had been cleared for flight. I made a few test flights in the P-51H, but most of my flying came from scrounging time in multiengine aircraft. I was so desperate, I even tried helicopters. During that period I was checked out in the UC-64, the C-47, and the Stinson L-5, a small liaison plane. I didn't actually check out in the helicopters (fighter pilots please note that I still had some pride), although I made as many as fifteen landings during one flight. Brad Brown, the helicopter test pilot, and I surveyed the countryside and saw many herds of caribou and some magnificent moose. We would have enjoyed shooting them, but only with a camera.

There was another even more important reason that I was rapidly tiring of Alaska. I had heard from a friend at Eglin that the neo-Neanderthal that Glindel Barron, the lovely blonde from Panama City, had been dating had left Eglin and returned to his cave in the north. I wanted to get back to Florida and stake my claim before someone less worthy moved in.

Although we were unable to do much test flying in the P-80s, a lot was accomplished. We developed a system for starting jet engines in cold weather that eliminated the hesitant starts and consequent warping of the turbine wheel shroud. Colonel Muldoon, Barney, and I met with the Allison tech rep and the master sergeant maintenance chief in a series of discussions of the problem. The sergeant was a sharp and experienced mechanic, and it was he who devised the solution.

The fuel used in jets at that time was JP-1, which was close to pure kerosene. It was considerably less volatile and therefore harder to ignite than gasoline, but it produced more energy per pound. The sergeant reasoned that gasoline would make the start quicker and smoother but that JP-1 was needed to produce more thrust. Accordingly he installed a valve in the fuel system whereby gasoline from a drum on a truck next to the airplane could be used for the start, after which the gasoline hose was disengaged from the valve and the engine was run on its internal JP-1 fuel.

The system was tested, and it was immediately apparent that the problem had been eliminated. After a series of successful low-temperature starts over a period of a week, the P-80 was, at long last, declared ready for flight. On February 6, I made a soul-satisfying flight of one hour, during which the airplane performed perfectly, and I began feeling a bit jetty again. I was looking forward with great anticipation to a heavy flying schedule so that the test program could be completed before the test season ended, but it was not to be. In checking the engine to ensure that the turbine wheel clearances were unchanged, the maintenance crew found that the fuel was contaminated with small particles of some foreign substance, which in time could clog the filters and cause engine failure. The entire fuel system would have to be flushed repeatedly until completely free of contamination. The sergeant estimated it would take more than a month to obtain the proper equipment and several additional weeks to do the job. As it turned out, he was overly optimistic. The P-80 did not fly again until early that summer, when Dick "Superhot" Scott flew it back to Eglin.

Based on our results, the Air Materiel Command ran a series of starting tests with gasoline and found that much smoother starts resulted at all temperatures. It later became standard Air Force procedure to fill the P-80 leading-edge tanks, which held 94 gallons, with gasoline and the remaining tanks with JP-1. The gasoline was used only for starting and for purging the system of JP-1 after a flight, although it could be used in emergencies. This procedure was followed for several years until JP-4, more volatile than JP-1, became the standard fuel.

With the P-80s grounded again, Colonel Muldoon decided there was no need for me to remain in Alaska. On February 14, Valentine's Day fittingly enough, I left the Yukon for Eglin, the sun, the beach, and, I hoped, the blonde.

10

Characters in Flight

arrived back at Eglin on the twenty-first of February 1947 and moved back into the BOQ. After a few days it was as though I had never left. Late February and early March are the start of spring in northwest Florida, or the Florida panhandle, as it is called. It was warm and sunny most of the time, so I had the sun, but it was a bit too cold for the beach, and to my great disappointment, there was no blonde. I called her office as soon as I arrived and found that she had just left for a two-week vacation, but I did learn that she had not yet been claimed.

I had missed out on so much flying while at Ladd that I decided to try to catch up as soon as possible. The first five days I flew fourteen hours in six different types, a B-17 Flying Fortress, an F-13 Superfortress (photo reconnaissance version of the B-29), a North American AT-6 Texan, a P-80 Shooting Star, a P-82 Twin Mustang, and a B-25 Mitchell. The next week I added twelve more hours in a P-51H Mustang, a P-38L Lightning, a C-47 Skytrain, and a C-45 Expediter. During the three months in Alaska I had flown only forty hours, twenty-one of them on one trip in a C-46 Commando.

Since I had not yet been assigned any tests, the group operations officer asked if I would fly with another pilot in a C-47 to Great Falls, Montana, to pick up some of the Eglin personnel returning from Ladd. I agreed to go, and thus began a trip that ended in one of the hairiest flights I have ever experienced, including combat. The other pilot turned out to be Capt. Joseph Arthur Lynch, a fighter pilot known at Eglin as Artie and later, when he left the Air Force and joined North American Aviation as one of its top test pilots, as Joe. By either name, he was one of the all-time characters and a first-class pilot. At this time he was assigned to the 611th Group headquarters.

I met him at base operations on the morning of March 10, where he was filling out the clearance for the first leg of the trip, from Eglin to Omaha. I was not impressed by his appearance because he looked like anything but a fighter pilot. He was somewhat overweight and jowly, with a generally unkempt look. I was wearing a flying suit, but he wore rumpled khakis. As long as I knew him he always wore rumpled khakis. The weather was not too bad, some clouds but no thunderstorms en route, but the airdrome officer told him to be careful as there might be icing along the way. Although the airdrome officer was a captain, Lynch drawled, "Wal, Lieutenant, don't worry, I flowed in ice before."

We climbed into the cockpit, with Artie flying as pilot for the first leg, started the engines, and taxied to the takeoff end of the runway. After checking the engines, we took off, and to my astonishment, as I was retracting the landing gear, Artie was engaging the autopilot. I was astonished because the autopilot is usually not engaged until cruising altitude is reached. I was certain we were not going to be cruising at less than one hundred feet. When I got to know Artie better, I would not have been at all surprised had he decided to cruise that low.

As we climbed through two thousand feet, he had to make an adjustment to the autopilot, which is located on the instrument panel in a C-47. As he leaned forward to make the adjustment, he complained that he did not have a long stick with a suction cup on the end so he would not have to reach for the control knob. He said that all Air Transport Command pilots had them.

The flight was slow and uneventful. When we arrived over Offutt Field near Omaha, Artie called the tower and asked that we be refueled as soon as possible, because we were on an important mission. I wondered if he knew something I didn't. While I was filling out the clearance for the next leg, to Great Falls, Artie got some sodas and sandwiches, which we ate after takeoff.

After landing at Great Falls in the late afternoon, he asked me to get the passengers and their baggage loaded right away while he filled out the clearance. They were eager to get back to Florida and were all aboard, ready to go, when Artie arrived with the clearance. He said the weather had closed in behind us and that we would return via Denver and San Antonio to get around most of it. Just as we were getting ready to climb into the plane, a worried-looking captain came running up and identified himself as the Air Transport Command weight and balance officer. "Where is your weight and balance form? This plane looks overloaded," he yelled.

Since we were not flying an ATC aircraft, we were not bound by its regulations. Lynch replied, "Wal, Lieutenant, you guess our weight within a thousand pounds, and I'll give you a box of candy." With that, he climbed into the cabin and shut the door.

I think the weight and balance officer knew whereof he spoke, because our takeoff run was a thousand feet or more longer than we had figured, but we staggered into the air and, as before, immediately went on auto-pilot. There were two pilots among the passengers—one was Brad Brown and the other Thad Blanton, who had been on the famous Doolittle Tokyo Raid in 1942—and we had invited them to ride in the cockpit. They were as astonished as I was by the autopilot bit but said nothing. Artie was first pilot and seemed to have everything under control.

The two Pratt & Whitney R-1830 engines labored as the overloaded Gooney Bird struggled for altitude. At about 12,000 feet it seemed to have reached its ceiling, and it refused to go any higher. This posed a bit of a problem. The minimum altitude on the airways between Great Falls and Denver is 14,000 feet due to the proximity of the Rocky Mountains, and our estimated time of arrival was well after dark. Artie said that we could get enough power from the engines to continue the climb if we could su-percharge the engines by switching to high blower. The blower controls, however, were safety-wired in the low-blower position. The flight engineer told him that all C-47 engines were restricted to operation in low blower by a recent AAF technical order. Artie told the engineer to get him a pair of dikes (wire-cutting pliers). With them he nonchalantly cut the wires and moved the controls for both engines to the high-blower position. I sug-gested that he try it on one engine until he saw what would happen, but he said, "In for a penny, in for a pound," and left them both in high. To every-one's relief both engines responded with enough additional power for us to climb to 14,000 feet. We kept them in high blower until we let down to land at Denver, with no apparent damage to the engines.

Again Artie asked to be refueled as soon as possible while he filled out the clearance. The meteorologist told him that the weather was extremely bad from Denver to San Antonio, with icing and thunderstorms all along the route, and strongly advised that he wait until morning to proceed. The operations officer gave the same advice and said he would not sign the clearance, but Artie had a green instrument card and was thus authorized to clear himself. The operations officer went so far as to call the base commander, even though it was after ten o'clock, and had him try to persuade Artie not to take off. Artie told the base commander that we had four pilots on board, all of whom were highly trained test pilots, and that one of them had been on the Tokyo Raid. I did not see what difference that could make, but the base commander was evidently impressed and withdrew his objection. I was grateful Artie did not offer him a box of candy.

As it turned out the weather was not bad: a few clouds but no thunderstorms and no icing. After a smooth flight, we landed at Kelly Field in San Antonio at about two in the morning. The weather for the leg from San Antonio to Eglin was forecast to be about the same as we had encountered en route from Denver. We took off for the final leg a little after three and settled on course, on autopilot, of course. Everyone relaxed, looking forward to an uneventful flight.

A bit later I began to have a difficult time staying awake. Besides my fatigue from having flown some eighteen of the last twenty-one hours, the darkness and the drone of the engines had a strong soporific effect, and also, I am very much a day person. I kept nodding off and then jerking awake. Finally Artie said, "Damn it, Lope, you're driving me crazy with that bobbing. Slide your seat back and go to sleep for an hour or so. Then I'll wake you, and I'll take a nap." That suited me fine, and I dropped off almost immediately.

After about an hour and a half I woke up and looked over at Artie. To my surprise, he was sleeping soundly. I looked back in the cockpit, and the engineer and the other two pilots were also asleep. In fact, the autopilot seemed to be the only thing awake on board the airplane. Looking out, I couldn't see any lights on the ground. The autopilot had held the altitude well, but the gyro had precessed (drifted off the selected heading). We were heading about 20 degrees south of our course, which should have been almost due east. I knew we were to have turned to the northeast at Houston to stay on the airway to Lake Charles, Louisiana. I realized, with a start, that the absence of lights on the ground was due to the absence of ground. We were about eighty miles out over the Gulf of Mexico.

I immediately disengaged the autopilot and turned due north. After twenty minutes or so I saw lights up ahead. I let Artie sleep till we were back on course and the darkness was beginning to fade, but I woke him when I saw a row of large thunderstorms ahead. I had seen a lot of lightning to the east, but in the dark I thought it was much farther off. The closer we got to the clouds, the more ominous they looked. For all of my short flying career I had been warned to stay out of thunderstorms. So far I had followed that advice. I was soon to find out what sound advice it is. I suggested to Artie that we land at Lake Charles and wait until the storm moved off our route. He was almost convinced, because the other two pilots agreed with me, when we saw a C-54, about a thousand feet below, come out of the clouds heading in the opposite direction. Regrettably, Artie assumed that it couldn't be too bad if the C-54 made it through. We found out later that the C-54 had just entered the clouds and, wisely, had made a 180-degree turn and gotten out of them.

We tiptoed into the cumulus clouds at our cruising altitude of 9,000 feet. For the first five minutes it wasn't too bad, just some medium turbulence and light rain. Then suddenly all hell broke loose as we penetrated one of the cells of a monstrous thunderstorm. It was like flying into Niagara Falls. Torrential rain hit the windshield and ripped off the windshield wipers. In the violent turbulence, we dropped more than 2,000 feet, accompanied by an increase in airspeed to near the red line. A few seconds later we shot up to more than our original altitude, slowing almost to a stall. We could not hold altitude even within plus or minus 1,000 feet. Every minute or so we were hit with a tremendous burst of hail, which made the cockpit sound like the inside of a boiler factory. I was afraid that it might break out the windshield, which would have been uncomfortable to say the least.

To maintain as much control as possible all four pilots were fully engaged. I struggled to hold a level attitude with the control wheel, Artie held the heading with the rudder and helped me by using the elevator trim, Brad Brown worked the throttles, cutting the power as we descended and increasing it as we climbed, and Thad Blanton lowered the landing gear to slow us down during each descent and retracted it when we shot upward. From the look on Thad's face, I think he would have preferred to be back on the Tokyo Raid. We kept hoping it would abate, but instead it got worse. Artie called traffic control repeatedly to ask for a lower altitude but got no response except the heavy static caused by the constant lightning. If it was that bad in the cockpit, I wondered how it was going in the cabin. Those poor souls had nothing to do but be terrified.

After about fifteen minutes Artie said, "To hell with traffic control, this plane will come apart if we stay here. I'm going down to three thousand feet. It might be better there. No one else would be stupid enough to be flying in this." Letting down was easier said than done, because we were constantly lifted several thousand feet by violent updrafts.

Finally, after what seemed an eternity, we reached the general vicinity of three thousand feet, and it was a bit smoother. The sudden altitude changes were now in the hundreds rather than thousands of feet. Although visibility was still zero, the battering hail had ceased. We were unsure of our exact position. The radio compass was religiously pointing to every lightning flash, and we could not hear the radio beam through the static. Artie decided to make a slow letdown, hoping to break out of the clouds. That was a reasonably safe action, since we were near Mobile Bay. All the country for miles around was low and flat, and we didn't expect to run into another airplane.

During the long, agonizing letdown, we strained our eyes for a glimpse of the ground. We broke out of the clouds at between four hundred and five hundred feet, still in light rain, on the west side of Mobile Bay almost exactly on course. We were home free if the ceiling stayed this high for the rest of the trip, because we were almost in our local flying area. Letting down to two hundred feet as we crossed the bay, Artie followed the familiar beautiful white beach past Pensacola until we spotted the officer's beach club and then turned north across Choctawhatchee Bay. With Eglin in sight, we landed from a straight-in approach, and as we parked on the ramp, everyone let out a thankful sigh of relief. I don't think I ever have been so glad, before or since, to be back on the ground.

As the engines stopped, the door from the cabin burst open, and a large, angry captain, an ordnance officer called Moose, stomped in and yelled, "That's the last time I'll fly with any of you damned humming-birds!" When I looked back into the cabin, I didn't blame him. Baggage was strewn all over the seats and floor, along with the limp, white- or green-faced bodies of our passengers. We wisely remained in the cockpit until they had staggered off and crawled into trucks.

When we climbed out, the engineer told us to come back and look at the tail. Large sections of the paint on the fuselage and tail were gone, and the right horizontal stabilizer was so badly wrinkled that it had to be replaced. We obviously had made the right decision when we let down to a lower altitude. It was quite possible that we would have lost the tail, and our tails as well.

A few weeks later, to my surprise, rumpled Artie showed up at fighter ops and announced he was now a member of fighter test. I found that he had flown P-40s in the Pacific during the war, surviving two crashes due to engine failures. He was a true character with a good, if rather morbid, sense of humor. His standard greeting when he entered the combination squadron operations and ready room was "Hot day, big crowd, balloon gone up yet?"—whatever that means. When asked where someone was, his usual reply was "He went out to shit, and the hogs ate him."

Whenever a pilot in the squadron was killed, Artie would often put on a half-hour act of an undertaker trying to sell the widow a more expensive casket, mimicking an unctuous voice and silent, mincing steps to perfection. I'm sure that much of this clowning was calculated to lift the gloom that hung over the squadron following a fatal accident. If so, he was quite successful. Each pilot had his own way of dealing with the sudden loss of a close friend, one who was engaged in the same kind of flying as he. Artie's shtick helped to ease the pain. Fortunately, test pilots and fighter pilots are imbued with complete confidence in their invulnerability.

A few months after our unforgettable trip, the captain who had warned us against flying in ice became lost in bad weather while flying a Mustang and suffered a fatal crash. At that time the Mustang's only navigation radio was a small, low-frequency receiver, called a Detrola, mounted on the cockpit floor just in front of the seat. It was notoriously unreliable. When he learned of the accident, Artie said he wished Captain So-and-So could come back and do a fifteen-minute Detrola commercial.

Later, when I met his family, I realized that Artie and his wife were vivid proof that opposites attract. She was a lovely, cultured Vassar graduate named Cyrene (pronounced serene, which described her perfectly, by everyone except Artie, who insisted on calling her sigh-reen). She had three children from a previous marriage, two boys and a girl, and Artie and Cyrene had two children, a girl and a boy called, typically enough, Pookins and Buddy Jones. The family's English bulldog, which bore a strong resemblance to Artie, was named Mr. George Turbo.

I recently heard another Lynch story from his days as a test pilot for North American Aviation. In early 1954 he and Bob Hoover, the now famous stunt airshow pilot, gave a cockpit check to an Air Force pilot who was picking up a new F-100 Super Sabre at Mines Field, now Los Angeles International Airport. The engine exploded just after takeoff, and the pilot ejected. Tragically, he was much too low and was killed as he hit the runway, still in the seat. The airplane continued on and crashed a mile or so away in El Segundo. It hit in an open field, so no one else was killed or injured. Lynch and Hoover went out to the runway with the ambulance. It was obvious the pilot was dead, and Hoover was leaving the area when he saw that Lynch had gone some distance down toward the takeoff end of the runway. He joined him and asked what he was doing there. Lynch pointed at the centerline of the runway, the pilot's seat, and the smoke from the burning plane and said, "Bob, there was a guy that knew how to hold a heading."

The flight to Great Falls had been bad enough, but the day after our return I received the chilling news that I had been transferred from the fighter test squadron to the climatic hangar, where I would be the project and test officer on the all-climate testing of the P-80. Although my recent experience in Alaska made me the sensible choice to run the test, I didn't want to give up test flying as my primary duty. Fortunately, Colonel Slocumb, the fighter C.O., agreed and said that I could be attached to the squadron for flying and do as much flying as I had time for.

The climatic hangar is a large structure that can accommodate a B-36 bomber along with several other aircraft. The temperature of the entire hangar area can be maintained at anywhere between minus 65 degrees and 120 degrees Fahrenheit. In addition, there are several smaller temperature-controllable compartments in which smaller items can be tested. At the time that I was assigned there, the functional acceptance tests of the hangar had just been completed and the first aircraft tests were about to be run.

Once I learned that my flying time wouldn't suffer too much, I warmed somewhat to the assignment. As I learned more about the hangar, I was impressed with the amount of cooling and, to a lesser degree, heating equipment required to control the temperature in such an enormous building. In today's parlance, it was totally awesome.

The entire P-80 project, including the preparation of the test program, the running of the tests, the data reduction, and the completion of the final report, took only four months, from mid-March to mid-July of 1947. I had so much free time that I not only was able to fly as much as before but I also continued as test officer on the A-1 radar computing gunsight in the P-38. Along with most fighter pilots, I rated air-to-air gunnery as one of my favorite occupations.

The cold-weather part of the test was done first, with hangar temperatures at approximately 10-degree increments from freezing down to minus 65. After the aircraft had been cold soaked at the desired temperature (held at a given temperature until the entire aircraft had reached that temperature), a series of starts were made using the gasoline injection system developed in Alaska a few months earlier. In addition to the starts, all of the aircraft systems, such as landing gear, flaps, and trim tabs, were cycled. The airplane was heavily instrumented, and a great deal of information was gathered on the performance of the various systems throughout the test range. The airplane performed well, and there was no trouble at all with the starts at any temperature.

I was in the cockpit for all the starts, dressed in suitable arctic clothing. The P-80 tail pipe was vented to the outside through a duct that penetrated the hangar wall. One of my duties, before each start, was to go outside through a door next to the duct to ensure that the area was clear. At the very low temperatures, I would emerge from the door like a wraith in a cloud of vapor into an instant temperature change of some 150 degrees. As I walked around in that 90-degree heat in a fur-lined parka and mukluks, people driving past must have wondered if this was the same character who had climbed out of a P-47 in the same outfit in the middle of a softball field last July. In any case, it was reported as the first sighting in Florida of the abominable snowman.

The hot-weather test went much faster, since we had only three temperature increments: 100, 110, and 120 degrees. In Florida summers most of our starts were at 90 degrees or above. The only problem in this phase was the vile concoction of salt water and God-knows-what that the flight surgeon forced me to drink to protect me from the effects of the heat. It was nauseating. I needed something to protect me from the flight surgeon.

Just about the time I moved to the climatic hangar, I was notified of another chilling move to come. The powers-that-be at Eglin had decided to convert all the bachelor officer's quarters into family apartments. During and immediately after the war, there were large numbers of bachelor officers who did not wish to be married in wartime, but by early 1947 most of them had married. Since there was a severe housing shortage in the Eglin area, the decision was made to move the bachelors out and the married folks in. It was a sensible decision in retrospect, but it did not seem so at the time to the displaced bachelors, as the off-base housing shortage applied to them as well.

Maj. Don Rodewald, or Rode, as he was called, had been an armorer in the American Volunteer Group, the Flying Tigers. When it was disbanded in July 1942, he accepted a commission in the Army Air Forces as an armament officer in the 23rd Fighter Group. In late 1943 he returned to the States and went through flying training, becoming a fighter pilot. After a short tour at Eglin he rejoined the 23rd Group as a pilot in the 75th Fighter Squadron, my former outfit. He served in Shanghai with the AAF

Second Lieutenant Don Lopez in front of a 75th Fighter Squadron P-40M in Hengyang, China, in December 1943. (Donald S. Lopez)

Top: Lopez with the Eglin Field commander, Col. John F. Whiteley, after being awarded the Silver Star and Soldier's Medal. (Donald S. Lopez)

Bottom: A North American P-51H Mustang, the type the author flew to test the hammock seat. (National Air and Space Museum, Smithsonian Institution)

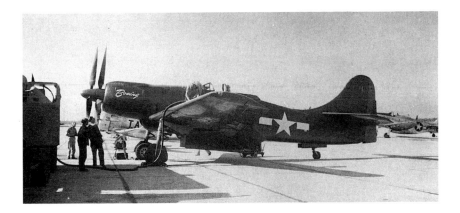

Top: Boeing XF8B, an experimental fighter-bomber tested at Eglin in 1946. Note the counter-rotating propellers and bomb bay doors. (National Air and Space Museum, Smithsonian Institution)

Middle: "Look, no hands!" The author flying a P-47N over central Florida. (National Air and Space Museum, Smithsonian Institution)

Bottom: A Lockheed P-80A Shooting Star undergoing cold-weather testing at Ladd Field, Alaska, in January 1947. (Donald S. Lopez)

Top: One of the Air Force Test Pilot School's North American T-6 Texans flown by the author in the flight performance course. (Donald S. Lopez)

Bottom: The flight test school's P-80A at Wright-Patterson. This was the first jet used in the school's program. (Donald S. Lopez)

Top: The cockpit of a flight test school P-80A. The three primary flight performance instruments—the engine tachometer, altimeter, and sensitive airspeed indicator—prominently located at the center of the panel. (Donald S. Lopez)

Bottom: Captain Lopez in a P-38 Lightning pulling up from a bombing run during a firepower demonstration. (U.S. Air Force)

Top: Napalm tanks dropped by Lopez from a P-80 are about to hit the target.
Bottom: Flames obliterate the target as he pulls up. (Donald S. Lopez)

Top: Eglin fighter test squadron pilots on the ramp. *Left to right:* Capt. Joe Young, Capt. Don Dessert, Lt. Bill Moore, Capt. Don "Lope" Lopez, Capt. Fred Belue, Capt. Ervine Pratt, Lt. Col. Emmett "Cyclone" Davis, Maj. Tom Hergert, Capt. Ray Evans, Capt. Tom "Hoot" Gibson, unknown, Capt. Joe Baglio. Despite the odd mix of uniforms, they were all in the same air force. This photograph was taken during the transition period from AAF to USAF uniforms and from winter to summer uniforms. (Donald S. Lopez)

Middle: Republic F-84 Thunderjet test team. *Left to right:* Captains Don Dessert, Fred Belue, Don Lopez, and Artie Lynch; Republic technical representative Artie Brown; nine members of the incomparable maintenance team; Capt. Hank Pashco. (Donald S. Lopez)

Bottom: Technical Sergeant Campbell and Captain Lopez in the fighter test squadron supply office. (U.S. Air Force)

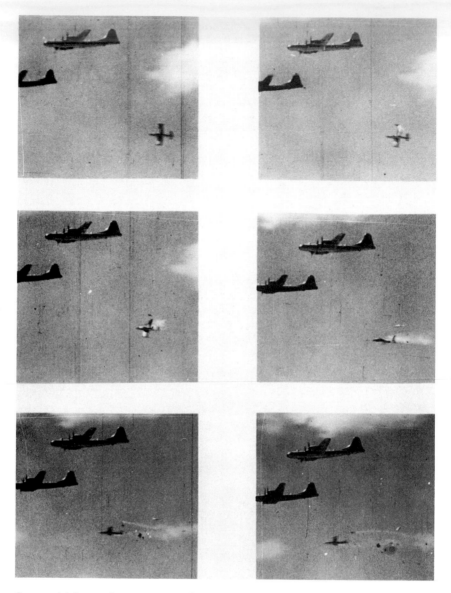

Sequential frames from 35mm motion-picture film showing Maj. Si Johnson's P-84B disintegrating in flight following a low-altitude pass at a flight of B-29s during a firepower demonstration. (National Air and Space Museum, Smithsonian Institution)

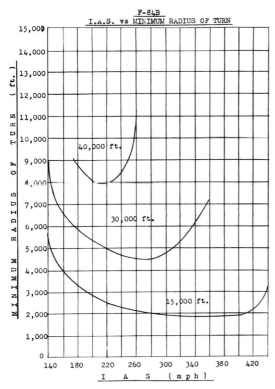

Top: The cockpit of an F-84
with special camera installed
to film through the gunsight.
(National Air and Space
Museum, Smithsonian
Institution)

Bottom: Plot of the F-84B
radius of turn versus airspeed
at various altitudes. (U.S.
Air Force)

Top: Drawing depicting a typical test combat mission for the F-84B. (U.S. Air Force)

Bottom: Four Eglin mechanics with a North American F-86A Sabre. Note the three gun-port retractable covers used on the early models. (U.S. Air Force)

Top: Maj. Joseph Tyler and Lt. Col. Dewey Slocumb, deputy squadron commander and squadron commander, respectively, of the 3200th Fighter Test Squadron. (U.S. Air Force)

Middle: An F-86A Sabre on ramp at Eglin. Note that the upper and lower gun-port covers have been removed. (U.S. Air Force)

Bottom: An F-84E Thunderjet loaded for a ground support test mission. (U.S. Air Force)

Top: Capt. Ray Evans in full regalia before a test flight in the F-86A Sabre. (U.S. Air Force)

Middle: A sight to make a World War II airplane buff cry: Northrop P-61s, Boeing B-17s, Consolidated B-24s, Boeing B-29s, and a Consolidated B-32 stored at Eglin Field 8, awaiting use as targets for armament tests. (U.S. Air Force)

Bottom: A Republic F-84C with APS-19 radar installed for night-fighter tests. (U.S. Air Force)

Top: Three F-80s pulling up after a napalm drop during a firepower demonstration. (U.S. Air Force)

Bottom: An F-80, having just dropped two napalm tanks on a row of simulated truck targets, flies over a burning P-61. (U.S. Air Force)

Top: A flight of three F-80s passing in review over a burning P-61. (U.S. Air Force)

Bottom: A Consolidated B-36 Peacemaker flying low in front of the stands at the close of a demonstration. (U.S. Air Force)

Top: A typical scene in the midst of a firepower demonstration, with napalm fires raging and several target aircraft on fire. (U.S. Air Force)

Bottom: A mixed flight of aircraft—a B-36, B-29, B-17, B-26, and P-51—passing in review. (U.S. Air Force)

Top: A flight of two F-80s, led by Lt. Wes Posvar, laying a smoke screen at the finish of a firepower demonstration. (U.S. Air Force)

Bottom: Glyn in the Lopezes' first house in Cinco Bayou, Florida—a great cook, then and now. (Donald S. Lopez)

after the war until being recalled to Eglin, where his young wife was dying of breast cancer. She died while I was in Alaska, and Rode, his two young daughters, and his mother were living in a big rented house about fifteen miles from Eglin near the small town of Mary Esther. I'll say more about Rode's courage later, but one mark of it was that he flew his wife's body back to Wisconsin for the funeral in a C-45, a plane so small and cramped that the coffin was constantly visible from the pilot's seat.

Barney and I were commiserating with Rode about our housing plight when he suggested that we move in with him, since his mother and daughters were to move to Tucson in a few days. We jumped at the chance and moved in as soon as his family left. The house was a far cry from bachelor quarters. It was a large, roomy two-story frame house surrounded by beautiful old oak trees situated on the inland waterway overlooking Santa Rosa Island. I could see that my life-style was about to make a dramatic change for the better.

Two more bachelors soon joined us. One was Lt. Col. Walt Glover, a handsome Virginian who was the base ordnance officer, and the other was Lt. Wes Posvar, a young redhead who had been graduated from West Point in June 1946 with the highest academic record compiled there by any cadet except Douglas MacArthur. After finishing flying school, he was assigned to Eglin and joined the cold-weather test detachment in Alaska in January. Upon returning to Eglin, he too was assigned to the climatic hangar, where we shared an office. We had been acquaintances in Alaska but became friends and roommates at Eglin and are good friends to this day.

Wes has the brain of a genius and the heart of a fighter pilot, a rare combination possibly attributable to his red hair. He loved to fly and party, and his favorite remark at about two in the morning, when festivities were beginning to wane, was "Let's start a brand-new party!"

Near the end of his first year at Eglin he was sent to the Air Tactical School at Tyndall Air Force Base near Panama City, Florida. He came back to Eglin regularly to fly and to visit, but at the conclusion of the four-month course he made a spectacular return to the area. Johnny Walker Red Label Scotch had just been put back on the market following the war. Wes had seen some of the advertising posters and obtained a large number of pennants proclaiming, "Red's back," which he plastered all over the town of Fort Walton and the base.

Although trained as a B-25 pilot, Wes was determined to fly fighters, another manifestation of his intelligence, and got himself attached to the fighter test squadron for flying. After flying with him in an AT-6, the only single-engine two-seater in the squadron, I was sure that he would have no problems flying fighters, and he soon checked out in the Mustang and the other propeller fighters. In those days few, if any, fighters had two seats. A pilot's first flight was, of necessity, solo. When the time came for Wes to make his first jet flight, in a P-80, I followed him in another P-80 as a chase pilot. I was astounded, to put it mildly, when at about 250 mph and 250 feet, he did a slow roll. At first I thought he was turning left and started to follow, but instead he went all the way around in a good roll. Even at Eglin in the forties, this was strictly verboten except in airshows. I was thinking that if he crashed out of the roll I had better dive in next to him. That would have been easier than trying to explain his roll. I thought no one had seen it, or if someone had, it wouldn't be reported. Wes knew better, but the sheer exuberance of flying a jet for the first time was too much for his restraint mechanisms. I really couldn't blame him. I felt much the same way on my first P-80 flight.

Artie Lynch expressed the feelings of most fighter pilots when he met Wes after that flight. He said, "I saw that roll, and I know why you did it— you had to!" Wes flew with the fighter squadron for the rest of his stay at Eglin. He was a fine pilot and flew on many tests and in firepower demonstrations in which he demonstrated his fighter-pilot skills in the most impressive way possible, that is, accurate weapons delivery.

Wes had a distinguished career after he left Eglin to accept an appointment as a Rhodes scholar. He held many important planning positions in Air Force headquarters, flew in the Berlin airlift, received a Ph.D. from Harvard, and was the first professor of political science at the Air Force Academy. Following his retirement from the Air Force, he served as chancellor and president of the University of Pittsburgh for more than twenty years. Despite his academic achievements, Wes still considers his flying days with the fighter squadron at Eglin some of the most enjoyable of his life, and we often reminisce about them with pleasure.

Barney was with us for only a short time. His request had been approved to return to college under a new AAF program in which officers whose education had been interrupted by the war could pick up where they had left off. He left almost immediately for the University of Florida in Gainesville, about 300 miles from Eglin. While Barney and I were in Alaska, Dick Jones was transferred to the 20th Fighter Group at Shaw Field, South Carolina, so the three irresistible bachelors at Eglin were now reduced to one.

Rode, Walt, Wes, and I plus Ted Shea, a civilian technician from MIT who was at Eglin to maintain the A-1 computing gunsight and to monitor the test, became the founding occupants of the house. We shared the rent and the housekeeping chores, but Wes, probably as a backlash from his West Point years, didn't make his bed for the entire six months we roomed together, although he did wash the sheets now and then. One of my chores, since I am an early riser, was to rouse the group in time for work. I did this by turning up the phonograph to its full volume and playing Red Ingle's recording of "Temptation." Then I would quickly vacate the area to avoid the missiles hurled from the balcony that encircled the living room. After a few weeks in the house, we decided it should have a proper name. After some thought I suggested Auger Inn, which was immediately and unanimously approved. To those not familiar with flier's euphemisms for "crash" and "death," words almost never used by pilots, to auger in means to crash and die. An auger is a type of drill, and a spinning airplane boring into the ground remotely resembles a drill boring into a plank.

Another euphemism for the same thing, "to buy the farm," has an interesting etymology. When a military plane crashed or crash-landed on a farm, the farmer would usually claim an exorbitant amount from the government in payment for his destroyed crops, forcing the government, in effect, to buy the farm. By common usage it became the pilot who bought the farm when he was killed in a crash.

Auger Inn became well known in the Eglin area, with many parties in the house and on the dock, which was complete with a canoe and a sailboat. As the original residents, or Auger Innmates, married or were transferred, other pilots moved in, until finally in 1949 the house was sold, and there was no longer any room at the inn.

Not only had the housing situation improved, but my personal life brightened considerably when Glindel Barron returned from vacation. I asked her for a date, she accepted, and after several more dates the realization slowly began to dawn on me that there just might possibly be something in life more important than flying.

11

Gunsights and Highball

During these months, March to October 1947, I enjoyed a stretch of some of the best and most interesting flying of my career. Despite being assigned to the climatic hangar for the first half of the period, I was able to fly with the fighter test squadron almost as much as I had before the transfer. I became the test officer on the A-1 gunsight in the P-38L and was one of a group of pilots on Project Highball, testing the interception capability of the P-80. On many weekends I flew in airshows in the Southeast and on other weekends flew on personal cross-country flights. To top it off, I made several long ferry flights and, wonder of wonders, was able to buy a new car.

Cars were hard to acquire after the war. Auto manufacturers had to switch from war production back to production of civilian vehicles, and it was late 1947 or early 1948 before cars could be bought without paying ridiculous premiums. Consequently, it was quite common for young people not to have their first car until they were in their mid-twenties.

My nonflying life was even more satisfying. After several more dates with Glindel I had fallen deeply in love, and we began to go steady ('gō 'sted ē: to date regularly and exclusively, usually a precursor to engagement and marriage). We dated almost every night and had lunch together as often as possible. Life was sweet, both in the air and on the ground.

The A-1 gunsight in the P-38 was the first radar-ranging, computing gunsight used by the Army Air Forces. The test version of the sight was called the Davis-Draper sight, after its inventors Col. (later Lt. Gen.) Leigh

Davis and Dr. Stark Draper of MIT. Dr. Draper later was instrumental in the development of inertial guidance, which made space navigation possible and which is used in almost all military aircraft today. The sight was developed in the MIT laboratories and was mounted in a P-38 because of the space available in the nose section of the pilot nacelle and the clear field of view for the radar resulting from the space between the propellers. It had been installed in one P-38 in early 1945, and by 1947 that P-38 was the only one remaining in active service in the AAF. The sight could not have been installed in any of the single-engine propeller fighters without some kind of a high-drag pod on the wing outside the arc of the propeller. That summer, Glyn (short for Glindel) told me she could always tell my plane when it flew over because it had two tails with a board in between, not a bad description for an airplane novice.

Flying the only P-38 in the Air Force prompted some interesting reactions from former P-38 drivers. Colonel Slocumb, the squadron commander, flew P-38s during the war and, like all P-38 pilots, loved the airplane and its distinctive sound, a throaty purr due to the turbosuperchargers. He told me to taxi by his office at the corner of the hangar on every flight and rev up the engines so he could enjoy the sound, which of course I did. Whenever I flew it up to Bedford, Massachusetts, to enable the MIT technicians to modify the sight, the airplane would be surrounded at each refueling stop by former P-38 pilots and mechanics lovingly renewing their acquaintance with it. It was lucky that the airplane was made of aluminum or it would have rusted away from the tears shed on it.

The tests went on for a number of years, as the MIT lab was constantly modifying the sight based on the test results. The sight was regularly maintained and modified by an MIT technician or technicians at Eglin, but the airplane had to be flown to Bedford whenever major modifications were to be made. There the gunsight would be removed and taken to Cambridge. All of the gun camera film shot during the test flights was analyzed frame by frame at MIT, and the targets were scored and hits charted by the MIT crew at Eglin.

The targets were flag targets, 6 by 30 feet, with radar corner reflectors. They were towed by the squadron's B-26 (later by Douglas A-26s), flown by the medium and light test squadron, at 200 mph at 8,000 to 10,000 feet a few miles offshore along the Gulf ranges. All firing passes were made toward the Gulf, but camera gunnery passes could be made in either direction.

The 20mm cannon and two of the .50-caliber machine guns had been removed from the nose to make room for the radar and sight. The two remaining .50s were fitted with hydraulic chargers, and the ammunition belts had dummy rounds after each ten live rounds, so only ten rounds could be fired per gun during a single pass. This precluded expending too many rounds on a single good pass and made the test more precise. The test ran for several years, and I was the test officer from early in 1947 until late in 1949, except for the period that I was at test pilot school. The last part of the test was flown in a Republic F-84 Thunderjet.

It is not especially difficult for a good fighter pilot to hit an enemy aircraft from within a narrow cone of about 40 degrees astern and a range of less than 200 yards. The problem becomes progressively more difficult as the range and angle off the target increase. (A fighter flying at a right angle to the path of the target is 90 degrees off the target; zero angle off the target is from dead astern.) The Davis-Draper sight was a radar-ranging, lead-computing sight designed to allow accurate firing from high angles off (more than 60 degrees) and long range (about 750 yards); therefore, the gunnery passes were set up to fire at 60 degrees angle off and 750 yards range. We did quite a bit of camera-only gunnery to test the tracking capability of the sight before the actual firing phase of the test. Two other pilots, Maj. Don Rodewald from the weapons test branch and Capt. Don Dessert from the fighter squadron, participated in the testing. Since all three of us were named Don, there could have been considerable confusion, but fortunately I answered only to "Lope" and Rodewald to "Rode," leaving "Don" exclusively to Dessert.

A typical firing mission went as follows: The fighter took off some twenty minutes after the plane with the target, to allow it time to get into position and trail the target. As soon as the fighter was airborne the pilot turned on the gunsight to warm up the sight and the radar. As he approached the tow plane he checked to see that the radar was locking onto the target, as indicated by a light on the side of the gunsight. When the tow pilot called that he was ready for firing passes, the fighter took a position flying parallel to the tow plane, about 1,000 feet higher and 1,500 to 2,000 yards away. If the fighter was on the right side of the tow plane, the pilot would depress the button on the control wheel that caged the gunsight, locking the pipper into a fixed position in the center of the windscreen, and then roll into a diving turn to the left, putting the pipper on the target as he rolled level before starting a tracking turn to the right. When the radar light indicated target lock-on, the pilot released the cage switch and held the pipper (which was now continuously indicating the proper, and constantly changing, distance to lead the target) as close to the center of the target as possible. At about 750 yards and 60 degrees angle off, which would occur simultaneously if the pilot had judged his approach correctly, the pilot pulled the trigger and fired a ten-round burst from both guns. He would then pull up and turn to the right to get into position for the next pass while activating the switch that recharged the guns and noting any comments about the pass on his knee board. (After the mission one of the most difficult tasks is trying to decipher these comments.)

Usually three or four passes were made in one direction, and then the tow plane reversed its course and passes were made in the opposite direction. If the tracking was not smooth or the range and angle off were not correct, the pilot did not fire. The tracking was recorded, however, since the camera that filmed the pilot's view through the gunsight was activated by the caging switch, not the gun trigger as is standard.

The P-38 was a good gun platform, and as my proficiency increased, I achieved some excellent results that were gratifying to the MIT team and to me. On some of the best passes my average tracking error was only half a mil (one mil is the angle subtended by a chord of 1 foot at a range of 1,000 feet). Since I was firing from 750 yards (2,250 feet), my pipper was within 1.125 feet of the target center throughout the tracking portion of the pass. On these passes 25 to 27 percent of the rounds fired were hits. A score of 30 percent was required to be rated an expert aerial gunner, but that was based on firing from a much shorter distance and lower angle off. The gunnery specialists at the Wright Field armament lab told me that with a six-by-thirty target mounted on a ground range, a .50-caliber machine gun firing from 750 yards would score only about 27 percent because of the muzzle waver while firing. In other words, the Davis-Draper sight was very effective in the hands of an experienced pilot.

The sight was designed to be a gun-bomb-rocket sight. We did not participate in the rocket-firing tests, but we did considerable dive-bombing with the P-38; later, with the P-84, we tested all three modes. The dive-bombing procedure was quite simple. The pilot climbed to 10,000 feet, set the sight to the bomb mode, held down the cage button, and rolled into a dive of about 70 degrees. When established in a steady dive with the pipper on the pyramid target (a four-sided wooden pyramid, about 20 feet on a side and about 10 feet high, painted to contrast with the ground), the pilot released the cage button, and the pipper was held on the target. This caused the plane to fly at slightly less than one g as the dive angle slowly increased. When the accelerometer-actuated computing mechanism in the sight calculated that the time was right, the bomb was released automatically, and a light on the sight signaled the pilot to pull out. The release occurred at about 4,000 feet, giving the pilot plenty of altitude to recover from the dive. The starting altitude and dive angle were varied throughout the testing, and the results were quite good, with many direct hits and near misses recorded. To eliminate as many variables as possible, it was necessary to enter each run at a precise altitude, airspeed, and dive angle.

During this period most of the pilots in the fighter squadron were flying on Project Highball, a series of tests to determine the most effective methods for intercepting incoming jet bomber raids with jet fighters using the P-80, the only jet fighter available in numbers at that time. It tested not only the aircraft but also the ground controlled intercept (GCI) system. Instead of jet bombers (none were available at that time), two P-80s with tip tanks were flown in formation to simulate the radar return from a jet bomber. They could not be detected by radar at long range, so they were equipped with AN-APN 19 radar beacons. During the first phase of this test we flew seven days a week, and on one of those days the squadron logged forty-two hours on Project Highball alone.

The target P-80s would take off and climb on the heading assigned by the project officer to 35,000 feet. At 150 to 200 miles from Eglin they would turn to the inbound heading and activate the radar beacons. In those days there was almost no traffic at that altitude, so we were not required to work with the civilian air traffic control system.

The interceptor P-80 was parked on the taxiway, just off the runway and facing it at an angle of 45 degrees. The pilot was strapped in and ready to go, with his eyes glued to the control tower. The external power unit for starting was plugged into the airplane and idling, with the attending crew chief also watching the tower. When the GCI operator picked up the target on his scope, he signaled the tower operator, who flashed a green light toward the P-80. The crew chief immediately powered up the starting unit, and the pilot engaged the starter switch. As soon as the engine reached 35-percent rpm, the pilot signaled the ground crew to disengage the starting unit. The pilot advanced the throttle as rapidly as possible without exceeding the tail-pipe temperature limit and started the takeoff run from the taxiway, curving onto the runway heading. As soon as he was airborne, about one minute after the green light flashed, he switched to the GCI frequency and was given a climb heading while he accelerated to climbing speed, which without tip tanks was 330 mph at sea level. The P-80 was flown at full throttle (100-percent rpm) until the pilot completed the interception, with a simulated firing pass at the simulated bombers.

The interceptor took about ten minutes to reach 35,000 feet, and during that period the targets covered some seventy-five miles. Quite often, especially when the GCI operator was so new at the job that he turned the fighter too late or at the wrong angle, the mission would terminate in a long stern chase, and the bombers would reach the target before being intercepted. We soon realized that to meet the threat of bombers with higher speed and altitude capability, we needed more powerful ground radar able to pick up the bombers farther from the target, highly trained GCI operators, better climb performance in the interceptors, and longer-range weapons than .50-caliber guns.

During this period the United States had no reason to expect a bombing attack, although it had become painfully obvious that our wartime ally the Soviet Union was an ally no more. The Soviets had taken control of most of eastern Europe by installing Communist governments in all the countries they had liberated from the Nazis. In early 1946 Sir Winston Churchill, in a notable speech at Westminster College in Fulton, Missouri, vividly defined the new situation when he said, "From Stettin in the Baltic to Trieste in the Adriatic an iron curtain has descended across the Continent."

President Harry Truman decided that the free countries, often referred to as the West, could not permit Russian expansion to go unchecked. In March 1947 he presented to the Congress a policy of resistance to international aggression that became known as the Truman Doctrine. We were engaged in what was called a Cold War, fought politically and economically with propaganda and displays of military strength instead of the usual weapons. Although the tremendous military power of the United States had been severely reduced at the end of the war, it had to be reestablished and maintained at a level high enough to be a credible deterrent to the Soviets. Despite the overwhelming numerical superiority of the Soviets, as long as the West alone had the atom bomb the deterrent was credible indeed.

During Project Highball the squadron had two near fatalities, both due to malfunctions in oxygen systems. In the first, Capt. Blackie Oliver, a Mangus Colorado Apache from Arizona, was flying one of the simulated bombers when he drifted out of formation and went into a spiral, almost vertical dive. The pilot of the other P-80 saw him slumped in the cockpit but could do nothing but try to call him on the radio and follow him down. He couldn't stay with Blackie without exceeding speed and Mach limitations (580 mph and 0.8 Mach) but managed to keep him in sight.

Blackie's plane finally pulled out at about 3,000 feet (the dive began at 35,000 feet), and he regained consciousness. Although he was a bit groggy, Blackie followed the other pilot back to the base and landed safely. Unfortunately, the rapid descent while unconscious had severely damaged both his eardrums, forcing him off flying status and requiring him to use a hearing aid.

Blackie was a popular member of the squadron. He was short and wiry with jet black hair and sparkling, almost black eyes. His locker was next to mine, and frequently as we changed into our flying suits he hung a blue and gray scarf around my neck and performed an Indian dance that he said made me a member of the blue and gray tribe of the Mangus Colorado Apaches.

The second incident was almost identical to the first, except that the pilot, Capt. Ray Evans, took longer to recover and came out of the dive much closer to the ground, after going through several uncontrolled gyrations. When he did recover he heard his wingman, who had followed him down, screaming over the radio for him to bail out. Ray finally heard him, jettisoned the canopy, and tried to pull up, since he was down to about 1,000 feet and descending, but he couldn't pull the stick back. He found that his seat cushion (we flew with backpack parachutes and seat cushions) had slipped forward during his wild descent and was wedged between the seat and the stick. He managed to rip it loose and throw it out, where it wrapped around the right horizontal stabilizer. Luckily it did not affect the controls, and Ray was able to land safely. Both incidents were traced to failures within the oxygen regulators. The pilots could easily have been fatalities, but the Eglin area has few farms, and neither pilot wished to buy one.

A pilot who had been in the fighter squadron but had been transferred to base operations, Maj. W. Wayne Patton, had an accident that I thought for a minute would involve me. I had walked out of the fighter hangar toward the parking lot on the way to meet Glindel for lunch. I heard a P-51 taking off to the south but didn't pay much attention until the sound suddenly stopped. A sudden silence is always cause for alarm at an airfield, and I looked up and saw the Mustang at about 800 feet starting a turn toward the hangar. The standard procedure when an engine fails on takeoff is to glide straight ahead and crash-land the best way possible. The risk of stalling and spinning in is too great in a low-speed, engine-out turn. Pat evidently thought he had enough height and speed to risk a 270-degree turn back to the airport. I didn't share his confidence. He barely cleared the hangar, and when he came over me, the airplane was shuddering on the edge of a stall. I was afraid he would spin and crash on or near me, but he went over at about 30 feet, clipped some pine trees in the parking lot, and hit the ground with a tremendous impact at the other end of the lot. The airplane skidded across the road, narrowly missing two cars, and smashed into a culvert, bringing it to a stop. Part of the engine ripped off and went down the central hall of the base library and out the other end without hitting anyone.

The whole area was flooded with gasoline, and Pat's feet were trapped in the cockpit, but miraculously there was no fire. The engine must have cooled sufficiently in the glide, and Pat had cut all the switches. The base fire trucks arrived within about thirty seconds, before I could reach the plane, and flooded the area with foam. Pat was extricated and rushed to the hospital. His ankle had been crushed, and although he was able to walk again, he was removed from flying status and left the AAF. He stayed in the Eglin area and established a successful insurance and real estate agency. That was real intelligence: instead of buying the farm, he sold it.

Three other pilots were less fortunate during this period. Two were from the fighter squadron. The other was Captain Robbins, a fighter pilot who held an administrative job but was attached to the squadron for flying. I knew him because he was also from Tampa. He was returning from a weekend cross-country in a Mustang and was nearing the field when his engine failed. He tried to glide to the field rather than bailing out, but he hit well short of the runway and was killed.

Capt. Lawson "Lippy" Lipscomb was flying a P-80 on Project Highball and had a flameout at 35,000 feet some seventy miles from the base. He made several attempts to airstart the engine without success as he glided toward Eglin. A P-80 can glide about seventy miles from 35,000 feet, so Lippy tried to make a wheels-down landing but stalled and spun into the ground about half a mile from the runway. Lippy was short, stocky, and blond and was one of the squadron's jokers. He had been in Alaska with me and was a good friend. Too many pilots are lost in trying to save an airplane instead of bailing out. Their effort is commendable in that it illustrates their high sense of duty, but it is much worse to lose both the pilot and the airplane. Airplanes are replaceable; pilots are not.

Capt. George Parker was a night-fighter pilot who had joined the squadron that summer, and because he was rather quiet I didn't know him too well. He had been flying one of two P-80s covering a buzz-bomb launch and had followed it for some fifty miles out over the Gulf. They were flying below 1,000 feet when Parker's engine flamed out. He had a lot of speed, so he zoomed up several thousand feet and tried a number of airstarts without success. When he realized the engine could not be restarted, he was too low to bail out. The early P-80s did not have ejection seats, and he was forced to ditch in the Gulf. Ditching in a P-80 is not recommended; the intake ducts fill with water upon impact, causing rapid deceleration and sinking. The other pilot said George made a good touchdown after jettisoning the canopy, but the plane went under almost immediately, and he was not able to get out of the cockpit.

I don't want to leave the impression that these crashes and near crashes occurred in close sequence. They stretched over a period of some eight months. If they had all taken place within a few weeks, all fighter flying would have been suspended while the accidents were investigated and the causes determined.

In April the fighter squadron was asked to provide two P-80s for a weekend airshow in Jacksonville. Barney and I volunteered to fly them. Late in the afternoon of the Friday before the show we took off in formation, bound for Jacksonville with me in the lead. As is standard for the leader in formation takeoffs, I used only 98-percent power so that Barney would have a little margin to use to stay in position. The flight was uneventful, and after landing we checked in with the officer in charge of the airshow. He requested that we, having the only jets, make an early flight the next morning over Jacksonville to draw attention to the show.

The following morning we taxied out for takeoff, with Barney in the lead, and were cleared into position on the runway. We ran up the engines to full power, 98 percent for Barney and 100 percent for me, and on Barney's head signal released the brakes and started down the runway. Even with my 2-percent power margin I was unable to keep up with Barney. All the instruments were reading properly, except that the tail-pipe temperature was on the low end of its normal range. Barney lifted off the runway and pulled ahead even farther, and I began to wonder if my plane would get off at all. Since I was too far down the runway to stop, I continued the takeoff. Just before the end of the runway the plane staggered into the air, flying just above stalling speed. I retracted the wheels and began to slowly milk the flaps up a few degrees at a time. Although I was only twenty-five feet off the ground, the airspeed was approaching a more respectable reading, and I was beginning to breathe easier when the silver-dollar-size fire warning light came on with an almost palpable impact. The correct response is to reduce power, look back for any signs of fire, and if there are any, bail out. At my altitude and airspeed, all I could accomplish was the second step, which I did immediately, and to my great relief there was no sign of a fire. Still, I had a problem. I began a slow climb gently turning back toward the field and called the tower to report that I had an emergency and would land on any runway possible.

Barney chimed in on the radio, "What's the matter, Lope? No guts?"

I replied, "I've got plenty. I just don't want them scattered all over Jacksonville."

With the added altitude I was able to reduce power, and the light went out. I lowered the gear, lined up with the runway, and landed, shutting down the engine as soon as I was off the runway. I scrambled out of the cockpit as the fire truck screeched to a halt alongside. The firemen and I found that the paint on the left side of the fuselage, over the point where the tail pipe is attached to the engine, was discolored and blistered, which indicated an exhaust gas leak at that juncture. That explained the fire warning light but not the lack of power. With only one jet operational, Barney performed at the airshow alone.

On Monday a C-47 flew over from Eglin with a new tail pipe and two mechanics to repair the plane. When the old tail pipe was removed they found that it had slipped through the production line without the welded ring at the aft end, called the pucker string, that decreased the diameter of the nozzle exit and increased the thrust of the engine. With the new tail pipe the engine regained its normal power, and I flew back to Eglin with no trouble.

A minor but embarrassing incident occurred at an airshow in Atlanta about a month later. Si Johnson and I were flying P-80s, and on the second day of the show, when we started our engines, my oil pressure continued to register zero. I immediately shut down the engine, and after I climbed out of the cockpit and removed my Mae West (an inflatable life jacket), Si beckoned for me to come over and explain the problem. I ran over to his plane, which was at idle power, and stood by the cockpit. As I yelled and gestured about my oil pressure, the Mae West was sucked out of my hand and into his engine intake duct, leaving me feeling a bit foolish, to say the least. The protective screen kept it from entering the engine, but Si had to shut everything down so the mechanics could open the engine compartment and remove it. No damage was done, and Si was kind enough not to say anything to our fellow pilots.

In early July, the base commander at Tyndall Field requested that

Eglin provide a P-80 and pilot for the Fourth of July airshow in Panama City, which is Glyn's home town. I immediately volunteered, because I knew she would be home for the holiday. I flew to Tyndall on the evening of the third and reported to base operations for the airshow briefing the next morning. The Tyndall pilots were flying P-51s and A-26s. After their detailed briefing, the meeting seemed about to break up, so I stood up, ostentatiously displaying my red jet helmet, and said that I was flying the P-80 from Eglin and asked for instructions. The operations officer said, "You can come in as soon as we have cleared the area and do whatever you want." There could be no sweeter words for a fighter pilot—especially for this fighter pilot with his girlfriend and her family to impress.

The crowd for the show was on a large pier that extended from the main street out into the bay as well as along the shoreline. I took off about fifteen minutes after the Tyndall planes, climbing to 10,000 feet and cir-cling about five miles from the bay end of the pier. When the Tyndall flight leader called to report that his planes had left the area, I started diving to-ward the end of the pier, crossed it at more than 550 mph at about 50 feet over the crowd, and zoomed into a steep climbing turn over the main street (aerobatics are prohibited over populated areas). Then I lined up par-allel to the shoreline and did a series of low-level Cuban eights and reverse Cuban eights (combinations of loops and half rolls) over the water, finish-ing with another high-speed pass over the pier. It was necessary to curtail the show, because there was no jet fuel at Tyndall, and I had to reserve enough fuel to get back to Eglin the next day.

Later that evening I joined Glyn at the ground festivities, which in-cluded a fireworks display. I was in civilian clothes, and it was enjoyable wandering through the crowd listening to the enthusiastic remarks about the jet in the airshow. The audience seemed to have enjoyed it almost as much as I. From Glyn's reaction, a combination of awe and fear, I thought I would have either a prospective fiancée or an ex-girlfriend. Of course I hoped for the former.

The following is the view from the ground as she perceived it.

The people were in a celebratory mood, as on all July Fourth holidays in this small northwest Florida town, but somehow the mood seemed height-ened on this particular day in 1947. Since the end of World War II, Ameri-cans seemed more conscious of their proud heritage, and there was a heightened sense of patriotism. The events began early, as happy families arrived at the park dressed in bright summer colors. By midafternoon the colorful high-school marching band, impressive military parade, and concert were over. Adults and children alike had been stuffing themselves all day on hot dogs, homemade pies, watermelons, and refreshing snow cones. Feeling somewhat lethargic, hundreds ambled the few blocks to the pier overlooking the bay for what was to be the highlight of the day—an aerial demonstration by the planes from nearby Tyndall Army Air Field. In recent years the local population had become familiar with men in uniform and conventional airplanes, but today was to be anything but conventional. Most of the citizens had never heard the roar of a jet, much less seen one, but by late afternoon they would have a spectacular introduction to the jet age. Relaxed friends and strangers made casual conversation as they stood on the pier facing the expanse of the beautiful bay. The azure sky filled with wispy white clouds formed a perfect backdrop as the airshow began. The show opened with a formation flyby of A-26 Invaders and P-51 Mustangs. This was followed by a series of loops and rolls by three Mustangs. The crowd responded enthusiastically as the show seemingly ended with another group flyby. As the people slowly began to disperse, an unfamiliar rumble was heard in the distance from over the bay, causing them to wonder if a typical Florida afternoon thunderstorm was to end this perfect day. All eyes were drawn to a fleck in the sky that within an instant was transformed into what appeared to be a streak of lightning thundering down main street. Microseconds later a beautiful, sleek silver bullet was zooming up over the bay at an incredible speed. The sight and deafening noise momentarily left the audience in a state of shock, mixed with terror in some cases. That fear was short-lived, as this exquisite piece of machinery performed rolls, loops, and intricate maneuvers that left even the birds envious and me wondering if Lope was really at the controls. As suddenly as it had appeared, it turned east and disappeared, leaving the exhilarated audience completely stunned. This was a Fourth of July they wouldn't soon forget.

The next day I took Glyn and three of her brothers out to Tyndall to have a closer look at the P-80. Before leaving for Eglin I made a low, high-speed pass over the runway at the tower's request, rocking my wings as I headed west. I like to think that the airshow and P-80 inspection were influential in her twelve-year-old brother Doug's decision to become a fighter pilot, even though that decision would lead to the harrowing incident off the coast of Vietnam described in Chapter 5.

Barney called from the University of Florida in Gainesville in early

September to tell me that the Packard dealer had a new 1948 convertible available. It was the first postwar Packard model, and it cost the then astronomical sum of $3,500, more than half a year's pay. I had saved quite a bit of money during and after the war, so I told Barney I would take it sight unseen. I was tired of constantly borrowing cars from my friends, and there seemed to be little prospect of getting one elsewhere in the near future.

Rode flew me to Gainesville in an A-26 on a Friday evening, and I picked up the car the next morning. It was bright blue with red trim and a white top and had the first push-button windows I had ever heard of, much less seen. Barney and I drove it around for a while trying to ignore the worshipful looks of dozens of coeds. It had passed the checkout. I headed out for Eglin, arriving at Auger Inn after dark.

The next morning I introduced my sensational new acquisition to my fellow Auger Innmates. After each had driven it and run the windows up and down to their heart's content (this was to be a constant problem) I drove to the base to show it to Glyn. She was as impressed as the coeds had been: I didn't just have a car, I had a sporty new convertible. Seeing her in the car with the top down—the blue car setting off her blond hair and deep tan—I began to worry that it might encourage competition and that perhaps I should have bought a black sedan.

Glyn was not completely checked out on driving and did not have a license, so during the next few weeks she practiced driving in a deserted area near beautiful Destin Beach, then took and passed the driver's test.

Later that month we learned that the squadron would soon receive two P-80Bs for testing. The P-80B was equipped with a desperately needed ejection seat, which would enable the pilot to get out of the aircraft safely, even at high speed. Accordingly all the pilots were flown to Wright Field in a C-47 to learn how to use this vital piece of safety equipment. After a few hours of classroom indoctrination on the operation of the seat and the proper body position for ejection, we were taken into a large hangar that had a track running up one wall. On this track an ejection seat was mounted. Each pilot in turn climbed into the seat, assumed the proper position, and squeezed the seat trigger. With a loud, echoing explosion, the nervous occupant was propelled rapidly up the track to a height of fifteen to twenty feet, depending on the pilot's weight and the vagaries of the explosive charge. After the first shot we all put a dollar in a pot with the sum going to the one who came closest to estimating how high the seat would go on his turn. On one of the shots the sergeant loaded a dummy cartridge. When the pilot squeezed the trigger nothing happened, but he was petrified for fear that the seat would fire while he was climbing out. He was left sweating for about thirty seconds before being told that it was a dummy round. He dismounted with a combination of anger and relief.

When I flew in a two-seat F-16 in 1988, I couldn't help but contrast the briefing I received with the P-80B training. For the F-16 flight I underwent more than two hours of detailed instruction on the use of the tilted ejection seat and the related emergency equipment.

12

Head-on Passes

September was my last month in the Army Air Forces and my first in the U.S. Air Force. On September 18, 1947, a long-held dream came true, and the USAAF became the USAF. For the first time in our history the Air Force was a separate service, no longer part of the Army. There was no immediate effect on the personnel except that our serial numbers were changed, Army air fields became Air Force bases, soldiers became airmen, the 611th Proof Test Group became the 3200th Proof Test Group, and we held our heads a little higher. It took several years to phase in the new blue uniforms, and they did not become mandatory for all personnel until 1950. In 1948 and 1949 it was sometimes difficult to tell we were all in the same service, since there was such a mixture of uniforms, especially in the optional period during the change from summer to winter uniforms and vice versa.

September is the hurricane season in Florida, and over the years at Eglin, one of our missions was to evacuate the aircraft when hurricanes threatened. In mid-September a hurricane entered the Gulf and headed toward the Eglin area. On the afternoon of the seventeenth, the last day of the AAF, we were ordered to move all flyable aircraft to Maxwell Field, Alabama, about 130 miles north of Eglin. I flew the P-38, and Don Rodewald flew the P-82 night fighter. Since both aircraft had special radar equipment, they were put into a hangar at Maxwell while the rest of the aircraft were parked on the ramp.

The crews were all housed in the visiting officer's quarters, and after dinner at the officer's club most of the pilots went into Montgomery, a onetime capital of the Confederacy, which seemed a cosmopolitan city compared to Eglin's "city," Fort Walton, where cows occasionally wandered across the main street. Rode and I, and a few others, were tired, so we went back to the VOQ, where we were rooming together, and went to bed. Around midnight, Rode and I were awakened by one of the operations officers and asked if we were checked out in the C-47. A silly question—he should have known that fighter pilots can fly anything, but we humored him and said that we were checked out. Since all the C-47 pilots were in town, he wanted us to fly one of the Eglin C-47s to Memphis to pick up some emergency equipment that might be needed at Eglin. The storm was building in intensity and appeared certain to hit Eglin. We dressed and went to the flight line after arranging for the P-82 crew chief, who had flown in with Rode, to fly with us as flight engineer.

We made the flight to Memphis without incident, and the emergency equipment (rations, bottled water, blankets, and tents) was loaded while we supervised the refueling and checked the en route and terminal weather for the return to Eglin. There were some clouds but no serious problems, as the ceiling and visibility at Eglin were still well above the minimums. Except for some heavy turbulence at times, the flight was uneventful, and we landed at Eglin shortly after dawn. While the aircraft was being unloaded, we were told it would be necessary to make another trip. After a quick snack, we took off again for Memphis and flew at higher than normal power settings so that we could complete the round trip before the hurricane struck.

On the ground at Memphis we were photographed and interviewed by the local newspaper because of our mercy flight. I don't know if the story ever appeared in print—probably not, unless it was an especially slow news day.

When we landed at Eglin the winds were quite strong and gusty, but Rode made his usual good landing. This time we were instructed to go to Gunter Field, on the other side of Montgomery from Maxwell, to pick up still more emergency gear. On departing I made one of the strangest takeoffs of my life. The wind velocity was 35 to 45 mph with higher gusts. Under the circumstances, we left the external rudder lock in place while we taxied, to keep the rudder from buffeting. When we lined up on the runway, the crew chief got out and removed the lock, and I lowered full flaps to reduce the wind and propwash on him. After he got back to the cockpit, the tower cleared us and I advanced the throttles to start the takeoff. The airplane was barely moving despite full throttle, and I thought something was wrong with the brakes, until I noticed we were about twenty feet in the air. I had forgotten to retract the flaps, and the combination of full flaps and the strong wind on an empty airplane produced what amounted to a vertical takeoff. Chagrined, I sheepishly raised the flaps and climbed toward Gunter. When we landed there we were told that the winds were too high for further landings at Eglin (no surprise to us), and we took our trusty C-47 across town to Maxwell. There we found that the rest of the Eglin aircraft had been flown to Atlanta, and we were relieved to see that the regular C-47 crew was waiting to take it there. Since both of our aircraft were hangared, it wasn't necessary to move them. It was late afternoon by then, so we had an early dinner and went to bed to catch up on our sleep. We had flown ten of the last fourteen hours. All in all it was a good way to end our AAF careers.

Soon after we returned from the hurricane evacuation, Colonel Slocumb notifed me that I had been assigned as test officer on Project Agate. Its goal was to determine the feasibility and best method of attacking bombers head-on with jet fighters. The high speed of the fighters would make the closing rate very high and the time between reaching effective firing range and breaking away very short. B-29s were to be the targets, as there were no operational jet bombers at that time; the fighters were P-80s. The tests would be flown at 30,000 and 35,000 feet at various airspeeds.

The first problem was to determine how to measure the range at the start of the breakaway and the miss distance between the two aircraft as they passed. The range at which firing began could be determined precisely from a movie camera shooting through the fighter's gunsight reticle (illuminated circle on the gunsight). The size of the reticle and the wingspan of the bomber were known, so the range at any point could be calculated easily. I and the project officer, along with the bomber crew and members of the measurement and analysis section, had long discussions before we settled on the following method.

The attacking P-80 would have a 16mm movie camera in the cockpit shooting through the gunsight and actuated by the machine gun trigger on the control stick. Inside the canopy, behind the armor plate, would be a series of flashbulbs actuated by the bomb release button on top of the control stick. A second P-80, to be flown by Maj. Si Johnson, the squadron operations officer, would have a 16mm movie camera mounted in the cockpit, shooting 90 degrees to the right of the fuselage. The B-29 would also have

At Eglin, Rode was in the weapons branch in the proof division, which provided oversight and guidance for the weapons testing done in the flying squadrons and other organizations in the Air Proving Ground Command. The project officers for the various tests were assigned to the proof division. As part of his duties, Rode flew with all the squadrons as a participant in the many weapons tests. After leaving Eglin he was assigned to the armament division of the Research and Development Directorate in the Pentagon. While in both jobs he flew combat missions in Korea on Project Gun Val, to evaluate the effectiveness of 20mm cannon in the F-86 Sabre as a replacement for the standard .50-caliber machine guns.

On Sunday, January 11, 1954, Rode was returning to Andrews Air Force Base, Maryland, from a trip to Wright-Patterson Air Force Base in Ohio, flying alone in a Lockheed T-33, the trainer version of the F-80 Shooting Star. The weather was terrible at Andrews, extremely cold with low ceiling and visibility and freezing drizzle (freezing drizzle is conducive to icing, which is extremely hazardous). He was making a ground-controlled approach (GCA), an approach under the guidance of a ground controller who monitors the aircraft's heading and glide slope by radar, when he dropped off the scope and hit the ground about 1,000 feet short of the runway. The impact broke the T-33 in two, smashed Rode's face into the stick, and severely damaged his spinal cord. Fortunately there was no fire, probably because of the extreme cold and the snow-covered ground.

He was rushed to Walter Reed Army Hospital in Washington, D.C., where the plastic surgeons did a remarkable job of repairing his face, and the necessary steps were taken to ensure there would be no further injury to his spinal cord.

Rode was held in such high regard that within a few days after it was learned that he would be a paraplegic, he received job offers from several of the major aircraft companies, including Republic and Lockheed, relieving his mind of the worry of how he would be able to support his second wife and four daughters. After considerable therapy, much of it at the Long Beach Veterans Hospital, he went to work for Lockheed in military sales, where he remained for the next twenty years.

In 1969 he learned of a device—a hand control for rudder pedals—that would allow him to fly without the use of his legs. He started using it to fly rented airplanes. Later he bought a Piper Comanche 260 and installed the hand control. He became very active, flying hundreds of hours a year all over the country, often carrying his octogenarian mother to visit her grandchildren and great-grandchildren. He helped found and was active in the Wheelchair Aviators, a group that is now international and includes about 150 pilots.

Rode's skill and determination in once again learning to fly inspired me to write the following poem commemorating his second first solo:

Ode to Rode
On the Occasion of His Second First Solo

The Viet Cong are feeling quite shaky these days.
I'm not sure they even know why.
The answer's as easy as A, B, and C:
Rode is back in the sky.

The Russians aren't up over Suez these days.
They say they just don't want to fly.
But that's not the reason; it's really the fact
That Rode is back in the sky.

Even deep in the Kremlin they're feeling the strain.
They're all in a bit of a stew.
Said Kosygin to Brezhnev, "I just got the word,
Rode is back in the blue."

The peace talks in Paris are active once more.
The Reds want to hurry them through.

They feel they had better while there's still a chance.
Rode is back in the blue.

Way over in China, the bad one of course,
Mao said to his men as he frowned,
"The American Tiger is paper no more.
Rode is off of the ground."

In England the new prime minister said,
"We'd better devalue the pound.
Things look so much better all over the world,
Since Rode is off of the ground."

It's great to have Rode back up there again.
His flying's even better than mine.
While I tried to do a good lazy eight,
Rode did a great lazy nine.

So Rode—stay up there as much as you can.
To all of your friends it's a treat.
Just one more great thing from a man we all love,
To fly with your hands is a feat.

In 1984, at the age of 65, he made a remarkable solo flight around the world in his single-engine Piper Comanche. In slightly over four months, he flew 230 hours, covering more than 35,000 miles and visiting friends in many of the countries. He started and ended the flight at Washington National Airport, where I was proud to be one of those who welcomed him. Possibly to him, that remarkable feat pales next to the untold effort that allowed him, with crutches and leg braces, to walk down the aisle with his daughter at her wedding.

a movie camera shooting through a gunsight in the nose. On each simulated firing pass the second P-80 would fly in line abreast formation about
fifty yards to the left of the attacking P-80. The pilot would activate his
camera well before the attacker reached firing range and would stop it after
the breakaway. I would simulate firing at the desired range by pulling the
gun trigger on the stick that started the gunsight camera. When the trigger
was released, the camera continued running for three seconds. As I released
the trigger and started my break, I pushed the bomb release button that
fired one of the flashbulbs so the camera plane's film would record that
point. At the speeds we were flying, 400 mph for the fighter and 230 mph
for the bomber, the closing speed was about 300 yards per second, so as an
added precaution, we decided to run the first series of passes with my airplane offset to one side of the bomber's course. I decided it would be advisable not to inform the bomber pilots that during the war I had collided
with a Japanese fighter on a nonsimulated head-on pass, knocking off its
wing and part of mine in the process. That collision, incidentally, was the
first of my five victories.

I had to hold a precise airspeed but couldn't look down into the cockpit when close to the bomber, so I read and recorded my airspeed on my
knee board about twenty seconds away from the bomber, and Si recorded
his at the time of the pass. Since we were in formation the airspeeds were
essentially identical. The bomber held his altitude at 30,000 feet for the
first half of each test and 35,000 for the second half. My passes were, of necessity, at the same altitudes.

Offsetting the passes turned out to be a wise precaution, because on
the first series I was breaking away by pulling up, and it was obvious to Si,
and to all of us when we viewed his films, that I would have collided with
the bomber on the first few passes. Although I pulled the nose up in time
to clear the bomber, the P-80 mushed momentarily at the same altitude before climbing. To miss the bomber I had to break off the attack before I was
in effective firing range—not much of a surprise, as most of us in the test
instinctively knew that breaking away downward was the way to go. Even
without the mushing, when I pulled up I could no longer see the bomber.
That might have been an advantage if we were going to collide, but that
was not the object of the tests. The problem would have been even worse at
35,000 feet, where the fighter would have mushed even more in the thinner
air. We decided, then and there, to use downward breaks for the remainder
of the tests.

A series of offset passes using downward breaks at both altitudes indicated not only that it was safe to begin actual head-on passes but also that firing could be accomplished within effective gun range. I found that a violent downward break was not necessary, gravity is always ready to help a pilot descend. Only a slight forward push was needed to go down the ten or fifteen feet required to pass below the bomber. It also allowed me to keep my speed up to get back into position for another pass at the bomber.

We ran three test missions at each of three different airspeeds—300, 350, and 400 mph—at both altitudes. I flew the fighter on two of the missions, then Si and I switched planes for the third mission. As expected, the firing could be done from shorter ranges at the slower airspeed, but it took longer to get ahead of the bomber for a second pass. If only one pass was to be made, it was desirable to make it at about 300 mph; otherwise 350 was better. At 400 mph the fighter had to start firing at about 1,200 yards to allow a one- or two-second burst and two seconds for the break. Twelve hundred yards would be out of range for a side or stern approach, but for head-on passes it was barely acceptable. The slower speeds allowed firing from closer in and left more leeway for the break.

Si and I had no problems with the head-on passes once we had worked out the method, but the bomber pilots said the passes were hard to get used to. They had nothing to do but fly straight and level and wait, and hope, for the fighter to break away. It could not have been a comfortable feeling to have a fighter pass about ten feet below you at a closing speed of more than 600 mph. I much preferred being in the fighter, where I could initiate the break and feel more in control of the situation. One of the bomber pilots told me that it was uncomfortable, to say the least, watching the fighter grow in the windscreen at an alarming rate, then dive away barely in time. He said he drew some comfort, especially on Monday mornings, from knowing that a teetotaler was flying the fighter. (Being a teetotaler was not too common a failing among fighter pilots.) In the final report we stated that head-on passes were feasible with jet fighters at the speeds tested, but that the advent of jet bombers and faster fighters would require the development of much longer-range weapons than .50-caliber machine guns. Today's fighters are armed with guns with higher muzzle velocities and consequently greater effective range, as well as long-range missiles. Also fighters and bombers are now equipped with excellent radar that allows them to determine range exactly. We had to eyeball it.

In October, one of my personal dreams came true when I was selected to attend the USAF Test Pilot School at Wright-Patterson Air Force Base near Dayton, Ohio. I looked forward to this trip with mixed emotions, since I would be moving about 600 miles from Glyn. Orders are orders, however, and on October 21, I headed north with all my worldly goods and chattels, in order of importance: car, record collection, and clothes. I wondered how my newly acquired convertible and its recalcitrant windows would fare in the ice and snow of an Ohio winter.

It may seem odd that I was sent to test pilot school after two and a half years' experience in testing. It would, however, improve my ability to evaluate aircraft by teaching me the techniques of performance testing, especially the effects on performance of different weapons configurations. It would also hone my reporting skills, a vital part of a test pilot's duties. Compounding the backwardness of my flight-testing career, ten years later I received a master's degree in aeronautics from Cal Tech. Today it is done more sensibly. The pilot first gets the degree, then attends test pilot school, and finally serves as a test pilot. Of course, my experience as a combat pilot made up in many respects for my lack of formal education and training. Despite my 180-degrees-off approach, test pilot school was to be a most valuable and interesting six months for me, along with another even more valuable and exhilarating change in my life.

13

An Education in Flight Testing

xcept for a strange encounter with the Kentucky State Highway Patrol, the drive from Eglin to Dayton, Ohio, was uneventful. Through Tennessee there was no speed limit on the highways outside city or town limits. When I passed into Kentucky I didn't see any speed limit signs, so I assumed that the same rule applied. On a four-lane section of highway near Louisville, I was barreling along at 70 mph when two highway patrolmen on motorcycles joined formation with me on the left side. Not thinking I was breaking the law, I nodded to them but did not slow down until they turned on their red lights and motioned for me to pull over.

When I came to a stop the older of the two dismounted and told me to get out of the car. I was surprised, because police usually tell you to stay in the car. He asked me if I knew that I had been going seventy, and I said that I did. "Do you know what the speed limit is?" he asked. When I said that I didn't think there was a speed limit, he said, "Well, there is, and it's thirty miles an hour." He was belligerent and said that he was sending for a police car to take me to a nearby small town where I could be jailed for a few days until I could appear before the judge.

Somewhat taken aback, I said that I had to report to the Air Force Test Pilot School in Dayton the next day. Seeing my uniform hanging in the window, he asked if I was in the service. When I said that I was in the Air Force, he became a little more pleasant and asked to see my license. Upon inspecting it he asked what I was doing with a Florida driver's license. After assuring him that I was indeed from Florida, he walked to the back of the car and looked at the license plate. He said, "Hell, this is a Florida tag. It's green and white, and I mistook it for an Ohio tag." His whole manner changed, and he patted me on the back and said, "You go on, son, but try not to drive so fast."

I suspected then, and confirmed later, that there was some animosity between Ohio and Kentucky, especially along the border between the states. It may have started during the Civil War when Kentucky, though it remained in the Union, had a large population of Southern sympathizers. I noticed that people in Cincinnati spoke disparagingly of the residents of Covington, just across the Ohio River in Kentucky, and vice versa, and therefore resolved that if I ever had an Ohio license plate, I would drive carefully in Kentucky.

Wright-Patterson Air Force Base comprises two airfields, Wright Field and Patterson Field, connected by the major headquarters complex of the Air Materiel Command. Patterson is by far the larger of the fields and is in more open country than Wright, being farther from Dayton. Wright-Patterson, at that time, was the technical center of the Air Force and still is for aircraft and related equipment. Wright is now closed to flying and is the site of the USAF Museum, one of the finest air museums in the world, featuring such spectacular aircraft as the supersonic North American B-70 Valkyrie and the giant ten-engine Convair B-36 Peacemaker. The major laboratories (propulsion, aerodynamics, armament, and equipment) were at Wright Field, and the flight test squadrons and the test pilot school were at Patterson. Chuck Yeager, a graduate of the school when it was at Wright-Patterson, later commanded the new school at Edwards. Despite his lack of formal engineering education, Chuck's flying ability and his innate knowledge of machinery made him one of the best test pilots. He was able to recognize problems and report them accurately, which was especially valuable in the days before telemetry and computers. Today, most test pilots have advanced degrees in engineering.

The flight test school was established by the AAF during World War II in 1944 to provide trained military test pilots for the rapidly expanding AAF. It remained at Patterson until 1951, when it was moved to Edwards Air Force Base in California (formerly Muroc Army Air Field), where the enormous dry lake bed, extremely long runways, and clear air provided ideal conditions for the testing of jets and rocket-powered research planes such as the Bell X-1 and North American X-15. The curriculum and the number of students have been greatly expanded over the years, and the school, now the Air Force Research Pilot School, is recognized worldwide as one of the best. Most of the Air Force pilots who became astronauts were graduates of the Edwards school.

The school at Patterson was located on the west end of the ramp and was housed in a single low building near a hangar. To the east on the ramp were the hangars for the fighter, bomber, and cargo plane test squadrons. The school building had two classrooms, one for the performance phase of the course and the other for the stability and control phase. The class ahead of mine had completed performance and was in the stability and control phase. Two Eglin pilots, Edward "Duke" Ellington and Artie Lynch, were in that class. Duke was as good a pilot as his namesake was a musician, and Artie was one of the best. In addition to the classrooms, there was a film-projection room, a locker room for personal equipment like parachutes and other gear, an instrumentation shop, and offices for the instructors as well as the school's commander, Lieutenant Colonel Moon, with whom I had worked on the .60-caliber gun tests.

Colonel Moon greeted our class and gave us a general briefing on the rules and the curriculum. He said that this class had two distinctions even before we started: it was the first USAF class, and it would be the first class to fly jets at the school. We would fly North American AT-6s, North American P-51s, Beech C-45s, and Lockheed P-80s. The principal instructor for the performance phase was Doc Nelson, a civilian engineer, who in addition to being pleasant was a first-class instructor. There were seven students in the class—three majors, two captains, and two first lieutenants. All were from Wright-Patterson except me.

Although fighter test pilots are, almost by definition, characters, the most interesting character in the class by far was Maj. Chuck Brown, who sat next to me. He had joined the Royal Canadian Air Force at the start of the war and had flown combat tours in Hawker Hurricanes and Typhoons before transferring to the USAAF. He insisted that he had never been taught to fly but had been born a pilot. Following the war he was assigned to the 1st Fighter Group at March Field, California, the first operational group to be equipped with P-80s. He, along with Lt. Col. Pappy Herbst (who had commanded the 74th Fighter Squadron in my group in China) and Maj. Robin Olds (a twelve-victory ace from the Eighth Air Force), formed an aerobatic team that had one of the hairiest finales that I ever heard of. They flew over the runway at 1,000 feet, opposite the direction of landing, in close three-ship vic formation with their wheels down. Just past the landing end, they pulled up to 1,300 feet, rolled over in formation, lowered the flaps, pulled through in a split S (the last half of a loop), and landed.

In early 1946, Chuck Brown was leading a large group of P-80s in a flyby during an open house at March Field. He had been briefed to stay well clear of the bleachers, but instead, he approached the bleachers from the rear and led the airplanes directly over them at minimum altitude. In the ensuing panic the bleachers collapsed. There were several injuries, but fortunately none were too serious. To keep Chuck from being court-martialed, the group commander transferred him to a P-80 group being formed in Germany.

Chuck stayed out of trouble until late in the year, when a friend in his squadron was killed in a crash. The body was badly burned, and the remains were cremated. Chuck was assigned the solemn duty of taking the urn with the ashes back to the pilot's family in the States. En route, he passed through London, where he had many friends, and in the course of uncounted toasts to his departed comrade in various London pubs, he lost the urn. The next day, a frantic search of the pubs (at least of those he could remember) proved fruitless. In desperation he prevailed upon an Army mortician to provide another urn, complete with ashes, which Chuck solemnly delivered to the family.

The transfer to Germany may actually have saved Chuck's life. On July 4, 1946, Pappy Herbst, who had been married the day before, and Robin Olds were performing their P-80 show at March Field as part of a recruiting drive. In their finale, Pappy flew into the ground and was killed, while Robin Olds successfully completed the maneuver and landed.

The remaining students were Major Bray and Lieutenant Day (from the labs at Wright Field), Capt. Ray Popson (a helicopter and airplane test pilot), Lt. Claire Whitney (a West Pointer who had just been assigned to the bomber test squadron and who became a close friend), and Maj. Tom Weldon (an engineer with a master's degree in aeronautics from Cal Tech, who was always ready to help us less-educated students with the mathematics required in the course). At no time, in my wildest dreams, could I have ever imagined that someday I would attain an M.S. in aeronautics, especially from Cal Tech, but in 1957 I was awarded the same degree from the same great institution. As Fats Waller said, "One never knows, do one?"

About half of the curriculum for the flight performance phase of the school consisted of classroom lectures; the other half was dedicated to planning and flying the various tests, then reducing the data and writing the reports. One tenet of flight testing that was drummed into us was that no matter how well we planned and flew the tests, they were of little value if they were not reported accurately and fully. Nothing that was observed during a test was too trivial to report. Several trivial items, put together, might reveal a performance flaw that would otherwise be overlooked.

To make the flight tests of the various aircraft seem as authentic as possible, the student was given a memorandum from a fictitious office at Wright Field requesting that a specific type of aircraft be tested and assigning the student as the test pilot. The North American AT-6 Texan was the first aircraft assigned, since it was an advanced trainer and relatively easy to fly. Also, it had been tested so often that the school had good benchmark data against which to evaluate the students' results.

The student would prepare a test program and submit it to the instructor in the form of a memo, outlining the goals of each phase of the test, the equipment and facilities needed, and the approximate number of flying hours required for each phase. When it was approved, the flight testing got under way.

For several days preceding each flight phase, the instructor would go over all aspects of the information to be obtained and the method of obtaining it, as well as how to reduce and plot the data. The first phase of the test was to calibrate the airspeed indicator (ASI) and the altimeter in the test airplane. The altimeter was a standard USAF instrument, but the ASI was a special test instrument that could be read to the tenth of a mile per hour. For all tests the altimeter was set to the local barometric pressure.

To calibrate the ASI, the aircraft was flown in a series of minimum-altitude (100 feet) runs over a two-mile measured course at 10-mph increments, from 95 mph to 165 mph. The airspeed and altitude had to be held with great precision throughout each run. The glass on the altimeter face was tapped lightly before each reading to ensure that the needle was not sticking, and the elapsed time in seconds for each run, timed with a stopwatch, was entered on the pilot's knee board. Two runs would be made in opposite directions at each airspeed to eliminate the wind effect, and the average time for the two runs would be used to compute the speed over the ground, which at that low altitude was equal to the airspeed. The indicated airspeed was then plotted against the computed airspeed, and the correction required at each speed was determined.

The altimeter was calibrated in a manner similar to the ASI calibration, by flying a series of runs at a fixed indicated altitude of 100 feet above the runway at 10-mph airspeed increments. Each run was observed through a theodolite in the control tower by a fellow student, who measured and recorded the number of degrees above or below the 100-foot line. Again the run data were averaged, and the student, by knowing the distance from the theodolite to the runway and the number of degrees of deviation, could compute his actual altitude. By comparing the actual altitude with the indicated altitude, the student could determine the altimeter correction.

The next task was to determine the power required to overcome the drag of the airplane at various altitudes and airspeeds. To do this a series of speed runs were flown, first at 6,500 feet, the critical altitude for the AT-6F. (Critical altitude is the highest altitude at which the engine can provide full power. In our tests a setting of 30 inches of manifold pressure and 2,000 rpm was presumed to be full power.) The manifold pressure was varied in 2-inch decrements, from 30 inches to 22 inches. On each run the cylinder head, free air, and carburetor air temperatures were recorded as well as the airspeed. At the start of the run the pilot climbed to about 300 feet above the desired altitude, set the power for that run, and descended in a gentle dive to the altitude. The plane was then held straight and level at exactly 6,500 feet until the airspeed stabilized. The readings were then entered on the knee board. The airspeed was read to the tenth of a mile per hour. Entering the run from a dive significantly reduced the time required for the airspeed to stabilize, compared with starting the run at the desired altitude and accelerating to the stable airspeed. This procedure was repeated for the remainder of the power settings.

On the next test mission a series of two speed points were flown at altitudes of 1,500, 3,500, 5,500, 7,500, 10,000, and 13,000 feet. Below 6,500 feet, manifold pressure was set at 30 inches for the first run and 28 inches for the second. Above the critical altitude of 6,500 feet, the throttle was wide open. The manifold pressure was recorded to the tenth of an inch on the first run and then reduced by 2 inches on the second. The same data were recorded as on the power-required runs.

Each flight mission usually lasted a little over an hour, but we would spend ten or more hours after the flight correcting the data for instrument error, temperature, and altitude and converting the readings to Standard Day conditions as set by the National Advisory Committee for Aeronautics (NACA): atmospheric pressure 29.92 inches of mercury, temperature 15 degrees centigrade (59 degrees Fahrenheit). Temperature and atmospheric pressure affect flight performance significantly; therefore, all figures must be converted to a standard so that data obtained under varying conditions may be compared. The resulting figures are then used to plot parameters such as speed versus altitude and horsepower versus altitude.

The next task was to determine the best climbing speeds at various altitudes using what are called sawtooth climbs. The climbs covered 1,000 feet, starting at 8,000 feet and at 16,000 feet. Power was set at 2,000 rpm and full throttle, since both tests were done above the critical altitude and 30 inches of mercury could not be obtained even with full throttle. A series of six climbs were made starting at 130 mph and repeated at 10-mph decrements through 80 mph. A seventh climb was made at 130 mph to allow a correction to be calculated for the decrease in weight due to fuel consumption during the climbs. For the low sawtooth a steady climb at the selected airspeed was established at 6,500 feet and continued to 9,500 feet. The time to climb from 8,000 feet to 9,000 feet was measured with a stopwatch and entered on the knee board. After diving back to 6,500 feet, the pilot made the next climb at 120 mph, and so on.

The high sawtooth was flown the same way, but the time to climb was measured from 16,000 to 17,000 feet. The high climb took about two and a half times as long as the low climb, since 17,000 feet is close to the ceiling of the AT-6 at the power settings used.

The term "sawtooth climb" comes from the tracing on the barograph (carried on all test flights), which records on a rotating drum the altitude on the vertical scale and the time on the horizontal scale. The climb portion of each run appears as an upward-sloping line, and the dive back to the lower altitude makes an almost vertical line downward. The tracing of the series of climbs and dives is serrated like the teeth of a saw. After the flight the barograph tracing is carefully measured to determine the time to climb the 1,000 feet, thus providing a second source of data.

The apparent rate of climb, in feet per minute, was easily calculated from both the stopwatch readings and the barograph data and then plotted against the corresponding airspeed. After applying the weight correction at each airspeed, the student drew a curve through the points. The high point on the curve was the best climbing speed for that altitude. The best climbing speed is constant up to the critical altitude, 6,500 feet for this test, and is a straight line above the critical altitude. The student used the two speeds from the low and high sawtooths to plot altitude versus airspeed, creating a graph of the best climbing speeds for all altitudes up to the ceiling.

The final performance missions for the AT-6 were check climbs to the aircraft ceiling using the climbing speed from the previous plot. Two climbs were made from 2,000 feet to 20,000 feet, recording the stopwatch time every 1,000 feet. Using both stopwatch and barograph data, students plotted the rate of climb versus altitude and time to climb versus altitude.

In the flight testing of new aircraft, tests such as these produced the data needed to prepare the performance charts used in the military pilot's operating instructions and in civilian pilot's handbooks. Without this information, accurate flight planning would be impossible.

The next phase of the testing was more subjective; the pilot had to assess the handling of the AT-6 including stalling speeds, control response, stability, and spin characteristics, as well as cockpit layout. No special mission was scheduled to evaluate the cockpit layout. Instead the pilot based his opinion on observations made during all the tests. The arrangement of the instruments, their readability, the accessibility of the controls and switches, and the range of adjustment for the seat and rudder pedals (to accommodate pilots of various sizes) were among the subjects covered.

At that time about the only thing that was standard about aircraft cockpits was that the pilot faced forward. Over the intervening years a great deal of research has been accomplished in this area, and standardization has been greatly improved. For example, the six primary flight instruments— the altimeter, airspeed indicator, vertical speed indicator, flight indicator (artificial horizon), directional gyro, and turn-and-bank indicator—have a standard layout in all aircraft equipped for instrument flight, from a Cessna 150 to a Boeing 747. More significant than the instrument panel layout have been the ergonomic, or human engineering, studies that determine where controls and instruments should be located, how they should be shaped, and how they should be operated for ease of use and to avoid confusion, especially in emergencies. For instance, the grip on the handle that controls the retractable landing gear is shaped like a wheel, and the flap control is shaped like a section of flap. Those two changes alone have reduced the incidence of accidents caused by retracting the wheels instead of the flaps on the ground after landing.

We flew all of our trim and stability checks with the aircraft loaded so as to move the center of gravity (c.g.) slightly aft of the aft limit. In the cruise configuration the plane was trimmed for 105 mph and checked at three airspeeds: 95 mph, 105 mph, and 125 mph. Aileron, elevator, and rudder response were noted as we performed simple maneuvers. At the off-trim airspeeds the control forces necessary to hold the target airspeed were recorded. The stability was checked by displacing and releasing each flight control separately to see if and how the motions caused by the control movements would be damped out. The AT-6 was quite stable; lateral and longitudinal oscillations (resulting from aileron and elevator deflection) were damped out immediately, and directional oscillations (rudder) were damped out in one cycle.

The tests were repeated in the approach configuration, with gear and flaps down and 50 percent of normal-rated power. From 1.4 times the stalling speed (75.6 mph) down to the stalling speed (54 mph), the airplane vibrated and porpoised badly, making it difficult to hold a precise altitude and airspeed. There was no warning before the stall, which was sudden and sharp with a pronounced right wing drop. In the landing configuration with power at idle, the aircraft handled well and was controllable down to the stall.

Following the handling tests, we performed six stalls, three with power on and three with power off, in the clean configuration (with gear and flaps retracted), with gear down and half flaps, and with gear down and full flaps. Stalling speeds, controllability, type and amount of stall warning, and the effectiveness of the standard recovery procedure were evaluated and recorded.

Next came one of the most interesting parts of the test program, the spin testing. We made six 5-turn spins, three to the left and three to the right, with ailerons neutral, ailerons with the spin, and ailerons against the spin. All spins were entered from a straight-ahead, power-off stall at 10,000 feet in the clean configuration with the propeller set at 1,500 rpm and the mixture at idle cutoff to prevent carburetor flooding. The standard NACA recovery—applying opposite rudder, waiting a half turn, and then applying hard forward stick (down elevator)—was used in all spins. The type of spin (steady or oscillatory), the number of turns required to recover, and the altitude at which level flight was resumed were recorded.

The steepest spins were encountered when the ailerons were held with the direction of the spin, and the most altitude (4,000 feet) was lost in these spins. The recovery from the spin to the right in this configuration required two and a half turns. It was difficult to enter a spin to the left with the ailerons against the spin, requiring about five seconds after the stall, since the AT-6 drops the right wing in all stalls.

I repeated each spin twice to confirm my findings. Also, to satisfy my curiosity, I climbed to 12,000 feet and did a ten-turn spin to the right holding the ailerons with the spin. The spin was steady, and the characteristics remained the same throughout the extra five turns. Level flight was resumed at 6,500 feet.

The AT-6 demonstrated no dangerous spin characteristics, recovery was positive in every instance, and it would be safe to spin any number of turns provided the entry altitude was high enough.

The spin tests were the final flying phase of the AT-6 test program, and only the most difficult part remained—writing the final report. The report included tables of the pertinent performance figures along with the graphs plotted from the in-flight data, a detailed evaluation of the aircraft's flight characteristics and cockpit layout, a separate report on the spin tests, a completed twenty-page Pilot's Observations questionnaire, and conclusions and recommendations for changes. I concluded that the AT-6 was suitable for use as an advanced single-engine trainer. I'm sure that conclusion was reassuring to the hundreds of thousands of pilots who had trained in it.

Following the tests on the AT-6, we ran similar but not identical tests on the North American P-51D Mustang, the Beechcraft C-45F Expediter, and the Lockheed P-80A Shooting Star. I won't cover them all in detail, but I will point out the main differences between them and the AT-6 tests.

The Mustang was equipped with a second instrument panel in the radio compartment, which contained the relevant test instruments and could be photographed with a movie camera operated by the gun trigger on the control stick. The camera was actuated whenever a reading was entered on the knee board.

The airspeed indicator was calibrated by the pacer aircraft method: the test plane was flown in close formation with a previously calibrated Mustang, and ASI readings were made (both pilot's panel and photo panel) simultaneously in both planes at 30-mph increments from 130 mph to 340 mph.

Since the Mustang's Merlin engine is supercharged with a two-stage, two-speed blower, the aircraft has two critical altitudes, one in low blower and one in high blower. Therefore, we flew a low and a high sawtooth climb in each blower stage, one below and one above the respective critical altitude. We also made a series of sawtooth climbs at the same airspeed with different settings of the coolant and oil shutters to determine the effect of their drag on the climb performance. Power-required runs and speed points also were flown in low and high blower and with varying coolant and oil shutter settings. Six low-blower speed points were flown at altitudes from 2,000 to 21,000 feet, and six were flown in high blower at altitudes from 12,000 to 31,000 feet.

Check climbs were made from 2,000 to 34,000 feet at the best climbing speeds. The climb from 2,000 to 18,000 feet was made in low blower, and then a climb from 9,000 to 34,000 feet was made in high blower. The power settings on all the performance flights in the Mustang were 2,500 rpm and either 42 inches of mercury or wide-open throttle.

As in the AT-6 test, we noted the handling and stability characteristics, stalling speeds, and takeoff and landing distances and evaluated the cockpit layout.

In the C-45 we flew in pairs; I was teamed with Lt. Claire Whitney on most of the flights. He was an excellent pilot and a pleasure to work with. We alternated as pilot and copilot, with the copilot being responsible for recording the data. The test C-45 had a photo panel and a special temperature gage that registered the temperature of each of the nine cylinders individually.

Most of the test flights were made to determine the effect of various settings for the cowl flaps and oil cooler shutter on the cylinder-head temperature and oil temperature. We found that the right engine exceeded the maximum allowable temperature in a climb with full open cowl flaps on an Army Hot Day (120 degrees Fahrenheit). In testing the handling characteristics, we determined that the minimum safe single-engine speed was 105 mph. This test was flown at 1,000 feet above the ground; one engine was shut down and the speed reduced until we could no longer maintain level flight. I was glad to finish the C-45 phase of the program, since it was and still is my least favorite of any of the aircraft I've flown. It wasn't difficult to fly, but the small control wheel combined with the small separation between the rudder pedals always made me feel as though I were flying a toy. Quite a few other pilots felt the same way. One weekend at Eglin seven pilots from the fighter squadron were going to fly to Maxwell Field in Alabama to visit a former squadron member. We rushed out to the C-45, and the last one in found that the only empty seat was the pilot's. In other aircraft the first one in would have grabbed the pilot's seat.

The P-80A was the last aircraft to be tested. Its program was abbreviated, because only four of the students had enough hours in the P-80 to participate: Majors Weldon, Bray, and Brown and I. Also, we were all ordered to other assignments before the tests were completed. Accordingly, Doc Nelson, the instructor, decided that we would make one consolidated report using the data the group had accumulated. Since this was the first class at the school to include jets in the curriculum, we were feeling our way.

The speed, rate of climb, and ceiling of the P-80 were much higher than those of the other test aircraft, and flying without external fuel tanks limited our flights to less than one hour on most missions. The high rate of climb, especially at the lower altitudes, required significant changes in the sawtooth-climb procedure. Instead of measuring the time to climb 1,000 feet, we had to use 4,000 feet, with a lead of about 2,000 feet into the climb and a 500-foot follow-through, because a small timing mistake in the short time to climb 1,000 feet would have caused a large error in computing the rate of climb. The same timing mistake on a 4,000-foot climb would produce an error 75 percent smaller. At high altitude, the rate of climb was considerably lower, and no modification was required.

We were able to complete the airspeed, altimeter, and free air temperature calibrations; a series of sawtooth climbs at intervals from 6,000 feet up to 40,000 feet; power-required runs at 5,000-foot intervals up to 40,000 feet; and timed climbs to 40,000 feet. When we had reduced and plotted the data, our figures were close to those determined by the Lockheed test pilots, which was gratifying but not surprising.

Jet aircraft do not have critical altitudes, since jet thrust decreases steadily with the reduction in air pressure at increasing altitude. Concurrent with the decrease in thrust is a decrease in fuel consumption as well as a decrease in aerodynamic drag on the airplane. Consequently, the most efficient cruise altitudes are quite high, usually in excess of 30,000 feet. The first P-80 cockpits were not pressurized, but later models had a 10,000-foot pressure differential.

Although we worked hard at the school, both in the air and on the ground, camaraderie was strong among the students and the instructors, all of whom were Air Force officers except Doc Nelson. We generally ate lunch together, and when the weather precluded flying, we often watched flight testing, combat, or training films together and exchanged exaggerated stories that illustrated our superior flying skills.

We also played Ping-Pong on lunch breaks and during bad weather. The stability class must have noticed that our performance class had only a few pingers and no pongers, because they challenged us to a series of matches. To no one's surprise, they wiped us out by 6 to 1. We could stand that, but then they issued this gloating pamphlet:

SKILL WILL OUT

2 Feb (SP) The barely willing forces (?) of the Flight Performance Course were overwhelmed 6–1 by the magnificent Stability and Control table tennis squad last Friday afternoon on the table of the ASTS pilot's lounge. This

lopsided score clearly shows the superiority of the Stability team in this contest (?), and fully indicates results to be anticipated as the two organizations meet in other athletic jousts. The results of the massacre were:

Singles:

Allan (S) over Whitney (P), 21–2, 21–7

Schleeh (S) over Brown (P), 21–15, 21–5

Munro (S) over Bray (P), 21–15, 14–21, 21–13

Northup (S) over Weldon (P), 21–10, 21–19

Nelson (P) over Ellington (S), 21–9, 21–8

Doubles:

Allan-Schleeh (S) over Nelson-Bray (P), 21–4, 21–10

Munro-Northup (S) over Day-Lopez (P), 21–9, 21–8

That was too much. We immediately challenged them to a basketball game to be played in the base gym on the first bad-weather afternoon, which came only a few days later. After a hard struggle we emerged victorious, primarily because Claire Whitney was several times better than any of the other players on either team. Following our victory we issued this communiqué:

BRAWN WILL OUT

5 February (SP) The Stability Weenies are listing their excuses today after the severe trouncing they received on the basketball court at the hands of the Performance Prestidigitators. The Weenies, flushed with victory in such nursery contests as Ping Pong and Hide the Feather, showed their true mettle when engaged in the manly art of basketball.

In the last quarter of the game, the Weenies (sometimes called the Stable Horrorlizers), cognizant of their impending defeat, made a last stab for victory by roughing up the valiant players of the opposition. With three minutes of play remaining, Whitney of the opposition had to be carried from the court bleeding profusely from this unwarranted foul play. The Prestidigitators, undaunted by this turn of events, continued on to the last whistle.

FINAL SCORE

Performance 24

Stability 23

I played an important role in this victory by sinking the foul shot that gave us the victory. It was the only point I scored, even though I played the entire game.

To break the tie, being pilots, we decided that the next competition would be dogfighting. We couldn't use the flight-test Mustangs because of the test instrumentation, but the base flight squadron at Wright Field had a few Mustangs that were available for proficiency flying. We decided to use them.

The standard dogfight initiation procedure was adopted: the two planes would approach almost head-on; as they passed on each other's left, the fight was on. Each plane tried to get on the other's tail, usually by turning to the left as steeply and with as many g's as possible. The fights would start at 20,000 feet, and 5,000 would be considered the ground.

The first two fights scheduled were Lynch of Stability versus Brown of Performance and Ellington of Stability versus me. They were also the last two fights. We were so evenly matched that no one could get on the other's tail long enough to claim victory, although we all did, and fortunately we had no gun camera film for proof. More important, the base operations officer happened to be flying at the time and saw us racking his airplanes all over the sky. After that he would no longer let us fly them.

I was the only one in the performance class who was not stationed permanently at Wright-Patterson, and since I was not married I lived in the bachelor officer's quarters. Most of my married classmates, as well as the Ellingtons and Lynches from Eglin, were kind enough to have me to dinner now and then so I could enjoy some home cooking. I visited the Whitneys quite often, as Claire and I had become good friends as well as flying partners. Frequent phone calls between Dayton and Eglin encouraged me to believe that my bachelorhood was soon to end, and I looked forward to home cooking in my own home.

Glyn and I wrote almost daily, which helped to eliminate a few of those calls. I was more than happy when Brad Brown called from Eglin and told me that if I could catch a ride back to Eglin for the Thanksgiving break, he would fly me back to Wright-Pat in a Douglas A-26 on Sunday afternoon, in time for my classes. Luckily, someone who had relatives in the Eglin area was planning to fly down in a B-25 on Wednesday evening and had room for me. Being apart had convinced me that I didn't want to be away from Glyn, and rather than wait any longer, I decided to ask her to marry me during my visit to Florida. After some searching in Dayton, I bought a nice diamond engagement ring, with the hope that she would accept it and me as a package deal.

When I arrived back at Eglin the day before Thanksgiving and moved into Auger Inn, Rode told me I could use Wes Posvar's car, since he had flown home for Thanksgiving. I called Glyn right away, and we made plans to drive to Panama City and have Thanksgiving dinner with her family. We drove back to Eglin early the next evening. The beautiful Gulf beaches seemed the ideal setting to propose, so I stopped on an overlook and asked her to marry me. When she said yes, I immediately did an Immelmann off the deck with a few vertical rolls thrown in. Although I had performed those maneuvers many times in the past, this was the first time I did them sans airplane. I proudly announced my engagement to my Auger Inn-mates, and Glyn told her friends in the dormitory. The next night the Inn-mates arranged an impromptu engagement party at a restaurant in Pen-sacola, where we enjoyed a memorable evening.

At that time I was not sure whether I would stay in Dayton for the sta-bility and control course after completing the flight performance course, because that training was not required for the type of testing done at Eglin. However, Lynch and Ellington had stayed for the second course, and I hoped that I could as well. At the least, I would remain there through mid-March, and if I took the second course, until mid-September. Because of the uncertainty, we decided to get married in January at Wright-Patterson, even though it was a long way from her family, rather than delay the wed-ding for an indefinite period.

When I arrived back in Dayton, I met with Chaplain Probst, the Protestant chaplain, and he agreed to marry us on Saturday, January 17, in the Patterson Air Force Base chapel. I also reserved a room at the officer's club for the reception. Glyn, through her good friend Ann Webb (the other blonde, whose husband, Spider, was stationed at Wright Field), arranged for the cake, flowers, and other incidentals. Much more impor-tant to us though, was Ann and Spider's decision to move to a larger apart-ment in the same building, since they now had a baby; and we would be able to rent their former apartment. Housing was in short supply in the area, and that eliminated a major concern. It would also be nice for Glyn to have her good friend in the same building.

With school closed for almost two weeks for the Christmas holidays, I drove back to Eglin to spend Christmas with Glyn and her family. After Christmas we drove to Tampa and visited my mother and brothers for a few more days of in-law indoctrination. While there, Glyn took advantage of the larger stores in Tampa and selected a wedding dress. Several of my friends were home, and while Glyn was shopping, I rashly joined them in a long game of tackle football on our old neighborhood field, the Toilet

Bowl. Although I was in good condition, the next day I felt a close kinship with the White Sox shortstop Luke Appling, who was known as Old Aches and Pains.

The days passed too quickly, and I was soon driving back to the school without Glyn. The two weeks until she was to arrive seemed like two years. She arrived by train in Cincinnati on the Tuesday night before the wedding. I drove her back to Dayton, where the Weldons had kindly invited her to stay in the interim. The next few days passed in a blur as we took our blood tests, got the license, and Glyn checked all the arrangements.

The night before the wedding, Spider, Duke Ellington, and Artie Lynch set up a bachelor dinner in one of the hotels for my friends at the school as well as the contingent that was flying up from Eglin. Unfortunately the weather between Florida and Ohio was terrible, with heavy icing, forcing Rode and the rest of the pilots to delay the takeoff and finally to detour by way of Washington. I still remember vividly the sight of the long table, set with shrimp cocktails, with less than half the seats occupied. Rode, Wes Posvar, and the others arrived early the next morning, and we drove them to the hotel for a bachelor breakfast. During the breakfast someone came up behind me and said, "I hate all pilots, but especially fighter pilots." It was Colonel Shanahan, who had lost a leg in Alaska and was now a civilian weapons consultant to the Air Force. He knew Wes and me from Alaska and Rode from his armament work, and we invited him to join us. He was on his way to a conference and could not accept, but he congratulated me on my forthcoming marriage.

The wedding that afternoon in the beautiful Patterson Chapel was everything a wedding should be. One of my best friends, Dick Jones, with whom I had roomed in China, was my best man. Rode and Duke were the ushers. Ann Webb was matron of honor. Spider gave the bride away, since Glyn's father could not attend, although her mother and sister, Helon, were there.

Colonel Moon had given me Monday off for a brief honeymoon in that little-known honeymoon paradise, Columbus, Ohio. Because the temperature was only a few degrees above freezing, my convertible was not the ideal conveyance. My hands were almost frostbitten when I had to remove the graffiti on my windows with acetone. I had tried to outwit my friends by leaving my car at a garage in nearby Fairfield and arranging for Dick Jones to drive us there after the wedding, but there was a leak, and with the full cooperation of the garage manager, the windows were covered with graffiti applied with soap.

Wes Posvar, whose genius extends to all fields, had filled my hubcaps with bottle caps, which made a lot of noise at low speeds but were silent at higher speeds. It took me quite a while to locate the source of the rattle. The trip to Columbus was less than romantic as we huddled in the noisy, frigid convertible; the car had seemed so perfect in Florida. I missed my Alaskan flying clothes. The Neil House, however, was warm and comfortable, and we quickly forgot the miserable trip.

After the honeymoon we settled into our small furnished apartment above McCloskey's dairy barn. We switched from honeymooning to honeymooing. Less than two weeks later, Wes visited Wright Field to attend a conference and became our first dinner guest. Glyn served a delicious dinner that night and has continued to do so for more than forty-six years.

Finally, in early March, I completed the flight performance course. Flight test headquarters at Wright-Patterson requested that I be allowed to remain for the stability and control course and then be assigned to its fighter test squadron, but Air Proving Ground Command turned down the request and directed me to return to Eglin. We packed our belongings and headed back to Florida.

14

The Joy of Flying Low

When we arrived back at Eglin, as an old married couple of almost two months, we did not have to search for a place to live, because Mary Etta Koehler had arranged for us to sublet a house in one of the areas of officer's housing. Her next-door neighbor was on temporary duty for three months, and his wife and children had returned to their hometown to visit relatives. Len and Mary Etta Koehler and Don and Fran Dessert were our neighbors on either side. Len and Don were both in the fighter squadron and were good friends of mine. Glyn knew and liked both the wives; they became close friends and remain so to this day. The Koehlers had a lovely year-old daughter, Kathy, for whom we happily became assistant parents. The Desserts had two boys, Don Junior and Terry, both of whom later attended the Air Force Academy and pursued flying careers in the Air Force.

The first weekend after arriving we drove to Panama City, only sixty miles away, for a visit with Glyn's family and friends. I was curious whether in-laws would be different from prospective in-laws. It was a trip we were to make many times, and we always enjoyed it because of the beauty of the pure white sand dunes, the beach, and the blue-green water of the Gulf. Sadly, that pristine stretch of beach is now almost wall-to-wall high-rise condos and restaurants.

Upon returning from Panama City, I reported to the squadron and renewed acquaintances with the pilots and the ground crews. Although I was eager to get back to work, there were no new projects available, so I helped out on the tests that were in progress. Most were weapons tests with the P-80 (the P designation for fighters was not changed to F until June 1948), which was by then the first-line USAF fighter. I spent the next few weeks happily shooting, bombing, napalming, and rocketing assorted targets, and soon I felt I had regained my weaponry skills.

Shortly thereafter, Colonel Slocumb informed me that I had been assigned to test high-speed, minimum-altitude navigation techniques in the P-80. The goal was to determine if a pilot could maintain an accurate heading and identify checkpoints while flying almost 500 mph at an altitude just high enough to clear obstacles on the ground. If successful, this technique could be used to evade enemy radar by staying under its beams. The testing would be both challenging and exciting, because most flying at such low altitudes was prohibited. I was scheduled to meet with the project officer, a navigator in the aircraft branch of the proof division, the next morning to plan the flights that would be required, but I requested and received permission from Colonel Slocumb to make a couple of practice flights to prepare for the meeting. I quickly discovered that I could make only the briefest glances at the map and the compass, since my full attention had to be devoted to not running into the ground or other hard objects. This was especially important now that I was a married man.

At the meeting I told the project officer, Capt. Hunter Harrell, that holding the heading would not be a problem but identifying checkpoints would be very difficult. Navigational checkpoints look considerably different at ground level than from several thousand feet, and the time to identify them is minimal at best. After some discussion we decided that Harrell would prepare narrow strip maps for each simulated target with the course line from Eglin to the target in the center of the strip. The compass heading and the estimated time of crossing roads, rivers, railroads, and other prominent features were marked next to the feature in large numbers. None of the targets was more than thirty minutes from Eglin. Because of the relatively short duration of missions and the high speed at which they would be flown (475 mph), crosswinds would not present a problem. The first missions would be flown using a single heading, but depending on our results, we hoped to try some doglegs (en route course changes) on later missions. On each mission I was to fly to a given point just short of the selected target and then pop up to about one thousand feet and make a simulated attack. All the flights were plotted to avoid flying over towns, which was not much of a problem in that part of Florida.

I arrived at most of the targets right on the nose, but even when I was slightly off, I was close enough to carry out the attack after the pop-up climb. The project officer was pleased with the success of the missions right from the start. He was pleased, but I was elated. It was pure joy to fly so low at such high speed. I would fly ten to fifteen feet above the ground or trees, climbing just enough to clear obstacles, which were often trucks driving along highways. I don't think I scared any of the drivers too badly—by the time they realized I was there, I wasn't. Still, it must have startled some of them to see a jet cross the highway just ahead of them, only slightly above eye level. At least, I hope it did.

One reason I enjoyed the low flying even more than my usual flying was the feeling of freedom it gave me. During the past five months of precision flying at test pilot school, I had spent more time looking into than out of the cockpit. To hold altitude and airspeed with the precision required at the school meant keeping my eyes glued to the instruments most of the time. At minimum altitude, anything more than a quick glance at anything other than the approaching terrain would have been fatal—spectacular, but fatal nonetheless. The heads-up displays in modern fighters, which project pertinent flight data on the windscreen, would have been most welcome. The much higher airspeeds that today's fighters can maintain have made such devices vital. I also got a thrill from the much greater sensation of speed I felt when flying on the deck. The same airspeed at 30,000 feet would produce almost no sensation of speed, because the distance from visual reference points was so much greater. The only way to appreciate high speed at that altitude was to notice how quickly I would arrive at my destination.

The success of the first missions led us into the next phase, the inclusion of doglegs. This type of approach was designed to mislead the enemy as to the intended target. I learned that some precision was lost if the change in heading was much more than 30 degrees, since the plane covered a fair amount of distance in the turn itself. Also, it reduced the range, or fuel reserve, if I went too far in the wrong direction on the way to the target. A lesser, but irritating problem was the size of the map—a dogleg made the strip map too wide to handle easily. When we chose an easily identified feature as the turning point, the dogleg missions went quite well.

Next we tried missions with formations of three and four planes. Some preliminary flights confirmed what we instinctively knew, that tight formations were not the way to go. There was no advantage in flying a tight formation that close to the ground. Besides being pretty hairy for the wingmen, the flight would have to climb to more than 100 feet before turning to ensure ground clearance for the plane on the inside of the turn. We found that a loose echelon formation inclined to the side opposite the intended dogleg turn was the safest and easiest to fly. The leader navigated, and the wingmen were responsible for avoiding obstacles in their flight paths.

One of the last missions in this project didn't turn out exactly as planned. Barney Turner was visiting from the University of Florida for a few days to get in some flying, so he and Rode went along as wingmen. The weather wasn't too good at Eglin but was better to the north. After the briefing, we took off and headed out on the course indicated on my strip map. We hit the early checkpoints right on time but were a little off on the last two. Even so, when I pulled up I expected to see the target, a dam on the Chattahoochee River, in front of us, but there was no damn dam in sight anywhere. In fact, to quote one of my former commanding officers, "Didn't nothing on the ground look like nothing on the map." I immediately tuned my radio compass to the range station for Columbus, Georgia, which I thought would be the closest military airfield with good weather. The signal was strong, and we reached the base in less than fifteen minutes. The tower notified Eglin that we had landed, and after refueling we flew back at normal altitudes. The project officer met us on the ramp and sheepishly informed us why we had missed the target area so badly. He had put the wrong heading on the strip map, and none of us had noticed it, as we would have on a full map. That is what testing is all about, to discover potential problems and eliminate them. The need to check the headings carefully by comparing them with a full map before the mission was added to the final report.

At that time pilots were permitted to take their wives up in an Air Force plane for a thirty-minute flight once a year. Since all the fighters in my squadron were single seaters, I arranged to take Glyn up in an A-26 from the medium and light bomber squadron, whose ramp adjoined the fighter ramp. She donned one of my flying suits and a Mae West and then climbed up onto the wing, where I helped her into a parachute and carefully explained how to operate it. Despite the baggy flying suit and the bulky equipment, she still managed to look great. She climbed down into the copilot seat (this was a dual-control model), and after strapping her in, I began briefing her on emergency procedures. I explained that if we had to bail out, I would jettison the canopy, and she should release her seat belt, turn around, and dive headfirst onto the wing, slide off the trailing edge, count to three, and pull the ripcord. She said, "Forget it! There is no way I am going to dive off that wing. If anything goes wrong, I'll just stay in the airplane. I'm not about to make my first flight and first parachute jump on the same day." Luckily, nothing went wrong, and we had a most enjoyable flight, sharing the thrill of seeing familiar landmarks from a different perspective. But I resolved never to take her up in a military airplane again. Lacking the formal training, she would probably not get out if something went wrong. Evidently the Air Force came to the same conclusion and dropped the practice the next year.

One of the pilots on the base really milked the program dry. He was the only pilot in the photo test detachment, although I sometimes helped him out. He was running a whole series of tests on a new camera mounted in a B-25, and most of the flights were flown along the Gulf shoreline at less that 100 feet altitude. He took his wife along on one flight, and she enjoyed riding in the nose so much, basking in the sun and watching the remarkable blues and greens of the water, that he took her along on almost all his flights. He filled out a permission form for each flight but never turned it in. I think she must have logged about twenty hours by the time he finished the tests.

While Barney was at the University of Florida in Gainesville, one or more of his friends from Eglin would fly down to visit and let him get some flying time. Because Barney was a close friend and since both of my brothers were at the university at that time, I was invariably one of the pilots. We flew P-51s, B-25s, or A-26s, usually leaving Eglin in the late afternoon, arriving at Gainesville in about an hour, and returning late that night. Air Force pilots are required to log a certain number of hours of night flying time each year, and we met a good portion of our required hours on those flights.

The airport at Gainesville, Alison Field, is named after Maj. Gen. John Alison, a graduate of the University of Florida, a World War II fighter ace, and a distinguished leader. He had commanded the squadron I served with in China, the 75th Fighter Squadron, before I arrived in China and was practically a legend for his exploits while in China. I didn't know him at the time, but since then I have been fortunate enough to get to know him quite well, and he still retains his legendary status with me.

Most of the university visits were routine, but one flight turned out to be eventful. Rode and I were flying A-26s in loose formation with Rode leading on the trip down. Both airplanes were single-pilot models without copilot seat or dual controls. The flight engineer flew in the jump seat to the right and aft of the pilot. We had taken off a bit later than usual, and it was almost dark as we approached Gainesville. My engineer had asked if he could ride in the glass nose compartment to have a better view of the ground, and I had agreed. Without warning, about ten minutes from Alison Field, there was a loud explosion from the left engine, and it began streaming flames and heavy smoke. I shut down the engine and feathered the prop instantly. To my great relief the flame disappeared, and the smoke began to dissipate. The engineer must have set a world's record for the kneeling broad jump; he was strapped back in the jump seat before I had completed feathering the propeller. Rode called immediately, asking what had happened and if everything was under control. I told him that the left engine must have thrown a rod, the fire seemed to be extinguished, and there were no other apparent problems. It was the first time I had ever lost an engine in a twin-engine aircraft, but the A-26 is easy to handle on one engine. I landed without difficulty and was able to turn off onto the taxiway, letting the airplane roll as far from the runway as possible before shutting it down. I wasn't able to taxi to the ramp because the A-26 does not have nosewheel steering, and it cannot be taxied in a straight line on one engine without burning out the brakes.

After making arrangements to leave the flight engineer with the airplane, Barney, Rode, and I went to dinner and then flew back to Eglin in Rode's airplane. All the seats were occupied, so I was floored. The next day a C-47 was flown to Gainesville with a new engine and a crew to help install it. Except for the engine, which had indeed thrown a rod, there was no damage to the airplane. I'm sure that if this engine problem had occurred before my flight with Glyn I never would have taken her up.

The Eglin-based crew from MIT's instrumentation laboratory completed some modifications to the Davis-Draper (later A-1) radar-ranging gunsight in the P-38 in early April, allowing me to take up where I had left off in its testing. Some of my flight test school training proved valuable in the sight calibration runs that had to be completed before the firing and bombing phases could begin. I had to make numerous runs at precise airspeeds and altitudes, holding the sight on a fixed point and filming through the sight for as long as sixty seconds per run. The film was developed and analyzed back at MIT, and we were given the go-ahead for the firing and bombing phases.

The air-to-air firing phase was brief, since we only had to confirm what had been previously accomplished. The modifications to the sight were primarily in the bombing mode. The sight's special features, radar ranging and automatic lead computation, were not used for air-to-ground gunnery, eliminating the need for firing at ground targets. I spent a good deal of time for the next several months diving toward the ground from various altitudes and at various angles. Again, precise airspeed and altitude at the entry to the dive were of prime importance in guaranteeing that any inaccuracy could be attributed to the sight and not to poor technique. The sight, however, proved to be remarkably effective. Using it, I was able to achieve many direct hits and an overall low CEP (circular error probable). In a dramatic firepower demonstration, the sight allowed me to score a direct hit on a pyramid target after releasing the bomb and completing my pullout above a thin overcast. Although the observers in the bleachers could hear the P-38 in the dive, they couldn't see it through the cloud layer, but I, obviously, could see the target well enough to hold the pipper on it.

One rainy afternoon I was shooting the breeze with Ted Shea, MIT's on-site technical advisor on the gunsight test, one of the original Auger Innmates, and a good friend. He told me about a habit of mine, of which I was unaware, that used to irritate him no end. Prior to my starting the P-38 engines for each test flight, he would kneel on the wing next to the cockpit and go over the objectives of the mission, briefing me on anything special he wanted me to record. During his briefing I would seemingly ignore him, turning away to hook up the seat belt, shoulder harness, and radio leads; setting the altimeter; turning on various switches; and whistling the entire time. It infuriated him so much, he said, that he considered reporting it to Colonel Slocumb, but he soon realized that I was accomplishing everything he asked for on every mission. After that, he confessed, he rather enjoyed the routine. My wife also complains that I still don't seem to be paying attention when she is talking, but at least with her I don't whistle.

The YP-84 had arrived at Eglin for operational suitability testing before I left for test pilot school, but I had not been checked out in it, as only pilots assigned to the test of a new airplane could fly it. Upon completion of the testing the rest of the squadron pilots were checked out. While I was away, the production model, the P-84B, had been delivered. The Republic P-84 Thunderjet (in June it became the F-84) was the second USAF operational jet fighter. It was larger and heavier than the P-80 and was powered by the Allison J-35 engine, which produced 4,000 pounds of thrust. This was an axial flow engine; it compressed the intake air in a series of stages rather than in the single stage used in a centrifugal-compressor engine like the P-80's J-33. The axial-flow engine is more efficient than the centrifugal because the air flows in a straight line through the engine (axially) instead of having to turn through 90 degrees as in the centrifugal. It also has considerably less frontal area, an advantage in aircraft design. The axial-flow engine is used in virtually all jet aircraft today.

The Thunderjet had a high landing gear to prevent the long aft fuse-lage from hitting the runway on landing, requiring a long ladder for cock-pit entry. It was a bit faster than the P-80, but the 80 had a higher ceiling.

The 20th Fighter Group, based at Shaw Field near Sumter, South Carolina, was to be the first group to be equipped with the latest model, the F-84C. Four pilots from the 20th (led by Capt. Jim Kunkle, the engineering officer for the 77th Squadron) flew to Eglin to familiarize themselves with the F-84 and its air-to-ground weapons delivery capability, since the 20th was a tactical group.

During the familiarizaton they encountered some difficulties with the retractable bomb racks and also with the landing-gear retraction system. The bomb racks did not extend far enough from the lower wing surface to avoid creating a wind-tunnel effect. The resultant low pressure between the bomb and the wing caused the bomb to hit the wing when released instead of dropping clear. The problem was corrected by lengthening the rack, thus moving the bomb farther from the wing. The landing-gear problem was due to the improper installation of a small part.

More serious was a sudden pitchup that occurred during a high-speed dive-bombing run. At about 600 mph in a steep dive, the nose of a P-84 suddenly and violently pitched up, imposing a high g-load on the aircraft. There was no apparent reason for the pitchup, and the Republic officials said that it had never been encountered by either company or Air Force pilots, including those at Eglin. Further tests were scheduled to find if it was a design problem or was something peculiar to that individual aircraft. That particular aircraft could not be flown again before the effects of the excessive g's on the structure had been determined.

On May 10 I was checked out in the P-84B, the test of that model having been completed. It was easy to fly, with good control feel and no bad characteristics that I could determine on that short first flight. The cockpit was much roomier than that of the P-80, and the gunsight was not right in the pilot's face. One feature I particularly liked was the variable aileron boost. It could be varied from high ratio (more sensitive) for aerobatics or low altitude to low ratio for high-altitude and cross-country flight. This relieved a lot of the strain on the pilot on long flights.

I had a personal interest in the pitchup problem. I knew I would be doing a great deal of dive-bombing in the 84, since the A-1 gunsight was to be installed in it, and I would be the test officer. The next day, however, I would be back in the P-80 for the firepower demonstration.

15

Firepower Demonstration, May 11, 1948

O ne of the missions of the Air Proving Ground Command was to demonstrate the firepower of the Air Force some three times a year for groups of about one thousand, comprising members of citizen groups, high-ranking officers of all services, and students of the various officer service schools such as the Air War College and the Armed Forces Staff College.

This particular firepower demonstration began for the participants at 6:30 a.m., as the pilots of the 3200th Proof Test Group filed into the head-quarters briefing room. In their crisp, starched, open-collared khaki uniforms they looked more alert than they felt. The firepower demonstration was scheduled to begin at ten, and some of the bombers would have to be off the ground no later than nine.

The 611th Air Force Base Unit (Proof Test Group) was made up of four squadrons: my squadron, fighter test; medium and light bomber test, flying B-25s, B-26s, and B-45s; heavy bomber test, B-17s; and very heavy bomber test, B-29s and B-36s. The group was not large, and most of the officers were friends. In fact many of us had been checked out in planes from the other squadrons.

Although we had practiced for several days to perfect our timing, this briefing was as detailed as the first. The firepower demonstrations were the Air Proving Ground's chance to demonstrate not only the latest Air Force weaponry but also the skill of its pilots and bombardiers, and not just by hitting their targets but by hitting them exactly on schedule. The thirty or so individual attacks would be completed in less than forty-five minutes total time. The spacing varied, depending on the weapon being demonstrated. Some of the fighter passes were only thirty seconds apart; precise timing was vital.

Col. Bull Curry, the group commander, entered, and we all sprang to attention. After we were seated he said a few words, stressing that the only thing more important than timing and accuracy was safety. Some fighter pilots need to be reminded of that regularly. He would rather have us be late than be the late. After telling us just to make it as good as the last practice, he turned the briefing over to the operations officer, Lt. Col. Joe Davis, Jr., who would be in the tower at the range, controlling the show.

Colonel Davis proceeded through the briefing, mission by mission, covering start-engine times, taxi, takeoff, initial point, targets, abort procedures, and radio discipline. He, like Colonel Curry, stressed safety above all. The demonstration was to lead off with a flight of six B-29s dropping ten 500-pound bombs each, followed by the heavy and then the medium bombers. Finally the fighters would strafe, dive-bomb, skip-bomb, rocket, and napalm a myriad of targets. The targets included small buildings, trucks, airplanes, and pyramids for dive bombing. No explosion was faked; all of the ordnance was live.

For this demonstration I took part in two events. I was leading a flight of three P-80 Shooting Stars that were to drop napalm on a wooden shack target, and then my flight would join up with Maj. Si Johnson, flying a P-84B, in a simulated attack on a flight of B-29s as they passed in front of the stands at an altitude of about 500 feet. That was to be the last event of the demonstration. At the conclusion of the briefing, we left the room in high spirits, eager to get the show on the road, and went back to our respective squadron operations rooms.

Once back, I changed into my flying suit and reviewed the operations schedule to see which P-80 I was to fly. I copied the order and times of events from the master schedule onto my knee board, underlining the event immediately preceding mine in black and mine in red. I checked with Si to be sure that I was clear on the altitude and location where I was to join up with him for our pass on the bombers.

Since our three P-80s were each carrying napalm in the two 165-gallon tip tanks, we would be flying on internal fuel only, which at low altitude gave us only about forty-five minutes' endurance. Therefore, we would not take off until fifteen minutes after the start of the demonstration, which, coincidentally, was fifteen minutes before our event.

About forty-five minutes before our scheduled takeoff time, Capt. Leonard Koehler and Lt. Fred Beluc, the pilots of the other two P 80s in the flight, and I went to the personal equipment shop to pick up our parachutes and Mae Wests, then hopped into a jeep and were driven across the field to the ordnance ramp, where our airplanes were parked. For safety, this ramp was some two miles from any building area, and aircraft carrying live ordnance of any type were armed and disarmed there.

Len, Fred, and I went over the details for the mission, including hand signals to be used in the event of radio failure and other emergency procedures. We then went to the planes, donned Mae Wests and parachutes (we wore backpack parachutes with separate seat cushions to fit into the bucket seats), and climbed up the ladders to the cockpits. In those days, at least at Eglin, we did not do a walk-around inspection of the planes before getting into the cockpit. The maintenance was so good and our ground crews so experienced that they would have taken it as a sign of mistrust and an insult had we done a preflight walk-around. Later, the USAF wisely made the pilot's preflight mandatory as part of the checklist.

Once in the cockpit, with the help of the crew chiefs we buckled our shoulder harnesses and seat belts, plugged in the radio leads and oxygen mask hose, and adjusted the seat height and rudder pedals to our liking. The P-80 had a small cockpit, and the gunsight was right in the pilot's face. A joke among the pilots was that you could always recognize someone who had crashed a P-80: "No hand hold" was imprinted in reverse on his forehead.

To make matters worse, most of our planes had 16mm cameras mounted on the sights, which further reduced forward visibility and obstructed the pilot's view of the instrument panel. When the seat was in the high position, as I liked it, my helmet rattled against the canopy in rough air.

At ten minutes after ten I circled my hand over my head as the signal to start engines. With the engine running in idle, the crew chief unplugged and towed away the starting unit. Len and Fred checked in on the radio, and I asked the tower for permission to taxi. We were cleared to runway one-nine, and I jerked my thumbs outward to signal the crew chief to remove the chocks from in front of the wheels.

We taxied into position on the runway in a three-ship right-echelon formation, lowered the flaps to 80 percent, and closed the canopies. I ran my engine up to 98 percent to give the two wingmen some rpm to play with on the formation takeoff, and nodded my head as a signal to release the brakes and start the takeoff roll. After we lifted off I retracted the gear and slowly milked up the flaps. When the airspeed reached 250 mph I started a gentle turn to the left, told the flight to switch to the mission control channel, and then reported in, "Mission control, Lopez airborne with three." Mission control acknowledged the call, and I continued my climb to the north toward Range 52. I leveled out at 5,000 feet and throttled back to about 80 percent to conserve fuel. By listening to control I learned that we had ten minutes to go before our run on the target. Once we were in the air, there was no casual chatter on the radio, as each pilot listened attentively to range control.

I made a few wide circles to the left, timing them so I would be over the initial point to start the run at T minus sixty seconds. At this point I turned due east to line up with the target, reporting to mission control that I was starting the run, and dipped my left wing as a signal for Len to slip over to the left side into vic formation and for the flight to arm the napalm tanks and the jettison switches. We approached the target, a wooden shack, in a 20-degree dive with my gunsight pipper on a point about 25 yards short of the target. On my signal, we released the tanks at about 100 feet altitude by pressing the button on top of the stick and immediately pulled up into a climbing turn to the left. Looking back I could see the flames obliterating the target and sliding far beyond it, a good hit.

Going back into echelon we climbed to the rendezvous point with Si. I saw his P-84 circling ahead and slowly brought up my flight to join him. Len slipped below me into formation with Si, and Fred and I joined them as the second element. Si waved and pointed to himself as a signal that he had control of the flight.

We circled for about ten minutes, listening to the subsequent missions report in; then the B-29s that were to be our target reported that they were two minutes out on their run. They were to cross the range at about 400 feet from west to east. We were about 4,000 feet above them and slightly to the south. We started our dive, timed to make the simulated firing pass at the bombers from right to left, just in front of the stands. Si timed it perfectly, and we curved toward the bombers at about 450 mph, then broke away in a steep climbing turn. That was the scheduled finish of the demonstration, and we loosened up the formation and headed back to Eglin to land, satisfied that we had completed another successful show.

Mission control came on the air and said, "Si, one of the visiting generals would like to see that again. Do you have enough fuel?"

Si replied, "Roger, if the twenty-nines can get back into position in time." The bomber leader said they could be on another run in about five minutes, so we climbed into position to start another pass, little knowing that the general had just unwittingly signed Si's death warrant.

We climbed to 5,000 feet, waiting for the B-29s to arrive over the range at 500 feet. A voice crackled in my earphones: "Si, this is range control. The B-twenty-nines are two minutes out, altitude five hundred feet, heading zero-niner-zero. You are cleared for your attack."

"Roger. We'll hit them just in front of the stands," Si answered. He started a slow descending turn to get into position. When the bombers crossed the boundary of the range, we nosed down into a steep dive to the north and then swung to the right into a curve of pursuit on the bombers. As we completed the pass, we began a steep climbing turn to the right. I thought that it must have looked great from the stands, because Si had timed it right on the money. It's always a good feeling when a mission goes like clockwork.

The good feeling was short-lived, however. My eyes were glued to Len's P-80 when, suddenly, from the corner of my eye, I saw Si's P-84 disintegrate. The pieces hurtled into the ground, sending up a tremendous cloud of dust and debris. It happened so fast that I couldn't believe my eyes. My first thought was that he must have collided with another airplane, but we were past the B-29s, and our three P-80s were intact. I yelled into the oxygen-mask mike, "What happened, Len?"

"Beats the hell out of me," he replied. "The plane just broke into pieces. Si didn't have a chance." Just then range control broke in and tersely ordered all planes to return to Eglin and land. I took the lead, and we proceeded back to the field in stunned silence.

We were still in a state of shock when we joined the rest of the pilots, who had already landed, and told them that Si had just bought the farm. Len, Fred, and I related what we had seen, but there was so little to tell. We didn't have the slightest idea what had caused the airplane to come apart. Republic Aviation, which built the P-84, was well known for the sturdy aircraft it produced, and there was no record of structural failure in 84s. There had been some pitch-up problems in earlier testing, but they had occurred at 600 mph, and we had not exceeded 500 mph. We knew the airplane hadn't exploded, because there was no fire either in the air or on the ground. This was the first time anyone had been killed during a firepower demonstration. In fact, no one could recall any type of accident during a demonstration.

Si was a skillful and experienced pilot. We were sure he hadn't erred in any way. He was the operations officer of the squadron and was acting as squadron commander in the absence of Lieutenant Colonel Slocumb. In addition to being highly respected as a pilot and leader, he was also well liked. We all had lost a good friend.

Si and I had flown together in many airshows. Glyn and I often joined him and his wife, Rachel, at the local boat races where Si raced his home-built motor boat, which, next to his newborn son, was his pride and joy. Driving home, I thought about the pleasant times we had shared and how in an instant one's future can be blown to hell. I wondered how I could break this to Glyn. Si was the first pilot to be killed in our squadron in the four months that we had been married. He would not be the last, and this was only the first of many times that I would be the bearer of such devastating news.

It was not until the next day that we learned exactly what had occurred. All the events in the demonstrations were filmed by high-speed motion picture cameras. The film clearly showed that Si's right wing had sheared from the fuselage and the remainder of the airplane had gone into the ground in a high-speed roll to the right. The airplane broke into pieces on impact, and Si was killed instantly. Some speculated that he had hit the propwash or wingtip vortices from the B-29s, but we knew that the three P-80s and Si were well clear of both of those hazards.

In the meantime, as soon as Si's death was officially confirmed, our group commander and the chaplain went to Si's home to inform his wife of the accident. I didn't envy the chaplain and the C.O. their duty that day, but I did wish there were something I could do to help relieve her sorrow. My wife didn't know a lot about flying and fliers before we were married, but she had worked at Eglin for a year and a half and knew well that airplanes crashed and fliers were killed. She also knew, though, how I felt about flying, and to her credit, she never suggested or even hinted that I take up a safer profession.

In combat, the death of a fellow pilot is easier to accept for two reasons: it is expected (after all, kill or be killed is the name of the game), and combat pilots are seldom acquainted with each other's families, which distances them from the family's suffering when a husband and father is killed. Death is an ever-present threat in flying and an even larger threat in test flying, but it occurred, fortunately, far less often than in combat.

Death is not the major fear for test pilots. What we fear most is screwing up in a way that causes the loss of the airplane or the loss of someone else's life. Alive or dead, the flier's image as an outstanding pilot—a precious commodity indeed—would be damaged or destroyed. It would be tantamount to an Oriental's losing face.

Test pilots are not daredevils who foolishly risk their necks by taking unnecessary chances. Quite the contrary, all the good ones do only what is required to get the job done, and they know their aircraft's systems so thoroughly that they are well prepared for emergencies. Chuck Yeager's motto is a good one for all test pilots, indeed for all pilots, to follow: "Always leave yourself a way out."

The reason for the structural failure that caused Si's death was not discovered until a few months later. Several of us were in Atlanta flying F-84s and F-80s in an Air Force Day airshow. Late in the afternoon, as we were preparing to take off for the second part of the show, we received a wire from Eglin stating that all F-84s were grounded until further notice. Two F-84s from the 20th Fighter Group flying in separate airshows (one in Fort Worth, Texas, and one in San Bernardino, California) had lost their wings that day in front of the spectators while pulling up from high-speed, low-altitude passes. By some miracle, both pilots parachuted to safety. Investigations determined that when the stick was pulled back for a moderate-g pullout at high speed with tip tanks installed, the F-84 experienced an aerodynamic phenomenon called stick reversal, probably caused by tip-tank oscillation. That is, after reaching a certain g-load the airplane would automatically tighten the turn until it exceeded the maximum structural g-loading, causing the wing structure to fail. It happened so quickly that the pilot could not reverse the stick force in time to prevent the wing failure. Republic Aviation, the builders of the F-84, solved the problem by adding small triangular winglets to the tip tanks.

I flew in many more firepower demonstrations during my remaining three years at Eglin, and I'm happy to relate that they were all accident free.

16

Big Airplanes, Big Year

While I was at test pilot school, a second model of the North American Twin Mustang, the P-82E, was delivered to the squadron. The radome and the radar controls had been removed and the right cockpit was now equipped with duplicate flight controls. It was not designed for use as a night fighter but rather as a long-range escort fighter for the Strategic Air Command. In theory, the pilot and copilot could relieve each other at the controls on long missions, thus reducing fatigue. In practice, it was found to be almost as tiring to ride in the small cockpit as it was to fly the plane, since there was no place to go and no room to stretch when not at the controls.

In the E model, the 1,380-horsepower Merlin engines had been replaced by 1,600-horsepower Allison V-1710-143s. Maximum rpm had been raised from 3,000 to 3,200, and takeoff manifold pressure had been increased from 61 to 72 inches of mercury. It had a top speed of 461 mph, a ceiling of almost 39,000 feet, and a range of more than 2,200 miles.

Artie Lynch was the test officer, and I flew in the right cockpit with him on my checkout ride. As was his custom, the checkout consisted entirely of aerobatics performed, and performed extremely well, by Artie, using maximum power for most of the flight. I never touched the controls. After some fifteen minutes of gut-wrenching maneuvers, while we were in a vertical climb at full power, there was a sudden jolt, and the right propeller went into full feather. It kept turning for a few seconds until Artie shut it down and rolled into level flight. I was thinking that whatever he was trying to demonstrate was surely dramatic, when he yelled, "Dammit Lope, don't screw with the controls when I'm flying!" I told him that I hadn't touched anything. He cooled down and said that the prop control must have failed.

We headed back to the field, and after Artie told the tower he had lost an engine, we were instructed to enter the downwind leg for a rectangular pattern and land. He replied that he was already on the initial approach for a standard fighter circular pattern, but the tower repeated the original instruction. Artie reluctantly complied, although he bitched at the tower operator until we were down and off the runway. He seemed to feel that the tower operator had somewhat less than the proper respect for his flying ability.

The crew chief confirmed that the linkage to the control had indeed broken, causing the propeller to feather, but at least the engine had not been damaged.

I was now a fully qualified graduate of the Artie Lynch Hands-off Checkout Method, so as soon as the linkage had been repaired I took the P-82E up and put it through its paces, albeit slightly more sedate paces than Artie's. I found it quite responsive and more enjoyable to fly than the night-fighter model. Also, the removal of the radome had eliminated the nose heaviness mentioned earlier, and power-off, four-point landings were now a piece of cake, or as the French put it, "C'est du gateau."

Sometime later, Wes Posvar told me about his checkout by Artie in the P-82E. Although an excellent pilot, Wes did not have much fighter experience at the time. Artie performed about forty-five minutes of aerobatics and then landed without letting Wes touch the controls. As they walked back to operations Artie said, "Well, I'm sure you can handle it now." And he was right. Soon after that, Wes was assigned to fly the F-82 in a firepower demonstration. He was to dive-bomb a target and then join two other F-82s for a flyby. He had never dive-bombed, so I flew in the right seat and made a few practice runs, with Wes observing through his gunsight. He followed with a few runs that were letter perfect. He must have mastered the technique on that short training flight, because during the demonstration he destroyed the pyramid target with a direct hit. Wes, with his remarkable academic achievements, helped dispel the general belief that brains were a handicap to a fighter pilot.

The heavy bomber squadron had received and was testing the Convair (Consolidated-Vultee) B-36, the USAF's long-range strategic bomber and the largest bomber ever in U.S. service. The requirement for a very-long-range bomber had been established back in 1941, when it seemed that Britain might fall and the United States might be required to attack targets in Europe from North America. When the British turned the tide, the urgency for such a bomber decreased, and the first flight of the XB-36 did not take place until August 1946, one year after the surrender of Japan.

The B-36 was an enormous airplane with a wingspan of 230 feet, 89 feet greater than the B-29, and a length of 162 feet, 63 feet longer than the B-29. (For comparison, the Boeing 747 airliner has a span of 196 feet and is 231 feet long.) Its gross weight was 328,000 pounds, and it could carry a bomb load of 72,000 pounds. Powered by six 28-cylinder, 3,500-horsepower Pratt & Whitney Wasp Major engines turning pusher propellers, its maximum range was more than 8,000 miles, and its service ceiling was 42,500 feet. A later model, the B-36D first flown in July 1949, had four 5,200-pound-thrust General Electric J-47 jet engines, two mounted on each wing, making it a ten-engine bomber.

The B-36, through no fault of the airplane or its crew, had a rather embarrassing debut at a firepower demonstration. As a blockbuster opening, the B-36 was to drop 144 five-hundred-pound bombs, not salvoed but in trail. It would start bombing as it came across the west boundary of the range and salvo the remaining bombs at the east boundary, covering a distance of 3.3 miles. This went off exactly as planned, except that most of the bombs failed to detonate—they were duds. It seems that the ordnance department had to use a lot of ancient bombs to make up such a large load. It might not have been so noticeable had they been salvoed, but the duds were painfully obvious when dropped in trail. The ordnance crews spent the better part of the next year locating the buried bombs and exploding them. I was flying a P-38 that day and, since I had plenty of fuel, had taken off early to watch the spectacular show. I was as disappointed as the spectators on the ground, but at least I was flying.

From time to time, when the defensive armament system was being tested (six retractable remote-controlled turrets plus a nose and a tail turret, mounting two 20mm cannon each), the fighter squadron was called on to make simulated attacks from various angles and altitudes with F-80s. I flew several of these missions, and in the beginning it was difficult to close to the proper firing range before breaking off the attacks; the B-36 was so large that it appeared to be much closer than it actually was. Like most things, with a little experience that soon ceased to be a problem.

Most of the base personnel were intrigued by the B-36 because of its size and its distinctive throbbing sound, caused by the inability to synchronize the six propellers. When the fighters were making high-altitude passes at the B-36 over the base, all the aircraft could be easily seen because of the contrails. Glyn said the crisscrossed contrails made it look like a game of aerial tic-tac-toe. With no bomb load and a light fuel load, the B-36 had a low wing loading and a high power loading, making it surprisingly maneuverable. The bomber pilots would constantly turn toward the fighters, making it difficult to complete a proper firing pass. It was quite a sight to see that monster making tight turns and apparently foiling the fighters, and it gave the bomber pilots a rare, but brief, opportunity to gloat. While it looked good from the ground and the fighter pilots were kidded about it, from the fighter cockpits it was obvious that many of the passes would have been successful, especially when the fighters split up and made coordinated attacks from different directions. Also, if the fighters caused the bombers to twist and turn on the bomb run, which must be straight and level to ensure accuracy, they would have accomplished their mission. The commander of the heavy bomber squadron realized this and, after letting his pilots enjoy themselves for a few days, told them to knock it off and fly standard bomb runs.

While they were testing the hemisphere gunsight in the nose turret of the B-36, I was assigned to make a series of head-on passes because of my experience on Project Agate. The tests were conducted at 10,000 feet, which cut down the time we spent climbing to altitude. Although I was now used to the size of the B-36, for some reason it looked much larger when approaching head-on, causing me to break off the attack at too great a distance for proper evaluation of the sight. After about three passes, each one closer than the last but still too far out, the pilot radioed, "What's the matter, Lope? Are you chicken?" Evidently he hadn't heard of my midair collision in China, or he wouldn't have been so rash. I didn't reply, but on the next pass I came so close that I instinctively ducked behind the instrument panel as I broke below him. He yelled, "Lope, you're not chicken, you're not chicken! I could read the numbers on both sides of your tail. By the way, I'm calling from the tail-gunner's position." The rest of the passes that day and later went well, with no further references to poultry.

The B-36 was the center of a major controversy between the Navy and the Air Force in 1949. In April, shortly after the Joint Chiefs of Staff had recommended and Secretary of Defense Johnson had approved cancellation of the plans to build the supercarrier *United States,* several documents were circulated anonymously in the Congress and among the press charging that corruption had influenced the selection of the B-36 by the Air

Force, that its performance was lower than claimed, and that the Air Force had exaggerated the effectiveness of strategic bombing. After a long investigation the House Committee on Armed Services concluded that there was no evidence whatsoever to substantiate the charges of corruption. The other charges against the B-36 and the effectiveness of strategic bombing were debated for many months afterward without any firm conclusion. Actually, the fight was really over roles and missions for the respective services and ultimately for a greater share of the defense budget. That fight is still going on. Despite the controversy, 383 B-36s were constructed, and the last one was retired from active service on February 12, 1959. Only one example of this giant aircraft exists today, dominating one of the hangars of the U.S. Air Force Museum in Dayton, Ohio. It is worth the trip just to see it.

I had a rather humbling experience during this period, causing me to believe, momentarily, that my flying ability was not as great as I thought. The only photo reconnaissance pilot on the base was enjoying a short leave, and I was asked to fly a few of his missions while he was gone. Flying an RF-80 (a standard F-80 with a modified nose containing cameras instead of guns), I was to photograph a resolution target from various altitudes ranging from 25,000 to 40,000 feet. A resolution target is a square of asphalt about 100 feet on a side, with black-and-white rectangular patterns painted in various sizes on its surface. It is used to evaluate the sharpness of the photographic images.

I thought it would be a simple task and, after learning how to operate the cameras, took off and shot the photos from the assigned altitudes. When I reviewed the film the following day I was embarrassed to find that the target showed up on only a few frames, and even on those I had barely caught the edge. I realized how difficult it is to fly precisely over a small target from high altitude without being able to see directly below the plane. Also, if the wings are not perfectly level the photograph will be off to the side of the target. I did a bit better on later missions, but it would have required a great deal more practice to master the art. I also did some aerial mapping in an F-82 in which the radar in the pod had been replaced with a camera installation. There was a camera operator in the right cockpit to handle the photography, but I had to fly a precise course over the ground, correcting for wind drift, for about ten minutes and then fly successive parallel courses adjoining the previous course. These flights were much more successful. My experience increased my already profound respect for photo reconnaissance pilots. I had always admired the courage and navigational skills required to fly unarmed deep into enemy territory, but I thought that taking the photos was quite simple. The pilot just flew over the target city in occupied France and yelled, "Dites fromage, tout le monde," and turned on the camera.

To me, one of the most beautiful large aircraft ever built was the Republic XF-12 Rainbow, built to meet an Army Air Force requirement for a long-range, high-altitude, high-speed photo reconnaissance airplane, for use in the Pacific theater. More than just a camera plane, it included a darkroom, where cameras could be reloaded and film developed in flight. The Rainbow was powered by four Pratt & Whitney 28-cylinder, 3,250-horsepower turbosupercharged engines turning four-bladed propellers, each sixteen feet in diameter. The exhaust was ejected from the rear of the engine nacelles to provide a small amount of jet thrust. The pilots sat well forward in the glass nose, which provided both good visibility and excellent streamlining.

The performance of the Rainbow was outstanding. In May 1946 it set a new speed record for four-engine aircraft on a flight between Wright Field, Ohio, and New York, averaging 426 mph. Although the AAF had ordered twenty Rainbows in October 1946, the coming availability of jet aircraft led to the cancellation of the contract in 1947, and only the two prototypes were constructed. A proposed airliner version ordered by American Airlines and Pan American Airways also was cancelled because of its high cost.

One of the Rainbows was delivered to Eglin in the fall of 1948 to test the concept of a flying laboratory, not to test the aircraft itself. Everyone admired its looks, both in the air and on the ground. The testing had been progressing well when it caught fire in the air a few thousand feet over the bay, not far from the field. Five of the seven on board bailed out successfully, but the two photographers in the rear were not wearing their parachutes and were killed in the subsequent crash.

In addition to my wedding, there were a great many other momentous events in the year 1948. In Czechoslovakia, a Soviet-backed coup ousted the legal government and replaced it with a pro-Communist one; the new Jewish state of Israel was formed and was recognized almost instantly by the United States; American athletes dominated the Olympic Games in London, winning thirty-eight medals; the first nightly television news program, featuring John Cameron Swayze, was inaugurated; the transistor, which revolutionized electronics, was invented; and Mahatma Gandhi was assassinated. Not as important but possibly more appreciated was the appearance of the bikini bathing suit, which was said to cover nothing atoll. Prosperity in the United States was the highest it had ever been, but there was trouble on the horizon.

On June 24, 1948, the Soviets imposed a blockade on all land and water traffic into Berlin, which was surrounded by the Russian occupation zone, in an attempt to drive the Americans, British, and French from the city. Within a few months the citizens of Berlin would be without food and fuel. President Harry Truman, with his usual courage, ordered that Berlin be supplied by air. At first, there was concern that it would not be possible to provide enough airlift capability to meet the requirements of 2.5 million people, especially in the winter, when the requirements for coal would increase markedly. But they were met. Aircraft and crews from all over the world were flown in, and an amazingly effective system of loading, unloading, and air traffic control was established. The massive Berlin airlift would continue until September 1949, although the Russians had admitted defeat and lifted the blockade on May 12, 1949. During the fourteen months of the airlift, more than 275,000 supply flights delivered 2,325,809 tons of supplies. It had shown decisively that the West would not cave in to Soviet threats.

Wes Posvar, who had been awarded a Rhodes scholarship and was now studying at Oxford, kept up his flying in a De Havilland Tiger Moth with the Oxford Flying Club. On several of his school breaks, however, he traveled to Germany and flew airlift missions.

Nineteen forty-eight was also the year of President Truman's famous whistle-stop campaign; against all odds and predictions, he defeated Thomas E. Dewey and won another term as president. That election has special meaning for me, since it was the first in which I was able to vote, and my vote helped to elect President Truman, who in my opinion was the most honest, straightforward, courageous, and down-to-earth president in this century.

Earlier I mentioned that after Si Johnson's crash, we had no more accidents during a firepower demonstration. That is true, but one of the pilots in the squadron, Ray Evans, came too close for comfort at two subsequent demonstrations. Ray was one of the pilots who had come to Eglin with the group from Pinecastle. He had flown P-47s in the Pacific during the war and had been assigned to Pinecastle when he returned to the States. Ray went balls out at whatever he did. He was an avid fisherman, and although he could not swim a stroke (he often said that the harder he swam the deeper he went), he regularly spent the day in small boats without a life jacket, standing up and casting his line. He fell overboard several times but always managed to grab the side of the boat, climb back in, and get on with the fishing. He and Frank "Radar" Smith were great fishing buddies and often spent hours in a T-6 searching out likely fishing holes and the roads or paths that led to them.

Ray had a close call during Project Highball when his oxygen regulator failed at 35,000 feet, causing him to pass out; he did not recover until he had descended to about 1,000 feet. But that was nothing compared to his dive-bombing misadventures during the next two firepower demonstrations. He was set up to dive-bomb a pyramid target with an F-80 early in the program and then join three other F-80s for a high-speed pass at the conclusion. In the practice the day before the event, he had missed the target by about 50 feet and felt he had lost a lot of face, which is anathema to a fighter pilot. He swore he would get a direct hit during the demonstration. He did, with the bombs and very nearly with the airplane. I didn't see it, because I was flying one of the other 80s, but several observers said that he came down absolutely vertical. He released the bombs so late that no one thought he would be able to recover, but recover he did, by pulling 11.8 g's. Even so, he barely missed the ground. Ray of course blacked out, as did many of the people in the stands. The F-80 did not fare as well, however. As he recovered from his blackout he radioed a bit groggily that the airplane didn't feel right. I joined formation with him to inspect it and saw why. It looked like an airplane drawn by a bad cartoonist. The right horizontal stabilizer was bent upward in the middle at an angle of almost 90 degrees, while the left one was tilted upward at somewhat less of an angle. The aft fuselage looked like one of those Shar-Pei dogs, with large wrinkles all along the skin. Luckily, he found he could maintain control, and he made a straight-in approach and landed safely. The F-80 was class-twenty-sixed (damaged beyond repair) and sent to the salvage yard. It was a tribute to Lockheed's sturdy construction that the airplane stayed in one piece, since he had far exceeded the 8-g design limit.

Ray was enjoined by the group commander and the squadron commander to begin the pullout in future dive-bombing runs much farther from the ground and to stay within design g limits. In the next demonstration a few months later, Ray obeyed half of the orders. He began his pullout a few hundred feet higher and this time registered only 10.6 g's on the accelerometer. The stabilizers didn't bend, but the fuselage was twisted enough to class-twenty-six another F-80. Ray was assigned to another type of mission in later demonstrations while we still had a few F-80s left. Artie

Lynch, in his inimitable fashion, said that Ray pulled out so late because Si Johnson was on the pyramid beckoning to him to come lower.

In the late fifties Ray commanded a squadron of Lockheed F-104 Starfighters at Hamilton Air Force Base, near San Francisco. He was making a practice ILS (instrument landing system) approach when his engine failed at very low altitude and he crashed into the ocean. After all his hairy escapades, he was killed on a fairly routine mission while doing everything by the book. Some problems are impossible to handle no matter how good a pilot you are.

In the summer of 1948, Artie Lynch was offered a job as a test pilot for North American Aviation. The lure of much higher pay and no requirement for an unwrinkled uniform was too much. He accepted, resigned his commission, and moved to California. On Saint Patrick's Day in 1954, he was killed during an airshow at Nellis Air Force Base in Las Vegas, Nevada, while demonstrating a two-seat version of the F-86 Sabre, which North American was hoping to sell to the Air Force. He had started a roll immediately after liftoff, but the rudder locked, and he crashed. Artie had once told us that when he died it would be on Saint Patrick's Day in front of a large crowd. He was truly one of a kind. I have fond memories of flying with him and of our time together.

I'm certain that Si and Ray and Artie are in that fighter pilot's heaven I mentioned earlier, where I hope to join them someday in the distant future, rat-racing among the mountains of sunlit cumulus clouds and buzzing a few feet above the beautiful white sand and blue-green water of a Gulf beach liberally sprinkled with bikini-clad blondes. With no regulations to restrict us, and no chance of getting killed, we will fly as close to the clouds and the ground as we wish. Surely, a merciful God will not have an FAA in heaven.

17

The Test of the F-84B

Late in 1948 I was able to fulfill one of my childhood ambitions by riding on the back of a fire engine. The operations officer asked if anyone wanted to fly a surplus P-61 Black Widow to Eglin Auxiliary Field 8, adjoining the bombing range where the firepower demonstrations took place, so it could be used as a target. It wasn't in first-class condition and had not been flown for several months, but it had been cleared for a one-time flight. I said that I would, gathered my flight gear, and went out to the airplane. When I looked it over I saw a good-sized tear in the fabric covering of the elevator. The crew chief said he had tried to sew it but the thread just ripped through the fabric. That wasn't reassuring, but he said he was certain it would hold together for a short low-speed flight. He also said that he would accompany me. That was reassuring, but I told him I would go alone, because if I had to bail out I did not want anyone in my way.

I made the flight, which lasted only ten minutes, with the wheels down; the wheels must be down to bail out of the main entry hatch behind the pilot, and I wanted to avoid possible problems with the hydraulic system. The flight itself was uneventful. After parking the airplane and getting the range officer to certify that the clock was still in it, I climbed aboard the fire truck that had been sent from Eglin to cover my landing. Rather than ride inside the truck, I chose to stand on the back platform, but like many childhood fantasies, the realization turned out to be far less exciting than anticipated. Perhaps tearing through the streets of New York City with the

168

sirens blaring would have been more of a thrill than sedately driving through the deserted piney woods of Florida.

In July 1948 we received the first F 80Bs, which were equipped with ejection seats, as all jet fighters would be from then on. It had become obvious that escape from a fighter at jet speeds was all but impossible without an ejection system. At first we worried more about the seat's firing accidentally than we did about getting out of a disabled plane. Many of us, myself included, left the ground safety pins in place all the time, figuring we would sacrifice the few seconds required to remove the pins for the reassurance they provided. We heard no reports of accidental seat firings, however, and after a short time, we followed the rules and removed the pins as part of the pre-takeoff check. As I related in a previous chapter, we had been given ejection-seat training at Wright Field several months earlier.

The 75th Fighter Squadron, in which Rode and I had served in China, held its first postwar reunion in September 1948 in Cleveland in conjunction with the National Air Races. We flew to Akron, where Wes Posvar, who was on leave in Cleveland, met us and drove us to the hotel. Wes didn't attend the reunion but joined us at the air races. There was quite a good turnout at the reunion, considering that so many of the squadron were still on active duty and were not able to make it. Our hotel bill was a bit higher than anticipated because one of our less-intelligent members, nicknamed the Talking Dog in China, poured a pitcher of drinks into a piano and threw a small table out a fifteenth-floor window. (It landed in an alley and didn't kill anyone. If it had, it would have been his first victory.)

The air races were of special interest to me because my friend from test pilot school, Chuck Brown, who had left the Air Force and become a test pilot for the Allison Engine Company, had entered a P-39 in the Thompson Trophy Race. I visited him in the hangar on the day before the race and inspected his Airacobra. It had been cleaned up aerodynamically to reduce the drag, and the wings had been shortened. What really amazed me was the engine. The normal takeoff power setting on a standard Allison, as used in the F-82, was 72 inches of mercury and 3,200 rpm. Chuck said that by using special fuel, he would pull 120 inches and 3,400 rpm at the start of the race and then reduce power in increments on each of the twenty laps. He said he planned to take off in first place and stay there throughout the race because the first-place plane is out of the rough air created by the propwash of the other planes, and its risk of collision is much less. Chuck was a superb pilot, and I was sure he would win if his engine held up, but it did not. Chuck, as promised, was the first off the ground and easily led the pack. Making picture-perfect turns around the pylons, he lapped many of the others. In the eighteenth lap, though, an overheated fuel line caused vapor lock, and his engine failed. He brought the Airacobra in for a dead-stick landing.

Not long afterward Chuck left Allison and became a test pilot for North American Aviation. The next year he was flying as the copilot in an AJ, a Navy bomber powered by two wing-mounted reciprocating engines and a jet engine in the aft fuselage. During some yaw tests, the tail came off and the AJ crashed into the ocean, killing both pilots.

We now had several F-84s, both B and C models, in the squadron, and I was flying them regularly. The C was essentially the same as the B except for 250 pounds of additional thrust from the engine and an improved electrical system. The F-84 was faster than the F-80 at all altitudes but had a lower rate of climb. Its range as a fighter-bomber was double that of the F-80 because the 84 could carry both drop tanks and bombs. The 80, which used the same racks for the drop tanks and the bombs, could not carry both at once. It was an easy airplane to fly, and the wide landing gear and the solid feel common to Republic fighters made it especially easy to land.

Three test programs on the F-84B were under way at Eglin during the period from March through December 1948: operational suitability, armament installation, and a brief test of the retractable bomb rack. The tests all were started just before I returned from test pilot school. Hoot Gibson was the test officer on the suitability test, Don Dessert on the armament test, and Si Johnson on the bomb-rack test. Many problems, some serious, were discovered in the course of this testing, requiring major modifications to the aircraft. I did not participate in the bomb-rack test, which consisted primarily of ground missions, or in the armament test, but I flew quite a few missions in the suitability test program. Don Dessert, as test officer, was the principal pilot, but he was ably supported by pilots from the 20th Fighter Group, which was to be equipped with the F-84. It was common practice at Eglin for pilots from operational groups to fly with Eglin pilots during tests of aircraft they were to operate.

The armament testing was to evaluate the gun installation, which consisted of six .50-caliber M3 machine guns, four in the upper nose section and one in each wing root, with 300 rounds of ammunition per gun. The gunsight was a K-14B with a hydraulic ranging mechanism. During the course of the program 62,533 rounds of ammunition were fired. In the functional phase the guns were fired in fifty-round bursts in straight-and-level flight, in pullouts and turns at 1 to 6 g's, and in minus-1-g pushovers at altitudes from 10,000 to 40,000 feet. Every malfunction, including cookoffs, was recorded along with the altitude, airspeed, and number of g's at which the malfunction occurred. A cookoff is caused by a gun becoming so hot that the round in the chamber fires without being struck by the firing pin. In combat a cookoff is startling to the pilot because it sounds as though his airplane has been hit. Although this was run as a separate series of tests, the results became part of the suitability test report.

Instead of summarizing the results of the tests, I have excerpted the following paragraphs from the final report of Air Proving Ground Project No. 6478-4—5, *Operational Suitability Test of the F-84B Airplane.*

3. CONCLUSIONS:

a. The F-84B does not perform satisfactorily any of the following missions:

(1) Fighter-Bomber.

(2) Escort-Fighter.

(3) Ground-support Fighter.

(4) Interceptor-Fighter.

b. Jet aircraft, as typified by the F-80 and F-84, have less utility of employment than conventional aircraft; i.e., excessive fuel consumption, especially at low altitudes, severely limits the tactical utilization of jet aircraft.

4. RECOMMENDATIONS:

It is recommended that:

a. A study be made to determine the feasibility of modifying the F-84Bs now produced to enable the airplane to perform satisfactorily a combat or training mission.

b. The structural integrity flight demonstration requirements for jet airplanes (AAF Specifications Nos. C-1803-E and F-1803-11) be revised to increase or decrease the maximum permissible "g" loading at low altitudes commensurate with the mission for which the aircraft is designed.

5. DISCUSSION:

a. General: Due to grounding orders and excessive time required to perform the many modifications made necessary by structural difficulties, the number of hours flown on the five aircraft available for service was small. A breakdown of total hours flown during all testing is as follows:

(1) Aircraft suitability 14 hrs. 35 min.

(2) Bombing 25 hrs. 30 min.

(3) Armament 35 hrs. 25 min.

(4) Electronics 17 hrs. 50 min.

(5) Transition 12 hrs. 10 min.

TOTAL 105 hrs. 30 min.

b. Structural Failures: The wing construction of the F-84B has been the main source of difficulty with the airplane. Pulled rivets, wing wrinkling and buckling were encountered when the airplane was submitted to loads greater than 6 "g" at speeds in excess of 400 mph IAS [indicated airspeed]. All aircraft exhibited these inherent weaknesses. Structural failures necessitated replacing the wings of three aircraft, and less severe indications of failure were apparent on the other two. The airplane was limited to a 6 "g" acceleration and speeds less than 450 mph IAS, which precluded any low-level, high-speed tactical operation because of the high wing-loadings encountered in the performance of such missions. It was found that pilots often inadvertently exceeded this limit during pullout regardless of their awareness of the restriction. Even in unaccelerated level flight at high speeds, loads as high as 6 "g" due to turbulent air at low-level have been recorded. Failure of the wing trailing edge brackets and wing fairing forward of the aileron cut-out area was apparent after early inspection of all aircraft. These failures are believed to have been a contributing cause of a fatal accident which occurred during the test, the aircraft disintegrating in flight at low-level. Resulting corrective action was to reinforce the brackets to prevent further occurrences. Only limited bombing and armament testing could be conducted because of the structural limitations and failures.

Pilot attitude toward flying the airplane was greatly affected by these failures. Pilots exhibited great reluctance to fly the aircraft and this prejudiced the airplane-pilot performance combination.

c. Pilot Observations: Detailed pilot observations were obtained from six pilots. A resume of unfavorable items remarked upon by the pilots is as follows:

(1) Cockpit Layout and Comfort: The listed cockpit installations were unsatisfactory for the following reasons:

(a) The circuit breakers on the left console are difficult to identify and operate during flight.

(b) The landing-gear handle is poorly designed in that it is difficult to operate and its location is poor because of its proximity to a number of switches. . . .

(e) The attitude gyro is on the opposite side of the instrument panel from the other flight instruments. . . .

(g) The dive-brake switch should be made more readily accessible; i.e., located on the throttle handle. . . .

(i) Only one fluorescent (ultra-violet) light is available for night flight. One light does not sufficiently illuminate the instrument panel and does not offer a safety factor in the event it becomes inoperative. . . .

(m) The instrument panel vibrates excessively; the "g" meter had to be reinstalled on the cockpit floor because readings as high as 3 "g" were recorded while taxiing. . . .

(2) Visibility: It was found that the forward visibility was almost completely obstructed by the gunsight installation, requiring the pilot to move his head from side to side in order to look through the forward side panels. This results in an increase in pilot fatigue. Rearward visibility is restricted by the installation of the head-rest cushion. It was pilot opinion that the restrictions to search visibility would seriously hamper pilot efficiency during a combat mission.

(3) High Speed Characteristics: On one flight, during a 0.80 Mach Number letdown the pilot inadvertently attained a speed of 0.82 Mach when his attention was diverted from the airspeed meter. At this speed a high degree of lateral instability, in addition to a nose-up pitching moment, was experienced. The instability noted was a strong rolling tendency to the right.

d. Range and Combat Radius: . . .

(3) At 100% rpm, fuel consumption at sea level (approximately 810 gallons per hour) is more than twice the consumption at 30,000 feet.

(4) Fuel consumption at 100% rpm is reduced approximately 140 gallons per hour per 10,000 feet increment of altitude.

(5) The decrease in fuel consumption at altitude, coupled with the increase in most economical airspeed, gives a maximum range at 30,000 feet (clean configuration) which is approximately two and one-half times the maximum range attainable at sea level. . . .

With a full ammunition and fuel load with external fuel tanks, the maximum radius of action at 35,000 feet was calculated to be 670 statute miles. . . .

e. Combat Comparison of the F-84B with the F-80A:

(1) General: Based on the results of combat comparison tests flown by the F-84B and F-80A-5 with full internal military load at 15,000, 30,000, and 40,000 feet, the F-84B was found to be slightly superior to the F-80A-5 in maximum speed in level flight, level flight acceleration, dive acceleration, and handling characteristics. The F-84B was considered a better acrobatic airplane and superior in formation flying because of greater stability, faster acceleration and deceleration, and the variable aileron boost system. . . .

(4) Turning Circle: Turning circle comparisons were begun from a head-on approach on parallel courses, using maximum power in both aircraft. At 15,000 feet, after approximately 7 turns the F-80A-5 was able to bring his sight to bear on the F-84B. At 30,000 and 40,000 feet approxi-

mately 5 turns and 3-1/4 turns respectively were necessary for the F-80A-5 to get into firing position. There exists an optimum speed range for minimum turning radius in level flight and for maximum rate of turn. As altitude is increased this region becomes more critical and changes of IAS have a pronounced effect on turning performance. Inclosure 3, pages 1 and 2, illustrates this more clearly. . . .

h. Armament: In APG Final Report, Project No. 6484-2—5, subject, "Service Test of the Armament Installation on the F-84B Airplane," dated 29 October 1948, it was concluded that the armament installation in the F-84B airplane is functionally unreliable and tactically unsuitable for Air Force use. 62,553 rounds of .50 calibre ammunition were fired. The following are a few of the discrepancies noted:

(1) Gun installation, ammunition loading, and boresight adjustment require excessive time and manpower. Approximately 2 man-hours are required to reload and install ammunition containers and properly service the gun access doors.

(2) Excessive fumes and noises from gunfire enter the cockpit and make it uncomfortable for the pilot. . . .

(4) A lateral oscillation was induced by over-controlling when pilots attempted to make sighting corrections during firing runs on air-to-air and air-to-ground gunnery missions. In tracking a moving or stationary target in rough air this effect is so exaggerated that maintaining the sight pip on the target is extremely difficult. Analysis of the gun camera film exposed showed that tracking errors of approximately 20 mils were the result of this lateral oscillation. [Six mils is considered an acceptable tracking error.] . . .

i. Bombing:

(1) The structural limitation of 6 "g" normal acceleration restricts the aircraft as a dive bomber. It was found that pilots often inadvertently exceed this limit during pullout regardless of their awareness of this restriction.

(2) In level flight while carrying bombs in excess of 250 pounds at speeds greater than 450 mph IAS a nose-up tendency was encountered. To counteract this moment, full nose-down trim and an additional push force of 10-15 pounds by the pilot was required. Upon release of the bomb a violent nose-down tendency was experienced and as high as 1.5 negative "g" was recorded on the accelerometer. This appears to be the result of a disruption of the flow over the tail by the bombing installation and bombs, and the full nose-down trim of the aircraft before bomb release. . . .

k. Maintenance: The overall maintenance of the F-84B aircraft requires approximately three times the number of man-hours required to perform similar maintenance on the F-80A-5 airplane. The requirement of special tools, lack of access doors, and location and installation of units and accessories make even routine maintenance . . . difficult.

The discrepancies listed above are typical of the teething problems encountered with new aircraft. In each successive model of the F-84 some of those difficulties were corrected, and the F-84E served throughout the Korean War as a fighter-bomber. The F-84 was also used by many of our NATO allies as a tactical fighter. In Korea the F-84 was considered the backbone of the Fifth Air Force's tactical operations, attacking targets with machine guns, rockets, bombs, and napalm. It proved relatively easy to maintain and could withstand enemy fire. In 86,408 missions, F-84s delivered 50,427 tons of bombs and 5,560 tons of napalm and were credited with destroying 4,846 gun positions, 167 tanks, 259 locomotives, 3,996 railway cars, 3,317 vehicles, and 588 bridges while losing 155 aircraft to antiaircraft fire and 18 to MiG fighters.

A test program's final report is prepared by the project officer and reflects the daily reports submitted by the test officer. The test officer's reports are compilations of the data from each mission and the comments of the pilots. In the F-84B program, pilots from Eglin and from the 20th Fighter Group at Shaw Field commented. Both the test officer and the project officer had to approve the content and wording of the final report before it was forwarded through channels for distribution. Informally, the pilots would discuss the day's missions with each other and pass on any information about the aircraft that might be useful or affect safety. The project officer, usually a pilot who flew a few of the missions himself, would sit in on these sessions several times a week.

In late March 1949, Eglin was invaded by Hollywood as Gregory Peck and a host of other actors, along with directors, cinematographers, and an enormous support crew, arrived to shoot the flying scenes for the now classic film *Twelve O'Clock High,* a story built around a World War II bomb group in England. The moviemakers came to Eglin for B-17s. The First Experimental Guided Missile Squadron (XGM) at Eglin was still flying a large number of B-17s, most of which were equipped to be flown as drones (unmanned aircraft), primarily for use in the testing of nuclear weapons. The XGM B-17s were the only ones still flying in the Air Force, except for a few individual test aircraft.

Twelve of the B-17s were painted in World War II markings and used exclusively for the film for about a month, flown by XGM pilots. Many of the ground scenes were filmed at one of the Eglin auxiliary fields and at the abandoned airfield at Ozark, Alabama, about eighty miles northeast of Eglin. The movie's flying schedule was published daily, and all other flights were instructed to keep well clear of the auxiliary field and the B-17 formations.

One of the scenes in the film called for a B-17 to make a wheels-up crash landing. Paul Mantz, the premier movie stunt pilot, had flown a B-17 to Ozark that he would crash. Some of the Air Force pilots heard what he was to be paid for crashing the plane and said they would do it for nothing. The director declined their offer. Paul Mantz was experienced in that type of work, and Air Force pilots spend much of their training learning not to crash. If you have seen the crash in *Twelve O'Clock High* you can appreciate the wisdom of the director's decision.

I don't know how long Gregory Peck was in the area, because he stayed in Fort Walton Beach in the best, and one of the few, hotels in the area, Bacon's by the Sea. He traveled directly from the hotel to the auxiliary field, and few, if any, of the Eglin personnel saw him. Many of the other actors, however, came to the officer's club occasionally, and they were quite friendly and outgoing. The remoteness of Eglin must have been a shock to the filmmakers, and I'm sure they were glad to return to the bright lights of Hollywood.

18

Sonic Booms and Radar

n March 1949, Dick Jones, then stationed at Shaw Air Force Base, near Sumter, South Carolina, asked me to be the best man at his wedding on Saturday April 2. He and Lois McConnell were to be married in their hometown of Lewiston, New York, near Niagara Falls. Glyn and I had met Lois a few months earlier, when she and her twin, Phyllis, visited Eglin for a few days while Dick was staying with us. I, of course, accepted. Dick had filled the same role for me a little over a year before, and I was glad to reciprocate.

The problem of how to get to Lewiston was neatly solved when I was asked to pick up a new F-84D at the Republic factory in Farmingdale, Long Island, on Friday the first of April. I was flown to Mitchel Field in a B-25 and was picked up there by a company car from Republic. At the factory airfield, I inspected and signed for the airplane, then took off and flew to Mitchel Field, all of five minutes away. Col. Ed Rector, who had been Dick's and my group commander in China, was now stationed at Mitchel and was to be an usher at the wedding. He met me at base operations and said he had a C-45 scheduled for the weekend and that we would fly to Niagara Falls that afternoon.

Following a quick lunch, we took off for what was planned to be a two-hour flight, but Robert Burns was right, our plans ganged a-gley almost immediately, as they aft do. As soon as we became airborne Ed (whom I always properly addressed as "Colonel" then) moved the landing gear switch to the up position, and the two green lights went out as they should. However, the lack of normal acceleration, airspeed, and rate of climb indicated that the gear had not fully retracted. Ed elected to continue on course while we attempted to correct the problem. None of the circuit breakers had popped, so we felt safe in cycling the switch several times, which we did to no avail. After leveling out at about 6,000 feet we tried to raise the gear by means of the hand crank on the right side of the pilot's seat. While Ed flew, I operated the crank handle. It was easy to turn at first because the airflow was helping the gear swing backward toward the up position, but after the halfway point it became increasingly difficult and then impossible, because I was lifting the total weight of the gear with precious little mechanical advantage. Ed tried to help by pushing over to create negative g to reduce the load on the crank, but the carburetors were not designed for negative g and caused the engines to sputter.

Since my unsuccessful attempts had been from the copilot seat, I decided to apply more leverage by standing up. It worked well until the last few turns of the crank. I was applying maximum pressure when the airplane suddenly nosed over into a dive. Ed yelled for me to stop, I immediately released the crank, and we leveled off. We tried to raise the gear again with the same result. We couldn't figure what was causing the dive until, on the third try, Ed noticed that I was bracing myself on the copilot's control wheel. On the last turns of the crank, I would force the control wheel sharply forward, and the airplane would obediently go into a dive. Ed decided we had fooled around long enough, so we lowered the gear with the switch, which worked properly going down, and landed at Stewart Air Force Base, near West Point, New York, where a mechanic located and replaced a defective relay. Reassured, we took off; the gear came up, and the rest of the trip was uneventful.

Dick picked us up at the airport along with Rode, who had arrived a bit earlier in a Mustang from Eglin. He drove us to the home of a neighbor who had volunteered to put us up for the wedding. After cleaning up and changing our clothes, we took off to see the Falls. I had never seen them except from the air, and while they were certainly impressive, I found them oppressive. I was uncomfortable standing against the rail only a few feet from that unbelievable torrent. I felt much safer in the air.

That evening after a short wedding rehearsal we all went to the home of the McConnells, Lois's parents. They were Scottish, and later in the evening I realized how Scottish. After tea, which was quite a ritual in itself, we held hands and sang "Annie Laurie" with the same reverence that most people accord "The Star-Spangled Banner." When we returned to our quarters, a new experience awaited us. Our twin four-poster beds were quite high and had feather mattresses about eighteen inches thick. I could have used an F-84's ladder to climb into it, and when we lay down we sank slowly out of sight into the feathery deeps. I could not see Ed, and when I said goodnight, he, as a former Navy officer, replied, "Up periscope." It was a weird but comfortable feeling, and I slept quite well, but at that age I always slept well, whatever the surface.

The next afternoon, the wedding went off perfectly. Lois wore a traditional wedding gown, and Dick, the groomsmen, and I wore our uniforms, which was also traditional for military weddings. Shortly thereafter, Dick and Lois left for their honeymoon, and after some mild celebrating by the wedding party, we retired, in Ed's and my case for another feathery night. In the morning we flew back to Mitchel Field with no landing-gear trouble. I stayed overnight with Ed in his BOQ, watching that new technical marvel television, which would not arrive in the Eglin area for several more years. I was mesmerized, even though the TV picture and the shows themselves were awful. The picture has improved greatly since then.

After breakfast on Monday I took off in the F-84 for Eglin. Because of the hot weather and the relatively short runway at Mitchel, I elected not to put fuel in the wingtip tanks and to use only internal fuel. That did not give me sufficient range for a nonstop flight to Eglin. I landed en route at Shaw Air Force Base. While the aircraft was being refueled I visited the operations office of Dick's squadron and told his friends that although they had one less bachelor, Dick's lovely new wife was undoubtedly a net gain for the base. Dick's new sister-in-law, Phyllis, later met and married one of the pilots in his squadron. Sadly, he was killed in a crash not too long after the marriage.

Shortly after I returned to Eglin one of the squadron pilots was killed in a crash that had a particularly tragic aftermath. Lt. Arnold Adams, who had been in the squadron for about a year, was on a low-altitude test flight one afternoon in an F-80C but failed to land at the scheduled time. After the tower had checked the other fields in the area without locating the aircraft, we took off in all the available planes to search for it. About an hour later a helicopter crew spotted the F-80 under about ten feet of water in Choctawhatchee Bay approximately fifteen miles from the base. A crash boat was dispatched to the scene, and the skipper reported that the pilot was still in the cockpit. We never did learn the cause of the accident, but as he hadn't reported an emergency, there was speculation that he had simply flown into the water. It is easy for a pilot to misjudge his height above the surface of calm water. His body was sent home for burial with the proper ceremony, and the airplane was recovered and stored in the base salvage yard. Some months later two mechanics were busy removing parts from its fuselage when the ejection seat fired, killing one of the mechanics. No one had thought to disarm the seat, possibly because it was a fairly new installation.

On the brighter side of events, our athletic fortunes took a large turn for the better when Capt. Jack Flack was assigned to Fighter Test. He was an outstanding athlete, a four-letter man at Ole Miss, the University of Mississippi. He had excelled in football, baseball, basketball, and tennis. Just before the war he had signed a contract as an infielder with the Saint Louis Cardinals, but after four years in the service, he thought his chances of a baseball career had diminished, and he opted to stay in the Air Force. Because Jack was a little over his best playing weight, he didn't look like the athlete he was, and he fooled a lot of people. At that stage of his life he might not have made it into the big leagues, but most of the rest of us wouldn't have been starters in the Jules Verne League (20,000 leagues below the majors).

Jack played shortstop on our softball team and, in addition to his outstanding fielding, immediately became the Babe Ruth of the base. His first few times at bat he hit towering home runs, far over the heads of the opposing outfielders. Then when they had moved back into the next county, he would drop a hit just over the infield for a triple. Toward the end of a game he often announced that he would hit a home run for the folks that came late, and then he would do just that.

He was not very tall, but even in basketball he was by far the best player on the base. He was the first person I ever saw dribble behind his back or throw blind passes. He was an accurate shot and a master at faking people out of their shoes. In one game he made one of the funniest plays I have ever seen. He had stolen the ball at about midcourt and was dribbling toward the basket, with two taller players in pursuit and closing fast. When he got to the basket he stopped abruptly and threw his arms up as if shooting. Both opponents leaped high with their arms flailing to block the shot. When they came down Jack calmly shot a soft lay-up for a basket. He had caught the final dribble between his knees and thrown his empty arms up. The would-be blockers were totally baffled by the fake, as were most of those who saw it, and probably don't know how he did it to this day.

Later, after I had left Eglin, Jack was one of the pilots on Project Ficon (Fighter Conveyor), in which F-84s were modified to be carried in flight by modified B-36s so that the bombers could carry their own fighter escort or ferry camera-equipped RF-84Fs on long-range reconnaissance missions. After a long period of testing, these hook-ups were found to be feasible, and a strategic reconnaissance squadron was equipped with modified B-36s and RF-84Fs in 1955.

Just before the end of 1948, Eglin received an F-86A Sabre to be tested in the climatic hangar. The Sabre, a swept-wing fighter built by North American Aviation and powered by the 5,200-pound-thrust General Electric J47-GE-13, was the first fighter capable of exceeding the speed of sound, albeit in a dive. Not until the F-100 Super Sabre came along in 1952 was an operational fighter capable of supersonic speed in level flight.

Colonel Slocumb arranged for several of the pilots in Fighter Test, myself included, to make short checkout flights in the Sabre before it began its climate tests. In addition to the swept wings, it had nosewheel steering and leading-edge slats that opened automatically when the airplane approached a stall. They allowed the F-86 to land slower and turn tighter than would have been possible without the slats. Adding to my eagerness to fly the Sabre was the world speed record it had set on September 15, 1948, just two months earlier, of 670.981 mph. On these brief checkout flights we were told not to go supersonic—just get the feel of the airplane. That I did, and it felt good; everything seemed to be just the way it should be, there was good visibility, and it was stable yet maneuverable—a joy to fly. As much as I enjoyed that first flight, there was a slight moment of anxiety as I landed. Because of the swept wing, the nose was higher at touchdown than anything I had flown. The touchdown was smooth, but as I slowed and began to lower the nosewheel to the runway, the time before it touched seemed so inordinately long that I had a second or two of panic, fearing that the nose gear had not extended. As I taxied in toward the ramp I realized the reason for my anxiety. I had been flying F-84s exclusively for the past several weeks, and in that airplane the pilot sits farther back from the nose. The angle of sight over the nose was therefore much less than in the F-86, and unconsciously I had expected the nosewheel to touch when I had the same view over the nose as in the F-84.

The Sabre still is my favorite jet fighter. My opinion is shared by many pilots. I couldn't wait to fly one again, but it was not until three months later, in February 1949, that we received several F-86s and I began flying them regularly. Since I had never flown faster than sound, the first thing I did on my next flight was to climb to 40,000 feet and roll over into a vertical dive. The Mach needle moved up to and then past Mach 1, but the only sensation other than being in a vertical dive was a slight dip of the left wing as the plane went supersonic. Once the speed brakes on each side of the aft fuselage were extended, the Sabre dutifully slowed and backed across the sound barrier. It was quite a thrill to go through this mythical barrier that for so many years had seemed to be the upper limit of mankind's quest for speed. There were no restrictions on causing the sonic booms that occur each time a plane exceeds the speed of sound, so we all did it as much as possible, but always over the Eglin ranges. Breaking the barrier later became one of the regular features of our firepower demonstrations.

It is interesting to compare those vertical dives required to achieve supersonic flight at that period with the flights I took in the Concorde in 1989. In the Concorde, passengers sat comfortably, eating and drinking, while the digital Machmeter on the forward bulkhead smoothly climbed through Mach 1 and then inched past Mach 2, finally settling on Mach 2.1. There was absolutely no sensation, and only the warmth of the cabin walls and the windows indicated the great speed at which we were traveling. The Concorde trips, from Washington to Paris and return, were made to celebrate the occasion of Air France's promise to donate a Concorde to the National Air and Space Museum when it reaches the end of its service life.

Also in February the squadron received its first TF-80Cs, F-80Cs that had been modified for use as jet trainers by lengthening the fuselage 38½ inches and adding a fully equipped second cockpit. In all but the few models used for gunnery training, the armament was removed from the nose. The airplane was much better known by its later designation T-33, assigned in May 1949, or by its nickname, the T-Bird. It became the standard jet trainer for the USAF and many of its allies, including the U.S. Navy. Almost 6,000 were built before production ended in August 1959. In the squadron the T-33 was used for instrument training, to check pilots out, and for taking nonpilots up for rides in a *jet*. Several other pilots in the squadron and I were made instructor pilots so that we could check pilots out (or transition, as it was called officially) in jets. I did quite a bit of this and gained a lot of experience in flying the T-Bird from the backseat.

One of my first tasks as an instructor was to check out one of the pilots from the Experimental Guided Missile Squadron, which was scheduled to receive some drone F-80s in the near future. He was an experienced B-17 pilot as well as a drone pilot (who flew the radio-controlled drone by means of special controls in another aircraft). In the case of the drone F-80, he would have to control it from a T-33 since a nonjet would not be able to keep up with it. He had not flown small single-engine aircraft since basic flying school five or six years earlier, and it took several flights for him to get accustomed to the sensitivity of the T-Bird's controls, especially the ailerons. For the first hour we went through the air rocking the wings, which is the signal to join formation. Had there been any other planes around we might have ended up leading a large flight.

After a few flights, when he had a good feel for the airplane, he said he would like to try some loops and rolls. I showed him a few loops, and then he did one. He did it pretty well except for easing off the back pressure on the stick as we went over the top, causing us to float into the second half of the loop. He did much better on later loops, and I showed him a few rolls, which are quite simple in jets. The pilot just pulls the nose up and moves the stick to the side, and the plane rolls smoothly with the nose on a point. It takes little if any rudder, unlike a roll in a primary or basic trainer, which requires the pilot to coordinate the rudder and stick movements through-out and to use a lot of forward stick when inverted to hold the nose up. I thought I had explained it well, but his primary instructor must have im-pressed him more. As we rolled inverted he jammed the stick forward so hard that the accelerometer registered minus 1 g, my head hit the canopy, the air filled with debris from the cockpit floor, and the engine flamed out as the fuel, which feeds from the bottom of the tank, stopped flowing. I stopcocked the throttle, grabbed the stick, and pulled through the horizon into a shallow dive to keep the engine windmilling, then rolled upright. We had plenty of altitude, so I let him make the air start and then let him try a few more rolls, which he performed well with absolutely no forward stick.

Maj. Gen. William E. Kepner had been named commanding general of the Air Proving Ground Command and Lt. Col. Emmett S. "Cyclone" Davis had assumed command of the fighter test squadron in August 1948. Now that we had the T-33, General Kepner told Colonel Davis that he would like to fly it. Colonel Davis assigned me to fly with him and check him out. During the time I was privileged to spend with General Kepner, he told me a few stories from his remarkable career. He had quit high school to enlist in the Marine Corps, where he served for four years. He left the Corps to return to school in 1913. In 1916 he was commissioned in the Indiana National Guard and served in Mexico. The next year he was ac-cepted into the Regular Army and was promoted to first lieutenant. Later that year, as a captain and company commander in France, he fought at Château-Thierry and Saint-Mihiel and was decorated for heroism. He became interested in flying while at the front and asked to be trained as a pilot. Instead he was given command of a battalion in the Meuse Argonne campaign and was seriously wounded.

After the war he applied again for pilot training but was sent to balloon school instead of to airplanes. He made the best of it and won several of the major international balloon races for the U.S. Army. He also was trained as an airship pilot and served as the test pilot on the Army's experimental metalclad airship. Later, after being rated as a naval aviator, zeppelin pilot, he flew as assistant navigator on the Navy's rigid airship *Los Angeles*.

In February 1932, at the age of 39 with the rank of major, he finally received his airplane pilot wings, but he made one final balloon flight that was almost fatal. As part of a National Geographic Society and U.S. Army project, he and two crew members were launched in the balloon *Explorer I* in July 1934 to investigate the ozone layer, in which there remains a great interest today, in the upper atmosphere. The balloon envelope ripped open, and they descended rapidly, but under control, from 60,000 feet to 4,000 feet, where the balloon exploded. They all managed to bail out successfully, with General Kepner going last at 500 feet.

He held several fighter commands, culminating in August 1943, when he took over the Eighth Fighter Command in England, with the primary responsibility of providing escort for the Eighth Air Force bombers. Under his leadership the successful tactics of aggressive escort were developed, attacking enemy fighters wherever and whenever they could be found, in the air or on the ground. Among his postwar assignments was that of deputy commander for air of Operation Crossroads, the nuclear bomb tests in the Pacific.

Although he seemed awfully old to me at the time, at 51 he was an excellent pilot with a lot of fighter experience, and he had no trouble mastering the T-Bird. I was a little nervous watching him change glasses a couple of times on final approach, but it didn't seem to bother him or the airplane.

I made a slight faux pas when we had parked after the first flight. I was filling out the Form 1, the official record that must be completed following every flight. I knew his name and rank, but after recording them I asked him for his serial number. He replied, "Six A."

Incredulous, I exclaimed, "Six A!" I had never known anyone with fewer than four digits in his serial number.

He laughed and said, "A bit lower than yours, eh?"

"Yes, sir, 18,158 lower to be exact." When new serial numbers were assigned after the formation of the U.S. Air Force, he was the sixth ranking officer. I felt honored to have the opportunity to fly with a gentleman of such stature.

A few months earlier I had learned that I would be the test officer on a test to determine the suitability of the F-84 and the F-86 as night fighters. All previous USAAF and USAF night-fighter crews had comprised a pilot and a radar observer, and the Air Force wanted to determine if the pilot of a single-engine jet fighter could accomplish both roles. Since I had no previous experience with airborne radar, the project officer, Lt. Frank "Radar" Smith, spent a good deal of time sharing the knowledge he had amassed in his years as a radar observer in night fighters, Douglas P-70s and Northrop P-61s, in combat in the Pacific theater.

Frank was one of the most popular officers in the proof division. Raised on a farm in South Dakota, he was six or seven years older than most of the pilots when he entered the Army. In addition he was balding and rather portly, and this made him appear even older. Although a first lieutenant at the time, he could easily pass for a full colonel if his rank insignia were not visible, and he made every effort to keep them not visible. He said he was the terror of the visiting officer's quarters latrine. When he came in to shave in his underwear, young officers who actually outranked him deferred to him so that he could use the basin first. He always wore the billed garrison cap that does not display rank rather than the more comfortable flight cap that does. Since he was not a pilot, when he attended conferences someone had to fly him there, and when he strutted into operations in his flying suit, carrying a briefcase and followed by his pilot, he was sometimes mistaken for a general. He had, and still has, a prodigious memory for jokes, or "old gags," as he called them, and could dredge up several to fit any occasion.

Because of my inexperience with the intricacies of radar, Frank arranged for me to travel to the naval air station on Boca Chica Key, near Key West, where the Navy had a few trainers, Beech SNBs (C-45s in the Air Force), for some in-flight indoctrination. Accordingly, I was flown to Boca Chica by the Marine liaison officer at Eglin and the head of the weapons branch in the proof division, Lieutenant Colonel Hubbard. We arrived too late in the afternoon to begin my training, so the three of us went into Key West, where I was introduced to turtle steak and Key lime pie, both of which were delicious.

They left for Eglin in the morning, and I spent the day in ground school learning the details of the APS-19 radar set and how to operate it. The next two nights were spent in the right seat of the SNB with a radar instructor behind me, running practice intercept missions on a target SNB. The instruction was first class, and I acquired at least a modicum of skill in tuning the set for maximum efficiency, identifying and tracking targets, and minimizing the effect of ground clutter. Although airborne interceptions were the primary goal of my training, I also learned a bit about radar navigation and locating targets on the water. The next day Lt. Fred Belue from my squadron came down in an F-82 and flew me back to Eglin.

A short time later the F-84 arrived with the APS-19 radar in a pod mounted under the belly just forward of the cockpit and the radar scope in the middle of the instrument panel. As test officer I did most of the flying on the test, with Capt. Don Dessert, the operations officer who had flown night fighters in combat, and Rode Rodewald flying some of the missions.

The early test missions were flown in daylight to familiarize us with the system and to check the radar in its various modes. We found out immediately that it was impossible to see the images on the scope in the bright Florida sunshine, or in any bright sunshine for that matter. To read the scope it was necessary to use a scope hood, a long opaque tube that fit around the face of the scope on one end and the face of the pilot, or at least his eyes, on the other; these were standard equipment for radar observers. This solved one problem and added another. The scope images were now clearly visible, but the horizon and the flight instruments were not. The pilot's eyes could not adjust quickly enough from the darkness within the hood to the brightness of the cockpit to allow for quick checks outside the cockpit or of the flight instruments to control the airplane properly. If the pilot kept his eyes in the hood he ended up flying on his back or in some other unusual attitude (for a while I was ready to go back to the hammock seat test), and if he didn't he could not read the scope. That problem was solved by cutting a small hole in the hood, positioned so that the pilot could see the attitude indicator while keeping his eyes in the hood. On all daylight missions a safety pilot flew behind the radar plane to ensure that the pilot, with his head in the hood, did not collide with the target plane or with another aircraft. Quite often a T-33 was used as the safety plane, which allowed Frank Smith to ride along and monitor the mission firsthand.

After we overcame the growing pains, the daylight missions went quite well. We were able to locate and track airplanes ranging in size from B-29s to B-26s, and we could find even jet fighters, but only at short range. On one tracking mission, the squadron commander, Cyclone Davis, was flying the B-26 target plane. After making several passes on which the radar was not up to snuff, I decided to cancel the rest of the mission but did not tell Colonel Davis. Instead, I waved off the safety pilot and told Cyclone that I was going to try a high-speed pass from his left rear quarter. I advanced the throttle to full power and climbed several thousand feet above the B-26; then, as I started diving toward the target with a closing speed of about 150 mph, I began a running commentary, saying that I had him on the scope and was closing in from the left. About five seconds away I told him I had lost him, then put my eyes against the hood and passed him on the left, missing his left wing by a few feet. He screamed, "Lope, you almost hit me. What do you think you're doing?"

"I didn't realize I was that close," I said. "The radar is acting up."

He told me to go back and land and get it straightened out, which I did.

After landing, I didn't know whether to tell him I had done it on purpose and have him think me a clown or pretend it was an accident and have him think me an idiot. I decided that clown was better than idiot and told him it was just a joke. To my relief, he had a good sense of humor, which I had suspected since he had "Cyclone Davis, the Mormon Meteor, no guts, no glory" painted on his helmet and also since he had nicknamed his son Typhoon. In fact, he has kidded me about it over the years. Cyclone was the third commanding officer that I served under at Eglin, and by coincidence all had flown P-38s in combat: Colonel Muldoon in North Africa, Colonel Slocumb in Italy, and Colonel Davis in the Pacific. Maybe commanding two engines imbues one with leadership qualities.

The night-flying portion of the tests that followed began with simple missions in which the interceptor and the target plane met at a predetermined altitude and location, and both aircraft operated with their navigation lights (on both wingtips and the tail) turned on. The goal was to determine how effectively the interceptor pilot could locate and track the target without using the navigation lights as an aid. All flights were monitored by the GCI (ground-controlled intercept) radar so that the range at first radar contact, which the interceptor pilot read off his scope and noted on his knee board and simultaneously radioed to the ground, could be cross-checked by the ground radar. In almost every case the figures were in close agreement.

Don, Rode, and I found it much easier to operate without the scope hood. The scope was clearly visible in the dark cockpit, and it was not difficult to watch the scope and monitor the other instruments. As expected, tracking large, propeller-driven aircraft was not a problem, since they provide such a large radar-reflecting surface; the jet fighters could not be picked up by the APS-19 radar except at very short range. The GCI radar could not track F-80s unless they were equipped with radar transponders (electronic devices that transmit, when actuated by incoming pulses from the ground radar, a signal on the same frequency that shows up strongly on the ground radar scope), but the F-80's transponders did not work with the APS-19 in the F-84. We ran a great many missions recording the ranges and angles at which we could pick up and track the different types of targets to determine the capabilities of the APS-19 as installed in the F-84.

In the next phase of the test we ran night intercept missions versus bombers and jet fighters in which the targets were blacked out, but for safety the interceptor's lights were on. On these flights we attempted not only to locate the target with our radar but also to get into position for visual firing. The airborne radar sets of that era were far less sophisticated than those of today, and it was not possible to fire at and hit a target by radar alone. We were usually successful in making visual contact with the bombers but had far less success with the fighters. If we were able to pick them up with our radar we could get close enough to fire, but picking them up was the problem. With the bombers we found it better to stay a little below them, for two reasons: they presented a much larger visual target from below than from directly behind; and we didn't have to fly in the turbulent propwash, which makes accurate firing difficult. With the fighter targets we could sometimes see a bit of light if we were directly behind the tail pipe.

One pitch-black night I had a near accident that bordered on the bizarre. Joe Cotton had taken off about half an hour earlier in the B-29 that was to be my target so that he would be at altitude when I took off. It was hot with virtually no wind, and I knew that with full tip tanks and the radar set, the takeoff run would be long. Since runway 1 at Eglin is 10,000 feet long I didn't anticipate any trouble, and I was right, for about forty seconds. The airplane had lifted off about 6,000 feet down the runway, and I had just moved my hand to the gear handle to retract the wheels, when a yellow light on the instrument panel came on, indicating that the main fuel pump had failed and the emergency fuel pump had kicked in. The engine rpm dropped from 100 percent to 96 percent. At a higher altitude or airspeed that would not have posed a major problem, but the airplane would not fly at 96 percent in this situation, so I put it back on the runway, stop-cocked the engine, stood on the brakes, retracted the flaps to put more weight on the wheels to help braking, and opened the canopy. I told the tower I was aborting the takeoff and continued to brake hard, hoping to stop before the plane ran off the runway. I knew there was a dirt overrun of about 1,000 feet, a perimeter road, and then a drop-off into a swampy area. I ran off the end of the runway still moving at a good clip, but once on the overrun the soft sand helped slow the airplane. I was not certain it would stop before the drop-off, and when the perimeter road appeared in my landing light I reached for the gear handle to retract the wheels, but the plane shuddered to a stop just before the road.

Seeing flames flickering under both wings, I cut all the switches and jumped to the ground, where I saw that the brakes had ignited both tires. Using a crude but effective method, I managed to extinguish the flames by throwing sand on them. Then I moved back from the airplane to be out of the way if the tires exploded from the heat. I could hear the sirens and the engines of the crash vehicles, but instead of getting louder they seemed to be fading in the distance. Apparently, the tower had sent them to the south end of the runway, about two miles away. I tried to jump and catch the edge of the cockpit in order to climb back in and inform the tower of the error of its ways, but the sand, while excellent for fire fighting, was too soft for good jumping. After several tries I gave up and piled some sand into a sort of adult sand castle. Jumping from its ramparts, I managed to grab the cockpit rim and climb back in. I was about to call the tower when a jeep pulled up on the perimeter road with my crew chief and his assistants, who, realizing immediately that I had not gotten off the ground, had driven to the north end of the runway as fast as they could. Luckily, the airplane was not otherwise damaged. After replacing the brakes, tires, and fuel pump, we were able to fly it the next night. Joe Cotton told me that he also knew that I was at the north end of the runway but was unable to get through to the tower.

I related my experiences in the operations room the next morning and, when I returned from lunch, was presented with a flashy cardboard medal with the inscription "Royal Order of the Flaming Sandcrab." It wasn't much, but I had not received a medal in some time, and since no one else had that particular medal, I wore it proudly.

The final report of this test concluded that it was possible and practical for a pilot to operate effectively as a night fighter without the assistance of a radar operator but that the F-84/APS-19 should not be considered for this role. A more powerful radar, designed for single-pilot operation, was required. The original test program called for additional testing of the concept using an F-86 equipped with the APS-19. That phase was cancelled because of the difficulty of mounting the APS 19 on the F-86 and because of the shortcomings of the APS-19.

A few years later, the single-seat F-86D entered production and became the USAF's first-line interceptor. It had a modified nose that housed a new radar and weapon system designed for a single pilot and was armed with twenty-four 2.75-inch folding-fin aircraft rockets. More than 2,500 F-86Ds were produced, and about 350 F-86Ks (an advanced model of the D armed with 20mm cannon) were produced for use by NATO countries. The F-86D Sabre Dog remained in the USAF inventory until 1960 and in the Air National Guard until 1965.

19

Target Practice in 1949

The bomber test pilots at Eglin felt a bit behind the times, because the fighter squadron was the only one equipped with jets. Although many of them had been checked out in the T-33, they longed for the arrival of the first jet bomber at Eglin. Whenever possible we added to their longing by demonstrating the great disparity in speed between our respective aircraft. The preferred method of demonstrating this point was very effective. Often, when we spotted a bomber flying alone, not over a bombing range, we dived on it from behind, with a closing speed of about 200 mph, passing just below it and then pulling up suddenly in front of it. Besides the visual shock, the bomber would lurch violently in the jetwash, and the crew said that it smelled as though they were inside a kerosene tank. We occasionally attacked another fighter, but only a propeller-driven fighter, since the jets were too fast to allow for sufficient closing speed. I have had it done to me several times, and it certainly got my attention. After the first time, I noticed that as the jet passed below I could feel a slight lift, which gave me a fraction of a second's warning.

In April 1949 the light bomber squadron was notified that it would be receiving its first jet bomber, and the Air Force's first operational jet bomber: the North American B-45 Tornado, powered by four 4,000-pound-thrust General Electric J47-GE engines. (Later models had upgraded engines with 5,200 pounds of thrust, giving it a top speed capability of 579 mph.) Shortly afterward, the squadron's commander and the operations officer went to Los Angeles for a familiarization course on the B-45 at the North American Aviation factory and then went on to Edwards Air Force Base to be checked out. After their triumphant return as the first Eglin jet-bomber pilots, they would check out the other pilots in the squadron. Well, things did not quite work out as planned.

The first B-45 was delivered a few days after they left for California. The group commander and the squadron's assistant operations officer could not bear to see it parked forlornly on the ramp, unflown. The temptation became overpowering, so after carefully reading the pilot's operating instructions, they decided to check each other out. They were both fine pilots with a lot of experience, and on the first flight the group commander flew in the front seat with the ops officer in the back. After landing, the ops officer signed the transition certificate, certifying that the commander was qualified in the B-45. Then they switched seats and repeated the process. They flew it a number of times after that, and I think they checked out a few more pilots before the return of the two from California.

To say those two were chagrined is putting it mildly. They were prepared to bask in the glory of being the first to fly the first jet bomber at Eglin, and instead they found that it had been flying regularly since a few days after they left. It was a bitter blow. They probably would have taken some disciplinary action had the prime culprit not been the group commander. Rank is a most effective armor in the military.

Shortly after that incident, I was fortunate enough to fly as copilot in the B-45 through the kindness of the assistant culprit Capt. Mac Greenamyre, a good friend and one of the best pilots in the light bomb squadron. I found it easy to fly and much more responsive to the controls than other bombers I had flown. Also, it felt more like flying a fighter because the seats were in tandem rather than side-by-side. One hundred and nine B-45s were built, and they saw service in the United States and Europe. A photo-reconnaissance version, the RB-45C, saw action in Korea. They remained in the inventory until 1958.

The light bomb squadron had a Consolidated OA-10 Catalina amphibian flying boat (famous in the Navy as the PBY) that they were using for air-sea rescue tests. One afternoon, the test officer met me on the ramp and asked if I would like to fly it. I jumped at the chance, and about an hour later, after a cockpit checkout and some words of wisdom on water flying, I found myself in the left seat of a flying boat taxiing out for takeoff. After a long run we lifted off and climbed toward the east end of Choctawhatchee Bay, away from the Eglin runways. The water conditions in the bay were perfect, with some gentle waves driven by a 10-mph wind. With my instructor's guidance I made two good touch and go landings (on water they are called, appropriately, splash and dash). After the second one the instructor suggested that we come to a full stop on the next landing and take a brief swim in the bay (yet another advantage of an Air Force career). After the next touchdown I cut the power, and we stopped in a short distance, without the gentle deceleration I was used to on runways. Once off the step, it stopped almost immediately and went so low in the water that for a moment I thought my next command should be "Up periscope." I had never been in a PBY at rest in the water, and I didn't realize how close to the pilot's window the water level rose.

A few months later the OA-10 was transferred to the heavy bomber squadron, and shortly thereafter it crashed into the Gulf with tragic results. The pilots had been practicing landings in the bay to gain familiarity with the aircraft, since none of them had any previous flying-boat experience. Besides the regular crew of two pilots and a flight engineer, there were several other pilots and a group of bombardiers and navigators aboard getting in some of their required flying time. After the pilots had made a few landings in the bay, they decided to try some rough-water landings in the Gulf, which was about as rough that day as the Gulf gets except during a hurricane. The first landing was successful, but during the attempted takeoff, before the plane reached flying speed, it bounced high off a large wave, and the pilot instinctively pushed the nose down to keep from stalling and dived into an oncoming wave. The fuselage ripped open, and the plane sank like a stone. Most of those on board managed to escape, but the pilot and several of those up front were not able to get out and went down with the plane.

One of the most spectacular weapons that we tested was the 11.75-inch rocket known as the Tiny Tim. It was developed and used by the Navy during World War II to attack and penetrate the concrete Japanese bunkers on the Pacific islands. The exhaust plume from the rocket motor was so large that the Tiny Tim could not be launched directly from a standard wing rack. When the firing button was pressed, the rocket dropped from the rack still attached to the airplane by a lanyard, then fired when it was about six feet below the wing. The Tiny Tim was a proven weapon, but we were testing the capability of the F-84 to launch it with accuracy. Lt. Jack Fallon, who had recently joined the squadron from the 1st Fighter Group, was the test officer and did most of the firings; I launched only one pair of the rockets, but I flew as chase pilot on several missions to check the under-side of the F-84 for possible damage. There was no damage on the first missions, so there was no further need for a chase plane.

Evidently the editors of *Life* magazine thought that a Tiny Tim launch was spectacular, because they sent one of their photographers, Jay Eyer-man, to Eglin to photograph a few launches. This was accomplished on regular test missions because Tiny Tims were too expensive to fire just for the magazine. On the *Life* missions, Jack Fallon flew the F-84, and Cyclone Davis flew an A-26 with the photographer and me riding in the glass nose. My job was to pass information back and forth between Mr. Eyerman, Jack, and Cyclone by radio and intercom. I was also to advise him what to expect during the firings.

I was amazed at the equipment the photographer loaded in the nose: about four cameras of various kinds, a wet-cell automobile battery to run one of the large cameras, and a bag full of lenses, filters, extra film, and many items I did not recognize. There was barely room for us in the nose, so I rode in the jump seat next to Cyclone, except when I had to be in the nose. We flew two missions in the A-26, and Jack flew four in the F-84, fir-ing a total of eight Tiny Tims. He landed to be rearmed while we remained in the air. When the photographer was satisfied with the position of the F-84 relative to our plane, I gave Jack the signal to fire. Eyerman used two cameras at once, the motor-driven large camera and a 35mm camera, taking a series of shots with each. Not being familiar with professional photogra-phy, I thought he was wasting a lot of film, but he said that film was the cheapest part of the equation. A few months later the photos appeared in *Life,* and they were terrific.

In 1950 Jack Fallon was transferred to Korea; he returned to Eglin the next year after completing his tour. We were stationed in Washington then, and we were greatly saddened to hear that while Jack was flying under the hood in the backseat of a T-33, making a practice ground-controlled ap-proach, an F-84 collided with the T-33 about fifty feet above the ground, killing all three pilots. The tower had cleared the F-84 for a simulated flame-out approach (a steep overhead approach) on the same runway but had not been notified by the GCA operator of the T-33's approach.

One of the major problems in aerial gunnery training is the lack of suitable targets, especially since the advent of jet fighters with their higher speeds and high-altitude operation. The standard six-by-thirty flag targets flutter so violently at high speed that they tear apart. In addition, the ex-treme low temperatures encountered at high altitude make the wire mesh of the targets brittle, increasing their tendency to rip. For years we had been hearing rumors that the armament laboratory at Wright Field was developing a much-improved target that would eliminate these problems and make for much more accurate scoring. So far no such device had materialized. One day, however, Rode called and asked me to attend a briefing at the armament branch on the new target device, which was finally ready for firing tests. The briefer from the armament lab described the device, which was called the firing error indicator (FEI). It was an acoustic receiver that was to be towed behind an airplane where it could record the sound of bullets passing through a 25-foot radius in a vertical plane centered on the unit. It used a rho-theta method of recording the location of the bullets, rho being the range or distance from the center and theta the angle (zero degrees, in a 360-degree circle, representing a point directly above the center). For example, a bullet that passed 15 feet in front of the target at the target level would be recorded as rho 15, theta 90, while one that passed 15 feet behind, at the target level, would be recorded as 15-270. The ground testing had been successfully completed, and the device was now ready for the aerial firing tests, which would be run at Eglin starting in about two weeks. I was selected to be the test officer.

As expected, about two weeks later, a task force arrived from Wright Field to run the preliminary phases of the FEI tests. Although the FEI would be towed in operational use and in the latter phases of the test, there was so much instrumentation in the first phases that the FEI had to be installed in a PQ-14 target drone. The bright-red PQ-14, adapted from the Culver Cadet, a prewar sport airplane, was a low-wing monoplane with a wingspan of thirty feet and a length of nineteen feet six inches, powered by a Franklin O-300 engine. It had a top speed of about 120 mph. The remainder of the task force comprised a Beech CQ-3 radio-control mother ship, a modified C-45 that would control the PQ-14, and a B-17 that carried the recording instruments and the observers from the armament lab.

In accordance with the test program, the first firing missions would be accomplished by two F-84s with only two of the six .50-caliber machine guns loaded. Two additional F-84s, with all six guns loaded, would fly as safety planes to shoot down the PQ-14 if it was damaged or malfunctioned and headed toward the shore. The firing would be done over the Gulf ranges and away from the shore, the standard practice for aerial gunnery at Eglin. On the first mission Thomas "Hoot" Gibson and I would do the firing, with Don Dessert and Joe Young flying the safety fighters.

Just before the first mission we were briefed in detail by the project officer from the armament lab. He explained again the function of the FEI and its importance to future aerial gunnery training. It would permit immediate and accurate scoring by eliminating the tedious counting of various colored bullet holes in the target, which I remembered so well from my days at fighter gunnery instructor's school, and would identify what hits were made on each pass, which would be a great boon to the gunnery instructors.

To minimize the possibility of hitting the PQ-14, we were instructed to fire at a range of at least 750 yards (almost half a mile) at an angle-off of no less than 60 degrees. We were also to fire short bursts to be sure that only a minimum number of bullets would be recorded on each pass. I asked if we were supposed to aim directly at the target and was told that we should, since the objective was to get the bullets as close as possible to the target.

At the conclusion of the briefing the fighter pilots remained in the operations room until the Wright Field aircraft had taken off, then we went out to the armament area where the F-84s were standing loaded and ready. As soon as we were notified that the target aircraft was in position and the equipment was functioning, we took off. I was leading with Hoot on my wing, and Don led the safety planes with Joe on his wing. I quickly spotted the red PQ-14 at 5,000 feet flying parallel to the shore with the CQ-3 and the B-17 about a mile behind.

After asking for and receiving permission to begin firing, I made my first pass, using a high-side approach from about 1,000 feet above the target and ahead of it to ensure a high angle off. I had misjudged my position slightly and could not lead the target enough to fire. Hoot, who was following my pattern, had the same problem and did not fire. I started the second pass not quite so far ahead and was able to fire a short but evidently accurate burst. The PQ-14 emitted a large plume of smoke and, nosing over, dived into the Gulf. After enduring some raucous remarks including, "That was the shortest test on record, Deadeye," "Whose side are you on, Lope?" and a brief rendition of "Smoke Gets in Your Eyes" from the other pilots, I led the flight back to Eglin, gloating quietly to myself over my latest victory. I eschewed a victory roll because the PQ-14 was small and unarmed, but I did indulge in a victory bank. After landing, we taxied to the armament area, where the ammunition was unloaded. Then we taxied back to the flight line, where the crew chief immediately stenciled a silhouette of a PQ-14 on my fuselage just below the cockpit. I never did find out how he had prepared the stencil so quickly. Later, back in operations, the chief armorer reported that I had fired a total of only seven rounds. The CQ-3 and B-17 did not even land at Eglin but went directly back to Wright Field. We never heard from any of them or of the FEI again, which seemed rather strange, although Rode later learned that all the bullets had hit the target so no data were recorded by the FEI.

The next morning someone had expanded on the "Smoke Gets in Your Eyes" theme by writing the following new verse to the song on the blackboard:

> They asked Lope how he knew, that PQ was through.
> Laughing he replies, when it's in my sights it dies,
> And smoke gets in your eyes.

No one took credit for the verse, for obvious reasons.

I was sorry that the major effort of aerial testing of the FEI had gone for naught but was not surprised at hitting the target. I had always been good at aerial gunnery, and over the last few years I had gotten a great deal of practice firing from long range and high angle off during the P-38 gunsight test. Although the F-84 at that time was equipped with a fixed gunsight instead of the radar-ranging, lead-computing A-1 sight, the practice in smooth, accurate tracking paid off.

It is likely that the armament lab was on the right track with the acoustic system. In May 1986, the 75th Fighter Squadron held its reunion in Alexandria, Louisiana, home of England Air Force Base, where the squadron was then based. Part of the 23rd Tactical Fighter Wing, it was equipped with the Republic A-10 Thunderbolt II, a twin-jet, armored, ground-attack fighter armed with antitank missiles and a 30mm GAU-8/A Avenger gun with seven rotating barrels capable of firing 4,200 rounds a minute. The squadron put on a firing demonstration that was quite impressive, with A-10s popping up from behind hills, firing from long range at a target, and then disappearing behind other hills. As soon as each pass was completed, range control announced the number of hits the pilot had scored. I didn't think much of it at the time, but much later I found out that the target had an acoustic scoring device that instantly recorded and displayed in the control tower the number of rounds that had passed through the target.

I add with pride that the 23rd "Flying Tiger" Tactical Fighter Wing performed well in the Gulf War (Desert Storm). It was good to see those shark mouths on the noses of aircraft in action again, although I'm sure that all of us old-timers would agree that nothing looks as good as a shark mouth on the nose of a P-40.

Eglin Field, especially back in the late forties, was in a sparsely populated area, perfect for its mission but without much in the way of entertainment except for the magnificent beaches. But one does not live by sand alone, so the base personnel had to search out their own entertainment. Of course, the base theater was popular, since it ran all the latest films, and the price of admission was only fifteen cents. There was a little theater group that produced two or three plays a year. We also attended and enjoyed the weekend dances at the officer's club, which often featured name bands. The major event, however, was the annual Mardi Gras, including a big parade with prizes for the best floats and a fancy-dress ball at the club with awards for the best costumes.

I never have been one to enjoy playing dress up, but I did want to attend the ball. I would have settled for a false mustache as a costume, but Glyn came up with a much better idea—better for her, that is. She decided we would go as the Tin Man and Dorothy. All she had to do was braid her hair and wear a pinafore dress and hair ribbons. I was to be encased in cardboard boxes, funnels, and foil. I resisted as much as possible and even offered to switch roles, but she said that my hair was too short to braid. Although I had to agree, I held out until I came home from work a few days before the event and found the back porch covered with cardboard boxes, rubber gloves, and old shoes, all painted silver. I capitulated. I even joined in by making a wooden axe and painting it silver.

On the evening of the ball I struggled into my costume with a great deal of help from Glyn. My body, from shoulder to knee, fit into a long rectangular box, similar to the ones the airlines now use to encase garment bags. Another box, a one-foot cube, with a large funnel on top and a smaller one on the front for a nose, went over my head. My arms and legs were wrapped in heavy aluminum foil, and my shoes and gloves were painted silver. On the back of the box on my head, Glyn wrote in red nail polish, "My wife made me wear it!" We ran into a problem immediately— I was not able to get into the car. I had to remove my head and body boxes, put them on the backseat, and climb gingerly into the front seat, trying to disturb the foil wrappings as little as possible.

Glyn kindly let me out at the side of the officer's club, and while she parked the car, I took my boxes behind some bushes and donned them once more. Carrying my axe, I emerged from the bushes, whereupon, because of my limited peripheral vision, I bumped into a man who was cutting through the open area next to the club. He sprang back and emitted something between a gasp and a scream. When I apologized, he said, "You scared me half to death, and I'm not afraid of anything." I judged from the smell of his breath that he was as well oiled as the original Tin Man, only with a different lubricant.

Glyn joined me, and we entered the club together. We met Don and Fran Dessert in the entrance, and right away I knew it was going to be a long evening. When Don finally stopped laughing, he blew cigarette smoke into my nose funnel and said, "Are you really in there, Lope?" As I was not able to sit down, I spent much of the evening standing against the wall drawing curious stares, raucous remarks, several more visits by Don and various squadron mates, and a bit more smoke. I could not drink anything until Glyn brought a Coke with a bent straw that would reach my mouth. I tried to dance a few times without a lot of success, but then I was not much of a dancer, even unboxed. I was standing for more than four hours, something that is especially difficult for fighter pilots, who even fight sitting down.

Finally, at midnight, the contest for best costumes got under way. After we all marched by the judges' table a few times, they announced the winners. Glyn's inspiration and labor and my ordeal had not been in vain. I won first prize for men's costume and the prize for best overall costume (overalls would have been more comfortable). Both prizes were twenty-dollar bills, which we used to begin a collection of Russell Wright pottery.

Meanwhile, the squadron had begun conducting tests with the F-84D, a much improved version of the earlier models. As part of the operational suitability testing, there was an extensive evaluation of the use of JATO (jet-assisted takeoff, sometimes more accurately called RATO, for rocket-assisted takeoff) on F-84s to allow takeoffs with heavier loads from shorter runways. Two JATO units, solid-fuel rockets providing 1,000 pounds of thrust each, were mounted below the fuselage just aft of the wing, one on each side. They were ignited together by activation of a cockpit switch and burned out in approximately fourteen seconds. The object of these tests was to determine the optimum point of firing in the takeoff run at various gross weights. Firing too late minimizes the effect of the JATO in reducing the takeoff roll, but firing too early can leave the airplane in a dangerous nose-up attitude at too low an airspeed.

For me, by far the most exciting part of a JATO takeoff was not when the rockets ignited, but when they burned out. The pilot must climb more steeply after liftoff than would be possible without JATO to ensure clearing obstacles at the end of the runway. If the pilot doesn't keep track of the burn time and lower the nose at thirteen seconds, the expression "Up the creek without a paddle" applies quite well to the situation, except in this case the canoe has about 800 gallons of flammable fuel on board.

We determined that the units should be fired so that one half of the burn occurred before liftoff and one half after. Applying this rule meant firing them at speeds ranging from 85 mph with no external loads up to 135 mph with the maximum load. With full fuel and ammunition, eight 5-inch rockets, and two 500-pound bombs, the takeoff distance was reduced from 5,500 feet for a maximum performance takeoff without JATO to 4,200 feet with JATO.

Before we leave the subject of JATO let me relate an incident at one of our firepower demonstrations. After the morning demonstration at Range 52 the dignitaries were transported to the officer's beach club for lunch followed by some additional events. One of these was a water landing and JATO takeoff by a Grumman SA-16 Albatross amphibian flying boat flown by Capt. Pete Branch, its test officer. The Gulf was rather rough that day, but Pete made a good landing and, after taxiing into position, started his takeoff run. At the proper time in the run the nose came up, the airplane bounced off a wave into the air, and slammed back into the water, nose high, with a tremendous splash. Then out of the splash the Albatross emerged in a steep climb with the JATO burning. It was a spectacular sight; the Albatross looked like a submarine-launched Polaris missile emerging from the deep. Later, Pete told us that just as he pulled back the wheel to start the climb and reached for the JATO switches on the cockpit ceiling, the plane hit a large wave, causing him to miss the switches. As soon as he hit the water he tried again and succeeded. We told him that it looked so good he should make it part of his act in future demonstrations, but he wisely demurred.

The deficiencies (a mild word for wing failure) encountered on the tests of the earlier models of the F-84 had supposedly been corrected in the D model. The major modification was the installation of a stronger wing. The test program for the F-84D was wide-ranging, as evidenced by the following excerpt taken from the Headquarters USAF directive authorizing the test: "This test should include an evaluation of the aircraft with respect to dive-bombing, ground strafing, aerial gunnery, range (both as a dive bomber and escort fighter), and instrument, night and formation flying. Also, the ease with which maintenance and inspection can be accomplished."

Three production F-84Ds were used for the tests along with seven J35-A-13 engines, five of which had been provided by Republic Aviation and which produced 200 300 pounds more thrust than the average production engines. This attempt to influence the test results did not have the intended effect. During the interceptor phase, actual intercepts of B-29s and of F-80s (simulating jet bombers) were run in the same manner as during Project Highball. The F-84 was scrambled from a position next to the active runway. Times were recorded from scramble signal to start of takeoff roll, to achieving best climb speed at sea level, to reaching target altitude, and to reaching best operating speed for the attack. The target aircraft flew missions at 5,000-foot increments from 20,000 to 40,000 feet. We immediately found that the ground radar was unable to paint (track) the F-84D, so the tests were delayed until a transponder beacon (AN/APN-19) could be installed on one F-84D. On the 40,000-foot mission the tail-pipe temperature exceeded the upper limit above 35,000 feet at 100 percent rpm. To remain within limits it was necessary to reduce the rpm, which materially reduced the climb and acceleration of the aircraft. Later it was discovered that this problem existed only in the higher-thrust engines.

The average time from scramble signal to start of takeoff roll was one minute and thirty seconds, and the time from start of takeoff roll to best climbing speed was one minute and fifteen seconds. The total time from scramble signal to 40,000 feet was twenty-three minutes, during which the interceptor covered 122 miles. (Today, an F-16 can climb to 40,000 feet in a small fraction of that time.) It was noted that improper pilot technique in holding the recommended best climbing speed at each altitude, which decreases from 370 mph at sea level to 235 mph at 40,000 feet, and failure to transition smoothly between these speeds can add three to four minutes to the climb. Also, on the return leg, descents for maximum range with minimum fuel consumption should be flown at 0.8 Mach, descending at 3,000 feet per minute. Later, shorter times to climb to 40,000 feet were achieved by leveling out at 35,000 feet, accelerating to maximum speed, and zooming to 40,000 feet.

The escort-fighter phase of the test was conducted in a similar manner to the interceptor phase in that simulated missions were flown escorting B-45s and B-29s at 25,000, 30,000, and 35,000 feet. Since only three F-84s were available for the missions, and escort missions usually involve large numbers of fighters, it was not possible to determine the effectiveness of the F-84 in defending the bombers from the intercepting fighters.

While escorting B-45s at 25,000 feet, the F-84D had a combat radius of action of 460 miles, and at 35,000 feet it increased slightly to 475 miles. The tip tanks were retained on these missions. On a theoretical mission with a B-45 at 35,000 feet, in which the tips were jettisoned when empty, the radius of action went up to 580 miles. On this mission part of the internal fuel was used during the outbound leg of the flight, so with larger tip tanks the range could be extended even farther. On all of the escort missions the fighters were required to be over the home base at 10,000 feet with no less than 100 gallons of fuel remaining.

Only seven practice missions to determine the combat radius of action in the fighter-bomber role were flown, because the results matched the calculated figures so closely that further missions were unnecessary. The major emphasis of the tests was to determine the capability of the F-84 to deliver the full range of fighter-bomber weaponry: guns, bombs, and rockets. Since a separate test of the A-1B gun-bomb-rocket sight was under way at Eglin, only the functional aspects of the weapons and their effect on the airplane structure were tested. Accuracy of delivery was not considered.

Approximately 46,000 rounds of ammunition were fired at various altitudes and g-loads. Few malfunctions occurred, and there was no damage to the airplanes caused by the firing. The pipper of the A-1B sight vibrated so much during firing (20 mils plus) that target tracking was impossible. One night mission was flown during which the glare from the fuselage guns was so intense that no additional night firing was attempted.

Seventy-four 500-pound and 1,000-pound general-purpose bombs were dropped at airspeeds ranging from 450 to 560 mph and dive angles of 0 to 45 degrees. No adverse pitching characteristics were encountered at bomb release with the fixed-pylon bomb racks that had replaced the retractable racks on the F-84B, nor were there any rack malfunctions. On several pullouts from high-speed dives, more than 7.5 g's were registered on the accelerometer. Despite the pullouts and several intentional hard landings with 500-pound bombs aboard, there were no pulled rivets, nor was there any skin wrinkling or other structural damage. When napalm tanks were dropped at speeds in excess of 430 mph, however, the right tank would bounce off the fuselage. This problem had been encountered earlier by Republic Aviation, but no solution had been found at the time of the final report.

The final report concluded that the F-84D was satisfactory as an interceptor up to an altitude of 35,000 feet, as a short-range escort fighter, and as a fighter-bomber but that it should not be procured beyond the present contract, because a more advanced model, the F-84E, was entering production. The A-1B gun-bomb-rocket sight was found to be unsatisfactory, and it was recommended that no further production be authorized until its deficiencies had been corrected.

The operational suitability testing of the A-1B sight in the F-84D overlapped the test of the airplane itself. The sight, manufactured by the Sperry Corporation, was the first production version of the A-1 (Davis-Draper) sight, which had been tested at Eglin for several years in a P-38 with good results. Most of the problems with the A-1B arose during the air-to-air gunnery phase. Although the sight was designed to use radar for its range input, radar was not yet available on the F-84D, so manual ranging was required, and the pilots found it difficult to range properly using the backup manual system. The computing unit of the sight used vacuum tubes, since transistors were just being developed and were not yet in wide use. Vacuum tubes are sensitive to vibration, and there was a great deal of vibration when the six machine guns were firing, so maintenance was excessive. Also, the firing caused the sight pipper to fluctuate so much that tracking was impossible. On nonfiring tracking passes on B-29s, pilots were able to track with about a six-mil error, which is acceptable. I did not participate in the gunnery phase; to eliminate the pilot variable, the test officer flew all those tests himself.

In the rocket-firing phase three pilots, with minimal experience in rocket firing, fired 118 rockets at speeds ranging from 202 to 512 mph and dive angles from 3 to 35 degrees. The sight functioned well in the rocket mode, since ranging was not required, and accurate results were obtained.

In the accuracy phase of the bombing test, ninety-four 500-pound general purpose bombs were dropped in pairs at various altitudes, entry airspeeds, and dive angles. All were released automatically by the sight. With the A-1B sight, the pilot rolled into the dive with the sight reticle caged. When the pipper, in the center of the reticle, was on the target the caging switch was released. The sight began tracking as the pilot held the pipper on the target while depressing the bomb release switch. The airplane flew a slightly negative-g path, and at the proper time the sight released the bombs, and the pilot pulled out of the dive. Bomb release was signaled to the pilot by a flashing light on the gunsight and by the reticle's going out. In the manual mode the pilot depressed the bomb release button when the reticle went out.

I flew about one fourth of these missions and was able to save considerable time by flying two missions without refueling. We were using a bombing range to the northeast of the field, so I took off to the north, climbed to the entry altitude en route to the range, rolled into the dive, released the bombs, let down on the way back, and landed to the south. The armorers, who were standing by at the taxiway at the runway's end, loaded the bombs with the engine running. Then I took off and repeated the process. It was safe to load the bombs next to the runway because they were inert, carrying only a small spotting charge.

Two pilots, experienced in dive-bombing (not Ray Evans), made comparison drops in F-84Ds using fixed sights. The A-1B sight in the automatic mode was generally superior to the fixed sights, especially at higher release altitudes. In rough air the A-1B had a tendency to release the bombs too early, causing them to hit short of the target, but the fixed sight bombing was adversely affected by rough air as well.

The final report stated that the A-1B sight was unsuitable for air-to-air gunnery for the reasons stated above, but it was suitable for air-to-ground gunnery, rocketry, and dive-bombing. Later, after considerable modification it became the standard USAF fighter gunsight.

On Friday, September 23, 1949, we learned that the United States' atomic advantage over the Soviet Union had been lost, thus increasing the fears of the Cold War. That morning, Colonel Davis called all the squadron officers together and announced that the Soviets had successfully exploded an atomic bomb. The United States learned of it when an Air Force reconnaissance plane detected intense radioactivity in the air over the Pacific. President Truman announced it to the country that same day. There never was any doubt that they would be able to develop the bomb, but it came four or five years earlier than expected. Later it was discovered that the development of the bomb had been expedited by the turnover of vital technical information to the Soviets by spies and traitors in England and the United States. The next month Communists completed the takeover of China, and the People's Republic of China was formed.

Also in 1949, thanks largely to the efforts of the newly appointed secretary of state, Dean Acheson, the North American Treaty Organization (NATO) was formed, linking the United States, Canada, and ten nations of Western Europe in a mutual defense pact that proved to be a remarkably successful deterrent to the Soviets' aggressive plans for expansion. The Federal Republic of Germany was organized with Konrad Adenauer as chancellor. Known better as West Germany, it later became a strong member of NATO. East Germany was a Communist state ruled by the Soviets. Ireland became the Republic of Eire. The Soviets and the United States withdrew their troops from Korea. Events in Korea and Vietnam would loom large in the future of the United States.

It was a good year for the arts. Rodgers and Hammerstein's musical *South Pacific* opened on Broadway, Arthur Miller published his play *Death of a Salesman,* and George Orwell published *1984.* The Christmas favorite "Rudolph the Red-Nosed Reindeer" was written by Johnny Marks. Albert Schweitzer published *Hospital in the Jungle.* The film version of the novel *All the King's Men,* based on the life of Huey Long, won the Academy Award for best picture, and its stars Broderick Crawford and Mercedes Mc-Cambridge won acting Oscars.

The Atomic Energy Commission announced the development of a breeder reactor that provided energy while creating more fuel than it used. In England, Geoffrey De Havilland introduced the first jet airliner, the ill-fated Comet. As the world entered the second half of the twentieth century, the U.S. Bureau of Standards forever abolished a prime excuse for being late to work when it developed an atomic clock accurate to one second in three billion years.

20

The Last Year of Heaven

ne of the major difficulties in instrument flying in fighters was the reaction of the primary reference instrument, the artificial horizon, to roll and pitch. If an airplane banked, climbed, or dived too steeply, the gyro tumbled, and the instrument became useless until the plane resumed straight and level flight and the pilot caged and reset it. Normally, a pilot performed violent maneuvers only in clear weather, and the gyro instruments would be caged to prevent damage. However, if because of vertigo or extreme turbulence the pilot exceeded the limits of the instrument, he would be deprived of its use when he needed it most. In late 1949 we began to test a new attitude indicator, the A-1 vertical gyro, that would not tumble regardless of the attitude of the aircraft; it would indicate correctly through 360 degrees of pitch and roll. The instrument's display was different from the artificial horizon's in that the horizon bar was replaced by a ball on which the equator represented the horizon. The upper half of the ball was gray, representing the sky, and the lower was black, representing the ground. It was immediately nicknamed the eight ball.

It was installed in the rear cockpit instrument panel of the T-33, and after some flights to familiarize us with the presentation, the testing got under way. The objectives were to determine if the gyro would remain erect, not tumble, regardless of the airplane's attitude and to evaluate its suitability for precision instrument flying.

To satisfy the first objective the pilot performed many aerobatic ma-

neuvers and combinations of aerobatic maneuvers while observing the instrument. In some of the most violent maneuvers the gyro did tumble, but
its self-erecting mechanism quickly restored it. In the second series of tests,
one pilot flew under the hood (a canvas cover that fits inside the canopy
blocking the pilot's view outside the airplane) in the backseat. The pilot in
the backseat closed his eyes while the safety pilot in the front seat rolled,
zoomed, and dived, leaving the plane in an unusual attitude—in a wing-
low climb approaching a stall; in a screaming, rolling dive; upside down;
or whatever the evil mind of the safety pilot could devise. When the safety
pilot shook the stick, the backseat pilot took control and tried to return to
level flight by reference to the attitude indicator and the other flight instruments (airspeed indicator, altimeter, rate-of-climb, directional gyro, bank-
and-turn). Sometimes in attempting to recover, the pilot under the hood
put the airplane in an even more unusual attitude, including a few spins. Of
course, the backseat pilot would get his revenge on the next flight when
they switched cockpits. Following that phase we flew a large number of
ground-controlled approaches and other precision instrument procedures
under the hood. Once we became used to the new instrument, we found it
a great improvement over the old one and were much more confident in
our ability to fly under all weather conditions.

The A-1 vertical gyro was approved for installation in USAF planes,
and although improved throughout the years, the same basic system has
been used in virtually all military planes ever since. In the latest "glass cockpits," in which the attitude indicator and other instruments are displayed
on cathode ray tubes, the eight ball is still used as a backup.

Although there were still a few F-80s in the fighter squadron, most of
our testing was performed in F-84Es and F-86As, both of which were undergoing operational-suitability tests. The F-84E was the latest model of
the Thunderjet and was a rugged, reliable plane. As usual we were doing a
great deal of bombing, rocketry, and gunnery to ensure that all the systems
functioned properly. The high-g gun firing was tiring, but at least the
F-84E cockpit was air-conditioned, helping to alleviate that wrung-out
feeling we had experienced in the F-80 when the cockpit temperatures
often exceeded 120 degrees. The tests went well with no structural or control problems, and the mechanics found the airplane much easier to maintain than the earlier models, a vital factor in combat aircraft.

On one of these gunnery flights I made a careless mistake that did no
harm but certainly focused my mind. I was letting down from 20,000 feet
on the way back to the field after expending my ammunition, and though

still over the Gulf, I was approaching the shore when I spotted a bright green splotch on the water about five miles from the shore and about five miles to the west of me. The splotch was the sea-marker dye that each pilot carries on his Mae West or life raft to make it easier for searchers to locate him. I started diving toward the splotch to see if a pilot was down in the Gulf and was about two miles away when there was a tremendous fiery explosion about 1,000 feet above the splotch. I pulled more g's than I ever had in combat with a Zero on my tail in turning back for shore. Then it dawned on me that a B-29 was scheduled to test airburst fire bombs over the Gulf that morning. Luckily no one saw me, and I haven't mentioned it to anyone until now, so please don't tell.

About two weeks before, Captain Hank Pashco, one of the squadron pilots, was engaged in a gunnery test in the F-86 when it caught fire, and he was forced to eject over the Gulf. The ejection seat and the parachute both functioned properly, and he landed safely in the Gulf. He had radioed that he was ejecting, and by good fortune another pilot spotted him descending in the parachute and circled his position until a crash boat arrived and picked him up. He was not injured and, aside from having swallowed a bit of the Gulf, was in fine shape. I think that his recent bailout led me to connect sea-marker dye with downed pilots instead of air-burst bombs, but that's not much of an excuse.

It has been said that flying is the second greatest thrill on earth; landing is the first. If that is true, the pilots in the fighter test squadron led an extremely thrilling life. Because of the high fuel consumption of the early jet fighters, especially at low altitudes, their speed in getting to and from the various ranges, and the nature of our weapons tests, we made an inordinate number of landings for the number of hours we flew. In looking over my Form 5 (official Air Force logbook) I found that in six months I made 176 landings but flew just 99 hours in ten different types of aircraft. That figures out to 1.77 landings per flying hour or 1 landing per 34 minutes. In addition, during the same period I flew twenty-five GCAs, all with simulated missed approaches, while testing the A-1 vertical gyro. I was fortunate to have made the same number of landings as takeoffs, which is one criterion for a successful flying career. One other criterion that I met was never being examined by a pathologist.

Ray Evans and I played a dirty trick on one of the flight engineers assigned to the base flight squadron. That squadron had a few C-45s, B-25s, B-26s, and C-47s to be flown mostly by pilots on the base who were not in flying jobs but still had to fly a certain number of hours per year to meet the minimum USAF requirements. Most were good pilots, but a few were a bit rusty. All of these aircraft had enlisted flight engineers who accompanied the planes on cross-country flights. One of them was a staff sergeant who was afraid of flying, but he needed the flight pay to help support his six children. His natural apprehension had been enhanced by some bad experiences with a few of the rusty pilots.

About three years earlier Barney Turner, Dick Jones, and I took one of the Base Flight B-25s on a weekend cross-country accompanied by that sergeant. Dick and I were flying the first leg, and as we climbed into the cockpit the sergeant said, "Major Turner, I hope you will do most of the flying, because Captain Jones and Captain Lopez are fighter pilots." When Barney noted that he too was a fighter pilot, the sergeant whipped out his wallet and showed us pictures of his children and implored us to please be particularly careful. We assured him that we were every bit as interested as he was in having a safe flight. Since the weather was excellent the flight was smooth and uneventful.

The dirty trick started innocently enough when the base operations officer asked me to find a copilot and fly a C-47 to Brookley Air Force Base in Mobile, Alabama, about 100 miles west of Eglin, to pick up some cargo. Ray Evans agreed to accompany me, and we went to Base Flight, filed the clearance, and went out to the airplane. Who should be waiting there but the nervous father of six; he became more nervous when he learned that fighter pilots would be flying his C-47.

All went well on the short flight to Brookley. While the cargo was being loaded, Ray and I grabbed a bite at the snack bar, and the sergeant went to visit some friends on the base. After filing a clearance for the return flight, I went into the cargo office and signed the manifest and the weight-and-balance form. We were loaded with some 2,000 pounds of lighting equipment for the softball fields, consisting mostly of large floodlights and some aluminum mounting fixtures, well below the C-47's load limit of more than 5,000 pounds. But when we arrived at the airplane it looked as though we had 10,000 pounds aboard. The cabin was jammed with large cardboard boxes, and there was barely room to squeeze through to the cockpit. Just about then, the sergeant returned, and when he looked into the cabin he almost fainted. He protested that we couldn't possibly get off the ground with that kind of a load. I told him that I was pretty sure we could, because the runway was fairly long. He did not seem at all reassured but climbed in and followed us forward to the cockpit anyway.

After we had checked the engines and were ready to take off, I told him to go to the back of the cockpit area and keep his eye on the cargo during the takeoff run, because we would be in real trouble if it shifted. After he went back I told Ray to lean toward the center of the cockpit so the sergeant couldn't see the engine instruments. I advanced the throttles slowly to about 80 percent of the normal takeoff setting. The acceleration was barely noticeable, and we used well over three fourths of the runway before lifting off. By the time he came forward, white as a sheet, I was using the standard climbing power setting, and he remained convinced that the long takeoff roll was due to the excess weight. He looked so worried that we were sorry to have added to his normal ration of terror. It wasn't quite enough to cause him to quit flying, but he did quit flying with fighter pilots.

I was doing a lot of flying on the F-86A suitability and armament tests, and whenever possible I sneaked in a sonic boom or two. The Sabre was a joy to fly, and the testing went smoothly with a minimum of problems. During the armament tests we encountered a design problem that was easily solved. The Sabre was armed with six .50-caliber machine guns, three on each side of the nose. To reduce drag as much as possible the gun ports had retractable metal covers that were flush with the fuselage skin, except when the guns were firing. When the pilot pulled the trigger, the aft ends of the covers retracted inward, leaving a clear path for the bullets. When the trigger was released, the covers returned to their original flush position. There were actually two related problems with this system. The gun-port covers cut off the airflow to the guns after firing, preventing them from cooling properly. In addition to reducing the life of the gun barrels, the overheating increased the number of rounds that fired spontaneously (cooked off). Normally, the round that cooks off doesn't hit anything and is not a problem. In this case, however, it shot off part or all of the metal cover. The solution was obvious: remove the doors and accept the small drag penalty, which was done.

One of the pilots on the F-86 tests was Flight Lieutenant Williams, a Royal Air Force exchange officer assigned to the squadron. Flight lieutenant is the equivalent in rank to captain in the USAF. During the accuracy phase of the armament test he was firing at a ground target in a 30- or 40-degree dive when he failed to pull out, flew into the target, and was killed. The accident was attributed to target fixation (waiting too long to start the pullout), which happens occasionally in strafing attacks and ground gunnery. During the next few years there were several similar accidents, also attributed to target fixation. A near accident in an F-86 brought to light a problem that may have been the cause of several or maybe even all of these crashes.

A pilot firing at a ground target in a Sabre had just begun his pullout when the stick grip broke off in his hand. He was high enough, and quick enough, to grab the stick below the handle and recover safely from the dive. Upon inspection it was discovered that extensive corrosion had weakened the connection. The corrosion was caused by electrolytic action due to slight leaks in the wiring that was routed through the stick to the controls in the stick grip (gun trigger, bomb release button, trim controls, and nosewheel steering button). Heavier insulation on the wires eliminated the electrical leaks, and to my knowledge the problem never recurred.

There was one test program that seemed pointless at first. Called Rockets for Interceptors, it involved the firing of rockets from F-84s and F-86s at high altitudes. It seemed pointless because there were no targets to shoot at with our five-inch HVARs. We were just to fire them and observe whether they ran straight. Shortly afterward the reason for the tests became clear when the first Lockheed F-80C arrived for suitability testing. It was essentially a T-33 modified for use as an all-weather interceptor, with radar in the nose and the radar operator's position in the rear cockpit. The armament was twenty-four 2.75-inch folding-fin aircraft rockets (FFARs) mounted around the circumference of the nose. It was the first use of the lead-collision sight, which aimed the rockets at a point ahead of the target, where the rockets and the target would arrive simultaneously. Before the system was tested for accuracy, a functional test of the rockets themselves had to be completed. A major discrepancy emerged in these tests. When the rockets were fired in salvo, all twenty-four at once, which was the standard procedure, the engine flamed out. The first occurrence was thought to be a coincidence, but it happened every time the rockets were fired. This did not inspire much confidence in the crew, since they were essentially shooting themselves down. No airplanes were lost, but in combat in bad weather, the potential was there.

The position of the rockets relative to the engine air intakes, which were on either side of the fuselage about five feet behind the rocket tubes, was responsible for the flameouts. When the rockets were fired, the oxygen-depleted smoke went into the air intakes and deprived the engine of enough oxygen to support combustion. After a great deal of agonizing, a team of Lockheed and Allison engineers came up with a solution. The engine control was modified to reduce momentarily, when the rockets were fired, the fuel flow to a level that could maintain combustion with the reduced supply of oxygen.

There was a great deal of testing of the lead-collision sight with 2.75-inch FFARs over the next year or so, much of it after I had left Eglin. It was the primary interceptor weapons system for many years and was installed in both the F-86D Sabre Dog and the Northrop F-89 Scorpion. Neither aircraft had the air intakes behind the rockets. Although the system functioned well, it had to be tested by firing at actual targets. Since towed targets were not suitable for rocket firing, drone aircraft had to be used. Accordingly, several firing tests with live rockets were flown against B-17 drones. The system proved to be quite accurate, with tragic results on one occasion.

On a hazy Florida afternoon, an F-86D followed by an F-86A chase plane took off for a firing test against a B-17 drone. Once the drone was in position over the Gulf with the B-17 mother ship about a mile behind it, the F-86D turned for a firing pass. The pilot was flying on instruments, guided by the lead-collision system, but he had unknowingly locked his radar on the mother ship instead of the drone. Because of the haze, the chase pilot did not realize what was happening and did not alert the F-86D pilot to the error. In the pilot's defense, it was difficult to tell what the target was because of the long range at which the rockets were fired and because the aiming point was not the B-17 itself but a point well in front of it. The F-86D pilot continued tracking the mother ship, and at the proper time the rockets fired automatically, blowing the B-17 out of the sky, with the loss of most of the crew and observers aboard. It was a costly way to prove a system.

In March 1950, Colonel Davis and I, both avid baseball fans, decided that we ought to try to see a spring-training game before the major league teams left Florida to start the season. My mother lived in Tampa, just across the bay from St. Petersburg, where the New York Yankees trained. Since the Yankees are my favorite team, I suggested that we fly to Tampa, borrow my mother's car, and drive to St. Pete to see the Yankees play the Cardinals. Cyclone agreed that it was a good idea, so on the morning of the game I flew a Sabre to MacDill Air Force Base and met my mother, who worked in the communications office on the base. About an hour later Cyclone arrived in a B-26 with a couple of our squadron mechanics who were baseball fans. I picked them up at operations, and we drove to the ballpark in St. Petersburg for the game.

I hadn't seen any big-league baseball since 1940, and my one and only minor league game had been a Birmingham Barons game two years earlier. It was a thrill to see the great players at close range rather than as minuscule figures in a giant stadium. I saw Joe DiMaggio, Yogi Berra, Gerry Coleman, Phil Rizzuto, Bobby Brown, Allie Reynolds, Whitey Ford, Vic Raschi, Ed Lopat, Johnnie Mize, and many others. We enjoyed the game as well as the atmosphere, but it ran a bit longer than anticipated, and we got back to MacDill rather late. Cyclone said he had a commitment at Eglin that evening that he could not make if he flew the B-26 back, but he could make it in the Sabre. Guess who flew the B-26 back. Since he hadn't worn a helmet and oxygen mask in the B-26, he had to use mine. I told him it would be dangerous wearing a helmet that did not have "The Mormon Meteor" painted on it, but he said he would take the risk.

In October I was able to complete the baseball cycle that started in spring training by attending the second game of the World Series in Philadelphia, between the New York Yankees and the Phillies. The Yankees had won the first game, 1 to 0, but the Phillies had surprised the Yankees by starting their stellar relief pitcher, Jim Konstanty. In the second game Robin Roberts opposed the Yankee's Allie Reynolds. With the score tied at 1 apiece, Joe DiMaggio ended it with a home run in the tenth inning. He also made a couple of great fielding plays and, as always, lived up to his reputation.

As a lifetime baseball fan I was flabbergasted, while a graduate student at Cal Tech, that Don Larson's perfect game in the 1956 World Series seemed to go unnoticed among the other students. Obviously they found Fourier series more exciting than the World Series.

In May, along with several others from Eglin, I began a four-month assignment to attend the Air Tactical School at nearby Tyndall Air Force Base in Panama City, Florida, Glyn's home town. We sublet our house in Cinco Bayou, and Glyn moved in with her parents while I shared a BOQ room with Joe Cotton from the heavy bomber squadron. He and his wife, who was expecting a baby, had rented a house near Tyndall, but he and I spent most evenings in the BOQ studying along with another friend from Eglin, Jim Colburn. Joe and I knew that the only planes available for students to fly at Tyndall were T-6s and C-45s, so we arranged to continue to do our flying at Eglin.

Tac School, as it was called, was a professional school for junior officers, up to the rank of captain. A few years later, after it was moved to the Air University at Maxwell Field, Alabama, its name was changed to

Squadron Officers School. The primary subjects of the curriculum were leadership, personnel management, logistics, public speaking, and writing. We attended classes about six hours a day and used the remaining hours for research, study, and softball. The school was divided into four sections, each represented by a team in the school softball league. Joe pitched for our section, and I played first base. We had a good season but lost the final playoff game and had to settle for second place.

Joe had finished flying school in June 1943, and all the graduates of his school, regardless of their choices, had been assigned to B-17s as copilots. That was bad enough, but on his first combat mission, with the Fifteenth Air Force operating out of Italy, his B-17 was shot down by the first burst of flak he had ever seen, and he was forced to bail out over the German-occupied Greek island of Corfu, where he contacted the underground and evaded capture until the end of the war. Back in the States he was stationed in Laredo, Texas, testing Bell P-63 Pinballs, which were to be used as targets for bomber gunners in training. He came to Eglin in 1946 when the P-63 program was terminated.

Joe loved to fly as much as or more than anyone I ever knew. He was devastated that he had amassed so few hours since flying school, and he was determined to pile up flying hours as fast as possible. He put up signs in base operations and at each squadron stating that he was available to fly anywhere anytime he was not flying with his own squadron. He often took T-6s up at night, flying at the lowest power setting that would sustain flight, and landing almost out of fuel. It all paid off for him. He graduated from England's Empire Test Pilot School, commanded the bomber test squadron at Wright Field for many years, and was a principal test pilot on the Convair B-58 Hustler and the XB-70 Valkyrie. After retiring from the Air Force he became chief test pilot for United Airlines. When he finally stopped flying he had amassed a total of 14,000 hours.

We signed in at Tac School together and as a consequence sat next to each other throughout the course. Once or twice a month we drove to Eglin on the weekend to do some flying. I could usually get a T-33 or a T-28, and Joe could get us scheduled for missions in the B-29. Although we didn't get as much flying as usual, we kept up our skills.

We worked hard at the school and did well; I finished number 5 out of 750 students, but I had a bit of trouble with the public-speaking seminars, primarily because of my abject fear. My experience had been limited to briefing pilots for missions, which is hardly public speaking. On the first day of the dreaded course, each student walked to the front of the room

and was handed a slip of paper with a word written on it. The student had
to make a five-minute speech on the subject. My slip said "euthanasia,"
which I now know means mercy killing, but I was a bit vague as to its
meaning then. I only knew that if the instructor had shot me dead at that
moment, it would have been an act of euthanasia. Since I had to say something, I started to tell about the youth in Asia that I had observed in India
and China during the war. The instructor, however, was not amused and
told me to stick to the subject. I mumbled for a while and then asked the
class to observe a few moments of silence for our war dead. At this point I
was told to sit down. The only positive comment I received was that I had
a nice smile. It came from one of my fellow students who had mistaken my
rictus for a smile. As the course progressed I did a little better. Joe, on the
other hand, did quite well with his down-home Indiana humor, which the
instructor obviously preferred to my Brooklyn-Tampa humor.

In late June 1950, North Korea attacked South Korea. President Truman and the United Nations made the decision to commit U.S. forces, and
later other allied forces, to defend South Korea from the Communists. Several of the students who were in units that were to be moved to Korea left
the school immediately, and many more were alerted that they would be
transferred at the end of the course in August. Several pilots and airmen
from the fighter squadron were either transferred to combat units or
alerted for transfer.

Tac School ended in mid-August, and we happily returned to Eglin
and full-time flying. All firepower demonstrations had been canceled for
the duration of the war, and almost all of our testing was aimed at the development of weapons and tactics for use in Korea. New underwing-pylon
bomb racks had been developed for the F-80C, the only jet fighter available
in Korea early in the war. Heretofore, the F-80 could not carry wingtip fuel
tanks and bombs at the same time, because the same racks were used for
both, severely limiting its range while carrying bombs or napalm.

Also under test were parafrag dispensers designed to be carried on the
wing racks of jet fighters. Parafrags are deadly antipersonnel fragmentation
bombs weighing about sixty pounds each; they are attached to small parachutes that open when the bombs are released, causing them to drop
straight down on targets. Long strikers on the front explode them about a
foot above the surface, hurling jagged shrapnel at tremendous speed in all
directions, vivid proof of the statement that it is better to give than to receive. I had used them a lot in China, and they were very accurate when released at low altitudes.

Both the light bomb squadron and the fighter squadron were developing tactics and techniques for night tactical air attacks in the mountainous terrain of Korea. Later Douglas B-26 Invaders (previously called the A-26) were successfully employed in this role.

My days at Eglin were about to come to an end. I was to be transferred to the Pentagon in mid-September. I was not looking forward to a Pentagon assignment, but at least I would be among friends. I would be joining Barney Turner and Frank Smith in the Air Defense Division of Fighter Requirements, which was headed by Col. Ed Rector, my former group commander in China who had been responsible for my assignment to Eglin. Our mission would be challenging, to study and recommend new aircraft and weapons for the air defense of the United States, but it was still the Pentagon, and who wants to read, or write for that matter, about the Pentagon?

Epilogue

Aviation has been the keystone of my life. It is responsible for almost everything that I have achieved, and all in all, it has been a great flight. As a young boy I read all I could about flying and was particularly fortunate in finding a generous pilot who occasionally would give me a ride. My dreams of becoming a pilot were fulfilled, and spending almost six years as a test pilot was the icing on the cake. While in the Air Force I earned bachelor's and master's degrees in aeronautical engineering and spent five years as a professor at the U.S. Air Force Academy.

Following my retirement from the Air Force I worked as an engineer on the Apollo and Skylab programs and, in 1972, joined the staff of the National Air and Space Museum as head of the Aeronautics Department.

Life has never been boring, and I have enjoyed a strong sense of accomplishment in every aspect of my career. I helped to test the first Air Force jets, taught the first classes at the Air Force Academy, was involved in NASA's Manned Spaceflight Program, and played an important role in the creation of the world's most visited museum.

My personal life has been equally satisfying. I have a wonderful wife, Glyn, and two children, a boy and a girl. Both my children have become successful and productive adults, and I now have a lovely granddaughter, Laura. Although neither our son nor daughter has any interest in flying, I still have hopes for the grandchild. Once when Laura was about three, she was in bed in our house when she yelled for me to hurry upstairs because there was a spider in the room. After some searching I finally located the tiny spider in the far corner of the room at the wall-ceiling juncture. I told her she had good eyes to be able to see such a small spider, and she replied, "Yes, I know. I can see air." What a good, and extremely rare, attribute for a pilot. Later when she was eight or nine, she wanted to know if I could fly upside down. When I assured her that I could, she asked me to take her up and fly upside down. I have taken her up several times, not yet in an airplane approved for inverted flight, but I will. The genes live on.

At times, things in life seem to go full circle. One of my first memories, and a lifelong inspiration, was seeing Lindbergh in a triumphal parade following his historic transatlantic flight in 1927. On the day of my retirement from the Air and Space Museum I was honored to escort Anne Morrow Lindbergh on a brief tour of the museum. Accompanied by her daughter Reeve, she arrived early, and I went with them to the second floor. There she paused at the *Spirit of St. Louis* and the exhibit of Lindbergh memorabilia. She then went to a bench opposite the Lockheed Sirius *Tingmissartoq*, in which she and her husband had spent so many hours exploring new air routes to Asia and Europe.

I stood a few feet away and watched as she sat, serene and lovely, with tear-filled eyes, quietly reliving some of their adventures together. I, of course, did not interrupt her reverie, but I hope that she realizes how universally she is loved and admired for her courage, devotion, and wonderful writing. It was truly a privilege to be with her. To me, she is unquestionably the woman of the century.

Index

U.S. Air Tactical School, 213
U.S. Army Air Force: becomes U.S. Air
    Force, 118
USS *Coral Sea*, 44

V-1 flying bomb, 10
Vandersteel, William, 28–30
Vermont Air National Guard, 55

Walker, Colonel, 89
Warner, Buster, 29
Webb, Ann (née Coleman), 59, 141, 142
Webb, Maj. Spider, 59, 141, 142

Weldon, Maj. Tom, 130, 137, 142
Whitehorse, Yukon Territory, 65-66, 77–79
Whiteley, Col. John F., 64
Whitney, Lt. Claire, 130, 137, 139
Whittle, Sir Frank, 8
Williams, Flight Lieutenant, 210
Wright-Patterson Air Force Base (Wright
    Field), 3, 14–16, 116, 125, 128–29, 141–43,
    214

Yak-11, 59
Yeager, Chuck, 15, 26, 128, 158
Young, Joe, 195, 196